ORGANISATIONAL BEHAVIOUR

Third Edition

Roger Bennett

BA, MSc (Econ), DPhil
London Guildhall University

M&E
PITMAN
PUBLISHING

London · Hong Kong · Johannesburg · Melbourne · Singapore · Washington DC

PITMAN PUBLISHING
128 Long Acre, London WC2E 9AN
Tel: 0171 447 2000 Fax: 0171 240 5771

A Division of Pearson Professional Limited

Third edition published in Great Britain 1997

© Pearson Professional Limited 1997

The right of Roger Bennett to be identified as author of this
work has been asserted by him in accordance with the
Copyright, Designs and Patents Act 1988.

British Library Cataloguing in Publication Data
A CIP catalogue record for this book can be obtained from the British Library

ISBN 0 7121 1069 0

10 9 8 7 6 5 4 3 2 1

Typeset by WestKey Ltd., Falmouth, Cornwall
Printed and bound in Great Britain by Bell and Bain Ltd. Glasgow

The Publishers' policy is to use paper manufactured from sustainable forests.

ORGANISATIONAL BEHAVIOUR

CONTENTS

Part Four
THE DESIGN OF ORGANISATIONS

PREFACE

My purpose in writing this book is to collect together into a single text all the essential topics connected with organisational behaviour and to present these in a clear, concise and informative way. The book is intended for use by business and management students in universities and other colleges and should be valuable also for students preparing for the organisational behaviour papers of the major professional bodies.

Organisational behaviour is today recognised as an important subject in its own right and is rapidly becoming an essential component of all undergraduate, professional institute and vocational courses in business and management. Unfortunately, however, the scope of organisational behaviour is so wide that students typically need to refer to an extensive range of source materials in order to keep abreast with their studies. Much of the source material, moreover, is highly specialised and contained in diverse, expensive and voluminous textbooks or in esoteric articles in scholarly journals and reports that are not easily obtained.

Accordingly, the text seeks to summarise this extensive literature, focusing on *principles* and *methods* rather than on particular empirical studies or organisational techniques. Early chapters emphasise scientific methodology and the role of the behavioural sciences in the analysis of organisations. These are followed by chapters on conventional organisational behaviour topics such as individual perception, motivation, theories of leadership, groups, and so on. Then there is material on the main principles and methods for structuring organisations and on recent developments (core and peripheral workers, networking, professional support groups, etc.) in the practice of organisation design. Additionally, there is an account of the Japanese approach to organisation and management, reflecting the enormous interest in this subject in Britain and other western countries.

The text refers to a substantial number of pioneering research studies and other seminal works in the organisational behaviour field. For convenience, bibliographic details of these works are gathered together in a single alphabetical list in Appendix 1 at the end of the book.

This new edition includes fresh material on, *inter-alia*: culture, organisational behaviour and strategic management, the impact of information technology, employee communications, anxiety and phobias, women in management, and the learning organisation. Sections on the nature of scientific method, participation, memory and learning, motivation and change management have been revised and extended.

Part One

BACKGROUND TO ORGANISATIONAL BEHAVIOUR

1

SCOPE AND METHOD OF ORGANISATIONAL BEHAVIOUR

INTRODUCTION

1. Definition of organisational behaviour

The subject of organisational behaviour concerns the study of how organisations function and how people relate to them through their conduct, perceptions and intentions – individually or in groups. As an academic discipline, organisational behaviour draws heavily on the social and behavioural sciences (especially sociology and industrial psychology) and on the theory and practice of organisational design (e.g. deciding how many divisions and departments the enterprise is to have, the human effects of the division of labour, techniques for allocating work, and so on).

2. Overview of the social and behavioural sciences in organisations

The main social and behavioural disciplines relevant to the study of organisational behaviour are psychology, sociology, anthropology, political science, history and economics. Of these, psychology and sociology are the most important. Sometimes a distinction is made between purely behavioural disciplines, i.e. psychology, anthropology and sociology; and the 'social sciences': politics, history and economics (plus certain aspects of geography and law). However, such distinctions are of little practical importance.

Psychology studies human thought and conduct either in isolation from social contexts, or in direct relation to a particular social environment. It seeks to determine the nature of individuals, their needs, motives, how they learn, how they modify their behaviour, and so on. Psychiatry is a specialised branch of psychology, dealing with mental disorders. Social psychology is a mixture of sociology (see below) and psychology. It is the study of individual behaviour in the context of a social environment and focuses heavily on interpersonal relations.

Sociology examines patterns of interaction among individuals and within and between groups. Thus it concerns, *inter alia*, the investigation of power, status, influence and authority within formal and informal organisations; the determination of group values and norms; communication systems, and social influences as a whole.

Managers need to make use of the behavioural sciences for several reasons, including the following:

(a) The fact that most aspects of management involve the administration of people and are thus necessarily concerned with interpersonal relations.

(b) The desirability of basing decisions about interpersonal relations on definite facts and analysis rather than idle speculation.

(c) The importance of psychological and social influences on productivity and the need to relate these to physical working conditions and organisational structures.

(d) The need to understand employee attitudes towards work, the causes of employee motivation, and how an individual's personality affects his or her relations with the organisation.

The problems

The application of the behavioural sciences to management involves a number of problems, as outlined below:

(a) Since the behavioural sciences draw upon so many diverse topics from psychology, sociology, administrative management, role theory (*see* Chapter 9), etc., it is difficult to integrate all these elements into a single body of knowledge immediately applicable to organisational design and analysis.

(b) People often behave in unpredictable and seemingly irrational ways, thus making the study of how they *ought* to behave seemingly irrelevant.

(c) Influences on human behaviour are enormously complex and wide-ranging. Any model of human behaviour is necessarily simplistic and will have to exclude many important considerations.

(d) Theories of human behaviour depend critically on the theorist's assumptions about human nature (*see* 13:8). If the underlying assumptions are wrong the theory will be useless.

(e) Interpretation of individual and group behaviour is itself subjective. Opinions about whether a certain mode of behaviour is good or bad may vary sharply from person to person.

WHY STUDY ORGANISATIONAL BEHAVIOUR?

The reason for studying organisational behaviour is that since an organisation consists of people, effective managers must be capable of relating individuals, groups, and formal structures (*see* Chapter 21) to the organisation's needs.

Behaviour of organisations

How an organisation actually behaves depends on the decisions and actions taken by its members. In order to understand the actions of organisations it is thus necessary to appreciate the fundamental factors that underlie human behaviour, notably:

- Perception (*see* 4:**14**)
- Past experiences and their consequences
- Learning (*see* 6:**1**)
- Motivation (*see* 8:**1**)
- Cognitive processes, i.e. the manner in which information is interpreted, thinking (*see* 4:**9**) and the use of language to communicate thoughts
- Personality (*see* 4:**5**)
- Social influences (approval or disapproval of peers, friendships, community values, etc.).

METHODS OF STUDY

A significant feature of organisational behaviour as an academic subject is its emphasis on the importance of logic and scientific method in the derivation of propositions and results.

3. Scientific method

The scientific method comprises a series of logical steps to be followed prior to drawing conclusions.

It begins with the specification of a *hypothesis*, which is a proposition that something is or is not true. Hypotheses are based on all the information currently available on the matter being considered and on the intuition of the person conducting the investigation. Thus, the fewer data available to support the proposition the more likely it is to be incorrect.

Next, the hypothesis is *tested* by predicting what will happen if it is valid and then taking observations and/or conducting experiments to see whether this is actually the case. Unfortunately, observations that seemingly confirm an initial hypothesis do not necessarily mean it is true, as the results might have been caused by an external influence unconnected with the matter being considered. Nevertheless, measurements and observations which are consistent with the original hypothesis at least enable the investigator not to reject it, while inconsistent results strongly suggest that the hypothesis is wrong. In the latter case the hypothesis must either be abandoned or modified in some significant way.

The above-mentioned procedures are sometimes referred to as the *hypothetico-deductive method*. Beliefs, hunches, past experiences or direct observations of possible relationships between variables progress from vague ideas towards formal propositions which are then checked against (perceived) reality via some sort of test. The basic assumption is that provided the researcher properly defines what needs to be measured, devises appropriate and accurate measurement methods and interprets the results objectively then correct conclusions should emerge. Measurements need to be valid, i.e. they should actually measure what they claim to be measuring; and reliable, meaning that tests should give consistent results when repeated in similar conditions. *Verification* of a hypothesis must always be regarded as *provisional*, because there is always the chance that someone will come along and disprove it. Hence the scientific method only produces hypotheses that are accepted 'for the time being' (which could be hundreds of years). The scientific method is itself said to be *positivistic*, i.e. it assumes that the best way to discover knowledge is through the application of logical thought and rationality, objective reasoning, and through scientific observation (rather than imagination and/or speculation). It is said, moreover, to presuppose that 'there is truth out there' which can be discovered given the application of the relevant scientific technique (Giere 1979). Advocates of the scientific method assert that it is by far the most effective means for destroying myths, superstitions and stereotypes and for promoting usable technology.

4. Facts and theories

A *theory* is a supposition concerning cause and effect. Note, however, that even within the natural sciences (*see* **6** below) there is no such thing as a 'scientific fact', since to assert the existence of immutable, absolute truths would itself be unscientific! This is because all scientific knowledge is *inferred* from human observations, and by definition only a finite number of observations – no matter how large the number – can be made. Uncertainties may be reduced through taking more and more observations, but can never be entirely removed.

Elements of theory

A theory provides a framework for determining what to observe; how to observe (and subsequently how to transform observations into data); and the procedures to be applied when drawing conclusions from data. Hence a theory involves a set of rules, themselves embodied in statements. Some of these statements have to be accepted without question prior to starting an analysis; others must be proven before they are believed. Statements accepted on faith and without proof are called the *axioms* of a theory. The term 'theorem' is sometimes used to describe a proposition that logically emerges from axioms. Statements proven to be consistent with observation and with axioms might be referred to as *laws*.

5. Arts and sciences

In practising an 'art', the individual attempts to create something of lasting significance. The creation could be a piece of music, a painting, a play, or anything of permanent value. Arts require imagination, discipline and extensive rehearsal before they are fully mastered.

'Science', on the other hand, is the attempt to explain nature by identifying relations between cause and effect, usually through observation, hypothesis testing and experimentation. Note that science and art are not mutually exclusive because arts themselves typically depend on underlying scientific principles.

Epistemology

This means the theory of knowledge: how people get to know things; the validity of the methods of investigation applied when searching for truth; and the frameworks used to describe and interpret discoveries. Thus it concerns the fundamental natures of experience, belief and understanding.

6. Natural sciences and behavioural sciences

Natural sciences such as chemistry or biology deal with material phenomena and are based on experiment, scientific method and observation. Three steps are involved in conducting analyses and investigations in the natural sciences:

(a) The development of a model (*see* **9** below) or theory to explain the state of nature.

(b) Calculation of the probabilities of the occurrence of certain events.

(c) Measurement of actual outcomes and comparison of these with the predictions of the theory or model.

Behavioural sciences, conversely, concern human thoughts and actions. Explanation and prediction are thus more difficult in the behavioural sciences because of the enormous variety of factors that affect human conduct and people's perceptions of events.

7. Induction, deduction and empirical research

Induction means generalising from one or several observations. This is necessary when an event or situation has occurred only a few times; but it is less than satisfactory because the outcomes observed might be untypical of what would happen on average if the observed event or situation were to be repeated very often. If a handful of people are seen to behave in a certain way in a certain situation this does not necessarily prove that everyone would behave similarly in that situation. This is particularly relevant to the study of leadership (*see* Chapter 13) and intra-group behaviour (*see* Chapter 12).

Deduction is the process of drawing conclusions about particular matters from large amounts of information. The problems here are:

(a) How to categorise and interpret the information.

(b) Deciding how to deal with occasional large divergences of certain observations from the general norm. Should these be ignored or taken as evidence that previous conclusions must have been incorrect?

> Note how all scientific enquiry is inductive to some extent, because there exists only a finite amount of observable information. There is always the possibility – however remote – that somewhere or other new evidence might be found that will disprove a particular theory.

Empirical science and non-empirical science

Non-empirical sciences (theoretical physics or pure mathematics, for example) rely on logic and are not tested against reality. Conclusions reached are (necessarily) regarded as self-evident. Empirical sciences, conversely, seek to describe and explain real life occurrences through examining real life events and data. Thus, all propositions are checked out against available information. Data might be collected through:

- questionnaires
- interviews
- historical records
- experiments
- personal observations.

The problems attached to empirical research include the following:

(a) Interpretation of data.

(b) Measurement problems (alterations in the definitions of data quoted in published government statistics, for example).

(c) Personal prejudices among researchers causing them to draw incorrect conclusions.

(d) Technical problems associated with survey design, statistical sampling, etc.

Grounded theory

This is a process of analytical induction based on the following steps:

(a) Collection of data and the formulation of generalised statements about possible relationships involved.

(b) Further data collection intended to check the worth of these general statements and the categorisation of results.

(c) Collection of yet more data to assess the plausibility of the categories of results stated and the provisional specification of the variables relevant to the phenomenon under consideration.

(d) Statement of an initial theory to explain cause and effect. This is extended and refined through further data collection.

Hence theories *emerge* from inductive reasoning about observed situations (Glaser and Strauss 1967).

8. Explanation and prediction in behavioural science

Human behaviour is difficult to explain and predict because human beings are extremely complex and potentially unpredictable animals. Their attitudes may change suddenly; their behaviour is sometimes illogical. Also, much human behaviour makes sense only in relation to social institutions. How, for example, is it possible to explain the observation of millions of people exchanging small pieces of paper and lumps of metal unless one knows about money and the principles and institutions of finance and banking? Further problems are as follows:

(a) Published data on human behaviour can be extremely inaccurate.

(b) People sometimes describe the reasons for their actions in a certain manner and then behave in ways completely at odds with the implications of their initial descriptions.

(c) Biases and personal prejudices within the individuals conducting an investigation can cause incorrect interpretation of information.

(d) It is rarely possible to examine and predict the consequences of every single aspect of a behavioural situation.

Nevertheless, the application of scientific method to behavioural studies does clarify fundamental issues, and it helps analysts to 'see the wood from the trees'. Without hypotheses and the theories they generate the researcher is confronted with a confusing, shapeless and unintelligible mass of disjointed observations. Other benefits are that:

(a) To the extent that general principles of behaviour actually exist, their discovery is more likely through rational scientific analysis.

(b) Analytical approaches to behavioural patterns are encouraged; it becomes possible to understand *why* as well as *how* things happen.

9. Models of behaviour

Axioms and theorems can be combined to form *models* of situations. A model is a representation of reality. It reduces an issue to just a few key variables, which the analyst may then study in great depth. Model building requires that a number of *assumptions* about the nature of the problem are made, for example that people are motivated by certain rewards, or that observations follow a normal probability distribution or some other prespecified statistical form. The model constructed will predict events and describe the circumstances in which they might happen. Model building has a number of *advantages:*

(a) Analysts are compelled to list and evaluate all the assumptions underlying their suggestions. Rational approaches to decision taking are thus encouraged.

(b) Problems are presented concisely, precisely, and in a clearly understandable form.

(c) Complex situations are reduced to a handful of manageable variables; peripheral issues are excluded from the analysis.

(d) Decisions based on the model may be taken quickly.

The *disadvantages* are as follows:

(a) Many human emotions that affect people's behaviour (fear, greed, discomfort, etc.) are extremely difficult to incorporate into a model.

(b) Usually, a model represents a situation only at a specific moment in time. In reality, however, business situations are constantly changing, so that the results from a model will be continually out of date.

(c) Important aspects of a problem might be ignored in order to make it fit neatly into the confines of a narrowly defined model.

Validity of a model

To determine whether a model is valid it is necessary to compare it against observed facts. If contradictions emerge the model is incomplete or false. A single exception can prove a theory wrong. Note however that no theory can ever be proven entirely true, as the possibility of finding contradictory evidence always remains (Popper 1963). 'Face validity' occurs when results appear to the researcher to confirm or measure what he or she intended to confirm or measure. The problem here of course is that observations might simply represent a compounding of errors or have arisen by chance. Hence the results should be logically as well as empirically consistent with all known circumstances of the situation before a model is regarded as valid. The validity issue is discussed further in 5:**3**

10. Experiments

Experimentation is rarely possible in the behavioural sciences, and even where it is the generalisations drawn from experiments involving humans might not be universally applicable.

Social science experiments typically occur under highly specific environmental conditions which may be neither permanent nor repeatable. Thus, laboratories are sometimes used for experiments because environmental factors may then be tightly controlled, recorded, and hence replicated in future investigations. Note, however, that if a laboratory is employed for an experiment on people, the laboratory conditions under which the experiment takes place might not truly reflect real life situations.

To be effective in discovering relations between cause and effect a behavioural science experiment should:

- be conducted in surroundings that are as natural as possible
- involve groups which are typical of the wider population
- be such that precise measurement of results is possible
- identify the actual causes of outcomes.

The *advantages* of experiments are that:

(a) They are much cheaper than widespread observation of entire populations.

(b) Precise measurement techniques may be employed.

(c) The environment in which the experiment is conducted may be easily altered (and the effects of the changes on participants observed immediately).

(d) Irrelevant complicating variables can be excluded.

Disadvantages of experiments include their *ad hoc* character, the difficulty of generalising from results obtained from small samples, the danger of excluding important influences that would exist in non-experimental situations, and the impossibility of knowing the true state of mind of participants at the time of the experiment (e.g. subjects might not be taking the experiment seriously).

Animals are sometimes used for experiments on behaviour. These might be extremely useful for learning about how animals react to certain stimuli, events and conditions; but the results cannot always be meaningfully extrapolated to humans. The fact that rats, dogs, or pigeons repeatedly act in a certain way in particular situations says much about the psychology of rats, dogs, and pigeons; yet may disclose very little about the psychology of human beings.

SCHOOLS OF THOUGHT IN ORGANISATIONAL BEHAVIOUR

11. What is a school of thought?

A school of thought comprises a number of writers, thinkers, and practitioners of a subject who all adhere to the same fundamental principles and doctrines and/or follow similar working methods where that subject is concerned. Members of the school may be separated geographically (proponents of the school might reside in different countries), or by time (new enthusiasts for a school can emerge many years after the death of its founders).

The main schools of organisational behaviour are normally defined as:

- The *classical* school (*see* **12** below and Chapter 2), usually (but not always) interpreted as embracing 'scientific management' (*see* **2:1–3**)
- The *human relations* school (*see* **3:1**)
- The *systems* school (*see* **3:16**), which includes contingency theory.

Problems can occur in deciding which writers belong to which school, especially if the writers are dead. Also, particular advocates of a school sometimes change the direction of their thinking during their own lifetime and thus publish material which directly contradicts their presumed allegiance to a specific approach to the subject. Nevertheless, it is usually possible to group people together into schools, using the following criteria:

(a) Members of a school make the same basic presumptions about human nature.

(b) They share a common perspective regarding the *objectives* of the discipline.

(c) Their methods of analysis are essentially similar.

(d) They share a common sense of purpose.

(e) Members recognise certain individuals as being the undisputed leaders of the school (e.g. it is not possible to belong to the Freudian school of psychology unless one basically agrees with the ideas and conclusions of Sigmund Freud).

(f) They hold similar opinions and usually come to similar and predictable conclusions about contentious issues in the field.

12. Classical, neo-classical and other approaches

There is a 'classical' approach to most disciplines (e.g. classical economic theory, classical architecture, classical management theory, etc.). It is not easy to define what a classical approach is. Often, the first few writers in a new subject are collectively referred to as 'the classical school' in that subject simply to enable the comparison of later writers on the subject with these pioneers. A better characterisation is to define the classical approach to any discipline as that which:

(a) rather than just being the first, is the first to analyse systematically the underlying *form* and *principles* of the subject

(b) uses facts (but *see* **4** above) and reason to arrive at conclusions, rather than imagination, feelings and intuition

(c) seeks to establish universal laws that can be applied to any problem arising in the field. The aim is to create order out of chaos and to resolve issues in methodical and economical ways.

Once initial standards are established, the people who subsequently adhere to them are typically categorised as belonging to the classical school. Note, however, that the word 'classical' does not necessarily mean 'best'.

Neo-classical approaches

Inevitably, certain followers of the founding pioneers will deviate from the latter's ideas while continuing to adhere to the classical school's fundamental principles, presumptions and methods of analysis. Often, such people are said to belong to the 'neo-classical' version of the school. Categorising individuals into classical or neo-classical schools (perhaps even a neo-neo-classical school, which is a further step removed from the original version) can be extremely problematic, and the confusion that arises can sometimes outweigh the value of the exercise. Note that neo-human relations and neo-systems schools of organisational behaviour have been distinguished (*see* 3:7).

13. Paradigms

A 'paradigm' is a conceptual scheme that lies at the heart of a field of study, representing basic assumptions about the nature of the discipline. As an academic subject develops (through fresh empirical research, reinterpretation of existing ideas, critical analysis of old data, investigations of anomalies that cannot be related to established theory, etc.) fresh paradigms emerge. These new paradigms require fundamental changes in how people think about the subject, and it is not surprising, therefore, that they are frequently resisted by existing writers and thinkers in the field. Old paradigms will have been discussed, refined, clarified and extended for many years, and those committed to them have much to lose if they are abandoned.

Thus, new schools of thought might emerge in response to fresh paradigms. The creation of the human relations school (*see* 3:1) and the development of the systems approach (*see* 3:23) are good examples of the process. (How these schools evolved is described in later chapters.) Thereafter various approaches compete with others in terms of their capacity to explain phenomena and to clear up problems that other approaches cannot handle.

Progress test 1

1. Which academic disciplines contribute most to the study of organisational behaviour?

2. Why should managers want to know about the behavioural sciences?

3. Explain the difference between psychology and sociology.

4. What is the scientific method?

5. What is an art?

6. Explain the difference between induction and deduction.

7. Why is human behaviour so difficult to explain?

8. How can the construction of models help the social scientist?

9. List the disadvantages of experimentation in the social sciences.

10. What are the major schools of thought in organisational behaviour?

11. What is the difference between a classical and neo-classical approach to a subject?

2

SCIENTIFIC MANAGEMENT AND THE CLASSICAL SCHOOL

SCIENTIFIC MANAGEMENT

1. Definition of scientific management

The term scientific management is used to describe the approach to management and organisation of a group of thinkers and practitioners led by F.W. Taylor (1856–1917) who published a highly influential book on the subject in 1911.

Scientific management is based on the philosophies of economic rationality, efficiency, individualism, and the 'scientific' analysis of work. Taylor believed that workers are motivated primarily by the prospect of high material reward. Thus, if employees' wages are closely related to the volume of work done, and if working methods are designed to generate high levels of output, then people will work as hard as their physical attributes allow and high quality production can be expected as a matter of course.

The fundamental principles of scientific management are as follows:

(a) Workers should be set relatively high targets to stretch them to their maximum capacities. Daily workloads should be specified by management following detailed examination of jobs and the most efficient ways in which they can be done.

(b) As far as possible, work should be completed under standard conditions involving the most efficient working methods. Working environments should be carefully controlled. The division of labour is recommended so that each operative is responsible for just a small number of tasks. Constant repetition of tasks develops speed, skill and, in consequence, high volumes of good quality production. No time should be wasted in fetching raw materials, arranging tools, or transporting finished work. Duplication of effort is to be avoided.

(c) Pay should be directly related to productivity, thereby stimulating effort and encouraging co-operation with management. Taylor even suggested the use of differential payments schemes by which employees who exceeded target performance would receive large bonuses whereas workers falling below target would incur significant cuts in wages.

Application of these principles required the measurement and analysis of work, including the study and timing of physical movements. Then, once a job had been evaluated the type of person most likely to succeed in its execution could be identified.

The training needs of selected workers were established through the systematic investigation of the skills necessary for particular types of work. Taylor believed that management should plan and direct all the worker's efforts, leaving little discretion for individual control over working methods. Job specifications should be detailed, clear, simple and precise; the fewer functions an individual is required to perform the better.

Management by exception

According to Taylor, organisations should be controlled through application of the 'principle of exception' whereby subordinates submit to their superiors only brief, condensed reports on normal operations, but extensive reports on deviations from past average performance or from targets set by higher management. Once established, standards would be monitored by picking out significant divergences from predetermined norms. Exceptionally good or bad results would then be analysed in depth and explanations offered, but slight deviations from normal performance would not be questioned.

2. Role of the individual manager

Scientific management emphasised planning, standardisation, close supervision and the detailed specification of employees' work. There is little or no scope for operatives to exercise discretion over how they complete their tasks. According to scientific management, there is but 'one best way' to manage, i.e. using 'scientific' principles.

Note (importantly) that scientific management is instrumental and utilitarian in orientation. It is far more concerned with mundane working methods than with organisational design and strategy.

3. Contributions of scientific management to organisation theory

The major contributions of scientific management to later approaches to organisation and management are as follows:

(a) It demonstrated the need to define clearly the patterns of authority and responsibility within organisations.

(b) It provided a rational basis for separating and analysing organisational functions.

(c) It emphasised the role of target setting and the need for logically determined standards.

(d) It stimulated interest in the design of incentive systems and the analysis of the role of money in the motivation of employees.

4. Labour relations under scientific management

Because the application of scientific management methods was genuinely expected to raise workers' incomes to unprecedentedly high levels, its advocates did not believe there could be any fundamental conflicts of interest between management and labour. The worker, it was assumed, would willingly accept the system.

In fact, organised labour and many individual workers did not share this view and many serious industrial disputes followed the introduction of Taylor's methods, both in the USA and in Britain. Unions saw scientific management as a challenge to their role, influence, credibility and position.

5. Work measurement

The timing of work was a principal feature of scientific management. Taylor himself would break down the cycle of a major operation into small groups of motions, which he called elements. These elements were then timed and analysed separately. Taylor's objectives were: (*i*) to cause work to become routine and easy to complete; (*ii*) to minimise physical effort; and (*iii*) to eliminate duplicated operations.

Followers of Taylor developed this approach. Of particular importance was the work of F.B. and L. Gilbreth, who conducted detailed analyses of human body motions in work situations. The Gilbreths began their investigations with a study of all the body movements required for bricklaying, extending the analysis to other types of work and eventually compiling a complete taxonomy of all the human body motions used in manual labour.

6. Objections to scientific management

Criticisms of scientific management include:

(a) Through its concentration on the mercenary and economic aspects of human nature the scientific school tends to ignore the social and psychological needs of employees. These psychosociological factors in fact exert powerful influences on behaviour.

(b) Attention is focused on efficiency on the factory floor rather than at higher levels within organisations. The existing environment in which firms function is assumed constant and accepted without question. In reality, however, business enterprises are microcosms of society as a whole, and if conflicts between owners and organised labour exist within society they may equally exist within firms.

(c) Division of labour creates boredom for those who must perform routine tasks. Constant repetition of simple movements dehumanises work. People become appendages of the machines they operate. In the longer term, excessive application of the division of labour could alienate workers to the extent that less is produced than otherwise would be the case.

On a wider level, opponents argue that the treatment of human beings as little more than adjuncts to mechanised production and the factory system is inappropriate in a modern democratic society which values personal development as well as the creation of physical wealth.

(d) Unemployment can result from increased industrial efficiency. Fewer people are needed to produce a given amount of goods. This, together with the loss of individual control over working practices and procedures implied by the scientific approach, naturally arouses distrust, fear and antagonism among organised labour. Moreover, the bulk of the additional wealth generated by the adoption of scientific management seemed always to accrue more to shareholders rather than to workers.

(e) Scientific management was devised and implemented when mass production was widely used in manufacturing industry, and it fitted well with the technological requirements of the period. However, contemporary technical, economic and social circumstances are so completely different from those prevailing during the early years of the century that the application of the approach may no longer be appropriate.

(f) The fastest way of performing a job is not necessarily the best.

(g) Although it is possible to measure how long, on average, a task takes to complete, there is no truly scientific way of estimating the time in which the task *ought* to be finished.

7. The scientific management revolution

Taylor stated that the effects of scientific management would be revolutionary. Everyone would have a job (eventually, if not in the immediate short term); incomes would be high and all the material benefits of mass production and a consumer society would be obtained. However, if scientific management was to succeed then, he argued, a fundamental change in managerial and employee thinking was required. Management and labour would have to:

(a) recognise the existence of a common interest in achieving higher productivity, and thus not engage in quarrels and industrial disputes over relative returns to capital and labour

(b) accept the need for a clear division between mental and manual work

(c) replace *ad hoc* rules and approaches with 'scientific' analysis of working situations.

8. Scientific management and the classical school

Scientific management is one of several components of the *classical school* of organisation and management. This school cannot be attributed to any one person, rather it is a conglomeration of ideas developed over many decades. The fundamental proposition is that people should be selected and trained to fit into the organisation; the organisation itself need not be structured to suit the human needs of particular individuals. Rigid organisation patterns are specified and people are allocated to particular positions according to their perceived suitability for those jobs. The classical approach is concerned with grand designs, seeks common causes of behaviour (normally assumed to involve mercenary and self-centred motivations) and looks for uniform principles that are equally applicable to the management of *any* organisation. It presupposes that the same mechanical laws of organisation and management can be applied to all businesses regardless of cultural and/or technical circumstances.

Central to the development of the classical school were the works of Max Weber (1864–1920) and Henri Fayol (1841–1925).

BUREAUCRATIC MANAGEMENT

9. Max Weber and the theory of bureaucracy

The term 'bureaucracy' was coined by the sociologist Max Weber to describe organisations exhibiting the following features:

(a) Extensive and binding systems of rules. Precedents are followed; procedures are standardised; interdepartmental relations are stable and continuous.

(b) Application of the managerial division of labour, specialisation of functions, precise definition of authority and responsibility structures.

(c) Hierarchical patterns of administration with unity of command (*see* 21:**3**).

(d) Complete separation of policy making from administration. Decisions are based on expert technical advice; control of staff is purely impersonal.

(e) Rules and decisions are always recorded in writing.

Bureaucracy is common in large organisations, and it is not necessarily a bad thing. It encourages rational approaches to management; and the formal procedures, specialisations, hierarchies and impersonal control mechanisms that it generates can sometimes be extremely effective, especially in very large and complex enterprises.

10. Advantages and disadvantages of bureaucracy

Weber regarded bureaucracy as the most efficient form of organisation. It was logical, self-perpetuating, and could resist external pressures of change. The practice of following existing norms and precedents meant that administrators could avoid having to exercise discretion, since relatively few unique problems would arise. However, bureaucracies are threatened by the large volumes of 'red tape' they generate, and the possibility that actual behaviour within the organisation might be influenced by charismatic leaders who are not part of the official hierarchy. Other problems include:

- slow decision taking
- excessively long chains of command
- discouragement of individual initiative

- possible failure to identify and remove incompetent individuals
- unthinking compliance with rules and procedures that become ends in themselves and detract from the achievement of organisational goals
- the possibility that people at the bottom end of an organisation may be more rational and better able to take decisions than those at the top. Hence, many activities may in practice originate at base of the organisation and effectively subvert decisions taken at higher levels of authority.

11. Theoretical criticisms of the Weberian approach to bureaucracy

Weber's general approach to bureaucracy has been criticised at the theoretical level on the following grounds:

(a) It ignores the roles and influences of informal groups within organisations.

(b) It does not explain the reasons for the *existence* of organisations.

(c) It implies that centralised organisation is superior to decentralised organisational forms, which is not necessarily the case.

(d) It has little to say about the influence of unofficial leaders.

(e) Weber offered no theory of how a bureaucracy would respond to external pressures for change.

12. Social implications of bureaucracy

Working in a bureaucracy has the following implications for employees:

(a) Work involves serving the organisation faithfully in return for security and a long-term career. Employees evaluate the significance of their activities according to how well they serve the needs of the organisation and not by other – possibly more objective – criteria.

(b) The organisation becomes the basis for the employee's entire way of life. Workers' self-identities (*see* 7:8) critically depend on their roles in the organisation.

(c) To the extent that an individual's career is crucial to his or her welfare, work and service to the organisation becomes a central life interest.

13. The work of Henri Fayol

Perhaps the most influential of all the classical writers is H. Fayol, a French mining engineer whose book *General and Industrial Management* (first published in 1916) has become a cornerstone of the classical school. According to Fayol, all business organisations are concerned with more or less the same types of activity; though which are the most important in particular circumstances will obviously vary from firm to firm. These activities comprise: finance and accounting, technical activities, commercial activities, security, and 'management'.
There are, he suggests, five aspects to management, as follows:

(a) Co-ordination, i.e. the unification of effort to ensure that all the organisation's members are pursuing the same goals.

(b) Control, i.e. specifying objectives, checking up on progress achieved and implementing measures to remedy deficiencies.

(c) Planning and forecasting, i.e. assessing the future and deciding what to do in the future if certain events occur.

(d) Organisation, i.e. splitting work into manageable units and then allocating work to departments, sections and individuals.

(e) Command, i.e. giving orders to make sure that decisions are actually carried out.

Fayol, unlike F.W. Taylor, was more interested in the general structure of administration than in questions of day-to-day operational control. He insisted there exist a number of fundamental principles of administration that should be applied to any organisation. The principles were:

(a) Unity of command (i.e. one person one boss, *see* 21:3)

(b) A fair internal disciplinary system

(c) Linkage of authority and responsibility, so that the occupant of a post possesses the authority needed to carry its responsibilities

(d) Specialisation and the division of labour

(e) Creation of stable work groups and job security for personnel

(f) Use of organisation charts and job descriptions

(g) The setting of objectives throughout the organisation, and the centralisation of plans to provide a 'unity of direction' for the entire firm.

SUMMARY OF THE CLASSICAL APPROACH

14. Contributions and problems of the classical approach

Classical theory emphasises formal rules, specialisation, the clear division of responsibilities and the achievement of high efficiency through the analysis of work, attaching relatively little importance to the personal and social needs of the people who operate within the organisation. The essential contributions of the classical approach may be summarised as follows:

(a) It introduced logically determined and rational theories where none existed before.

(b) Concern for productivity and quality of output was enhanced.

(c) It provided administrative mechanisms suitable for large organisations.

(d) Application of the division of labour, management by exception, etc., made mass production possible and thus generated the goods required to satisfy the rapidly growing consumer markets of the time.

(e) It laid a firm foundation for the subsequent study of the efficiency of working methods and organisations.

(f) Through its insistence on the existence of general principles of management, the approach created a recognition of the need for management training in order to equip individuals with the abilities needed to apply these principles.

On the other hand, classical approaches are rigid and the structures they imply are not usually capable of accommodating rapid technical, environmental and other change. Also, they create formal and hierarchical interpersonal relationships within organisations – perhaps out of step with the more liberal and democratic attitudes towards work relationships increasingly evident today.

Arguably, the classical approach was suitable for the nineteenth and early twentieth centuries, when technologies were simpler and organisational hierarchies more precise. Yet it may not be suitable for the complex and fast-changing modern business world, especially wherever interpersonal relations and possible conflicts of interest are involved.

Progress test 2

1. What are the fundamental philosophies upon which scientific management is based?

2. List the major contributions of scientific management to the theory of organisation.

3. What did F.W. Taylor assume about workers' attitudes towards scientific management?

4. Explain the contribution to scientific management of F.B. and L. Gilbreth.

5. Describe the nature of the revolution that Taylor regarded as essential for the effective application of scientific management.

6. Who were the main contributors to the classical school of management theory?

7. List the advantages of bureaucracy.

8. List the major problems attached to the classical school.

3

HUMAN RELATIONS, SYSTEMS AND CONTINGENCY APPROACHES

THE HUMAN RELATIONS SCHOOL

1. The human relations approach

Whereas the classical approach treats individuals *mechanistically* – regarding people as motivated almost exclusively by the desire to achieve high financial reward – the human relations school asserts that workplace behaviour is determined mainly by the *organisational* setting in which it occurs. Thus, social factors are regarded as influencing the actions and attitudes of workers at least as powerfully as incentive schemes and physical working conditions.

Leadership style, interpersonal and organisational communications, employee morale, group norms and cohesion (*see* 12:**3–5**), and job satisfaction are deemed especially important.

2. The Hawthorne experiments

Scientific management predicted that provided: (*i*) workers were 'scientifically' selected (so that their aptitudes corresponded with the requirements of the job); and (*ii*) the conditions of work were carefully planned, closely controlled and tightly supervised, then high productivity would result. Accordingly, scientific management theorists confronted with practical problems of inefficiency, poor quality of output, low employee morale, etc., would naturally seek to change the physical circumstances of work, and then monitor the effects of various alternations. Hence researchers would investigate such matters as how to choose the right workers for each type of job, how to predict the consequences of changes in workplace lighting, heating, humidity, noise, etc. and how best to divide and supervise the work.

In the late 1920s and early 1930s G. Elton Mayo and the Industrial Research team of Harvard University conducted a series of experiments at the Hawthorne plant of the US Western Electric Company in Chicago. At the outset of the study the researchers were disciples of the scientific management approach and thus believed that altering physical working conditions would affect the outputs of the work groups they investigated. In fact, entirely different conclusions emerged.

Details of the experiments

The studies began in 1924 when a number of engineers employed by the company conducted an enquiry into the relationship between workplace illumination and efficiency. Lighting levels were varied and the results on output observed. No clear relations could be discerned. Moreover, it seemed that output increased *whenever* a group knew it was being studied regardless of whether lighting was increased or turned down!

Elton Mayo was brought in during 1927. His brief was to analyse the causes of tiredness in work groups and the effects of variations in equipment and working conditions. He placed six female 'Relay Assembly Room' workers aged between 19 and 29 (average age 22) into a separate working area for a period of two years. Thirteen separate changes in working conditions, hours and incentive schemes were implemented at various times during the test period – each change lasting between four and 12 weeks.

Further experiments were applied to a 'Bank Wiring Room' comprising 14 specially selected male workers. A researcher sat in with the group for 18 months during 1930–32 and observed its behaviour. In addition to the experiments, over 21,000 employees of the Western Electric Company were interviewed between 1929 and 1932 in an attempt to establish employee attitudes towards their work.

Results of the study

Mayo and his associates reported the following results from their investigations:

(a) Significant increases in production occurred during periods when working conditions remained unaltered.

(b) Output sometimes continued to increase when physical conditions were made worse!

(c) The subjects of the study began to work as a team and wholeheartedly co-operated with the experiments. They felt they had become important employees and this of itself contributed to high team spirit.

(d) The social organisation of the work group and group norms and standards governed actual behaviour; not managerial directives and / or financial incentive systems.

3. Criticisms of the Hawthorne experiments

Mayo's investigations have been criticised on the following grounds:

(a) Observations of a small group of individuals should not be used to justify a general theory of human behaviour.

(b) The results obtained might have been nothing more than the consequence of operant conditioning (*see* 6:**3**) of the workers concerned (i.e. the subjects of the experiments *learned* to respond in ways they believed would meet with the approval of the investigators).

(c) Similar experiments have yielded different results.

(d) The later experiments were conducted against the economic background of the stock market crash and the onset of the depression of the 1930s. These conditions were unusual and bound to affect employees' attitudes.

(e) Western Electric was a non-union firm and at the time of the experiments was actively involved in preventing unionisation of the company. Attitudes of unionised workers might have been quite different from those recorded.

4. Major propositions of the human relations school

The fundamental propositions of the human relations approach are as follows:

(a) The amount of work a person does depends not so much on physical strength or dexterity, and not even on the physical conditions in which tasks are performed. Rather, it depends on the social conditions surrounding the work.

(b) Non-economic rewards can motivate workers more than high wages; feelings of happiness and security often result from factors independent of pay.

(c) Specialisation and the division of labour might not be efficient. Giving workers a wide variety of tasks – some of which require the exercise of initiative and discretion – can stimulate employees' interest in their work to the point where productivity actually increases.

(d) Individuals perceive themselves as members of groups. Norms of behaviour emanate from standards set by the group to which workers belong, and not from standards imposed by management.

5. Contributions of the human relations school

The major contributions of the human relations approach are that it:

(a) was the first to recognise explicitly the role and importance of interpersonal relations in group behaviour at work

(b) critically re-examined the relationship between wages and motivation

(c) questioned the presumption that society consists of a horde of mercenary individuals each attempting selfishly to maximise their personal self-interest

(d) showed how social and technical systems (*see* 20:**7**, **13–14**) interrelate

(e) highlighted links between job satisfaction and productivity.

6. Criticisms of the human relations approach

The human relations approach has been attacked for its seemingly unrealistic altruism. Organisational needs and objectives can vary enormously depending on current environmental circumstances. Against backgrounds of fierce commercial competition, ideological concerns for personal development and individual human rights (laudable objectives in themselves) can appear naive and implausible. In particular, the existence of conflicts of interest in industry has to be recognised. It is not necessarily the case that employees will feel they should pull together as a team. Other criticisms are that the approach:

(a) underestimates the effects of organisational structure on individual behaviour

(b) views organisations as closed systems (*see* **24** below) and ignores political, economic and other environmental forces

(c) does not explain the influence of labour unions on employee attitudes and behaviour

(d) overestimates the motivation, the desire to participate in decision making, and the occupational self-awareness of many employees. Not everyone wants to exercise initiative or to control their work. Indeed, many people have little idea of what they actually expect or desire from the employment experience and thus welcome directions imposed by a higher level of authority.

(e) focuses attention on the influence of small groups while neglecting the effects of the wider social structures within which groups are embedded.

Note also that the empirical studies upon which many of the conclusions of the human relations approach are based involved small numbers of subjects who themselves represented a particular culture at a particular historical moment. Social environments and perspectives have altered radically over the last half century and continue to change rapidly.

7. Neo-human relations approaches

A number of sub-schools have emerged within the human relations framework. The various sub-schools differ in respect of the following:

(a) The content of the material studied. Some insist that leadership style is the major determinant of employee behaviour, others emphasis individual psychosocial differences, the role of job design, etc.

(b) Whether they study the effects of external variables (political systems, for example).

(c) How they view the role of empirical research in relation to abstract theory, e.g. whether they believe that the basic forces that motivate workers can be observed and accurately measured.

(d) How they interpret the relationship between the way people feel and what people actually do, particularly as this affects patterns of interaction between individuals.

(e) The mechanisms that researchers believe contribute to the formation and change of attitudes.

8. Structuralism

The structuralist school is a derivative of the human relations approach. It regards conflict between individuals and their organisations as inevitable and (importantly) not always undesirable. In particular, structuralists argue that:

(a) Each organisation is to some extent unique and has therefore special problems requiring specific approaches.

(b) Large organisations are usually complex and contain many groups with disparate and incompatible interests.

(c) Frustrations and disagreements between factional interests inevitably arise.

(d) Formal procedures based on pluralistic assumptions (*see* 10:**17**) are necessary to resolve conflicts.

PARTICIPATION

9. Role of participation

Advocates of the human relations approach argue that the participation of employees in decisions that affect their working lives is essential for effective management. Participation can occur through:

- management/worker negotiating committees
- suggestion schemes
- worker directors on the boards of companies
- financial participation
- autonomous work groups
- joint consultation.

Purposes of participation

These include the improvement of the quality of working life plus increased business efficiency. Participation should enhance employee motivation and reduce industrial strife. At the national level, governments sometimes see worker participation in management decisions as a means for improving overall corporate productivity and hence for enhancing the nation's international competitiveness. The European Commission has always supported the involvement of employee representatives in management decisions on the grounds that it develops social cohesion, underwrites the principle of fair treatment for labour and acts as a counterbalance to the concentration of power in the hands of a small number of business organisations. Hence the Commission has proposed a number of schemes for involving employee representatives in the management of firms.

Other purposes of participation include:

- Increasing workers' job satisfaction
- Providing employees with a means for relating their own self-interests to those of the firm

- Inculcating in workers the belief that management wishes to be fair and just, and that management is taking employee welfare seriously
- Enhancing workers' feelings of job security. Decisions on new equipment, rationalisation, mergers, etc., can create great anxiety among the workforce. Involving employee representatives in these matters helps remove the fear of the unknown as workers will at least be kept fully informed of the latest developments.

10. Joint consultation

Here, management retains control over the decision-making process, but seeks to utilise the energy and initiative of the workforce by involving it in decision-making activities. Management informs employees of its plans and opinions on various issues, and invites comments from workers' representatives. The advantage to management of joint consultation is that expert advice is obtained from employees who possess detailed knowledge of shop-floor procedures and conditions. Also, workers who, through participation, are able to exert limited control over their working environments are likely to be more co-operative, with resulting benefits to efficiency. Further advantages are that:

(a) The implementation of new methods might be facilitated as the need for change is explained and discussed.

(b) Employees are given the opportunity to draw management's attention to their concerns (including grievances) in a forum not connected with (possibly confrontational) collective bargaining machinery.

(c) Management/worker communication is generally improved.

(d) Management and labour come to see issues from each other's points of view and to understand each other's problems.

(e) It provides management with valuable information from the workforce.

Employees frequently complain, however, that managements commonly desire consultation during periods of crisis when economies have to made, but are reluctant to consult the workforce when firms are experiencing success – for fear of provoking demands for higher pay and better conditions.

Objectives of joint consultation include:

(a) Creation of a forum for exchanges of views on matters of mutual interest to management and the workforce

(b) The critical examination of problems and the determination of solutions acceptable to all the parties involved

(c) Provision of an efficient channel of communication for management to announce its future plans and to receive workers' comments on them.

Drawbacks to joint consultation

Problems with joint consultation can include:

(a) Managements might raise issues at a joint consultation meeting that should really be the subject of collective bargaining.

(b) Employee representatives may wish only to discuss immediate workplace problems whereas management might want only to discuss long-term plans.

(c) Management may see the consultation process as little more than a device for passing on information, while employee representatives might want the opportunity to examine various options and recommend a decision.

(d) Bureaucratic joint consultation procedures are perhaps outdated in the modern world where progressive companies apply a range of more sophisticated means for involving employees in management decisions (group problem-solving, quality circles, etc.).

(e) Joint consultation might be used by management as a device for minimising union influence within the organisation. Arguably, joint consultation becomes redundant in firms with comprehensive and effective collective bargaining machinery.

Joint consultation, moreover, is not suitable for discussion of issues where management and unions have fundamentally conflicting interests.

11. Techniques of joint consultation

Techniques for joint consultation vary from consultative committees containing employee representation, through to briefing groups with two-way communication. To succeed, a joint consultation system requires from management a genuine willingness to listen sympathetically to divergent views, to explain and justify proposals and to enter into genuine discussions. Obviously, a joint consultation scheme will fall into disrepute if management persistently listens to employee representatives' opinions and then proceeds to ignore them. Joint consultation must not be seen to *compete* with normal management/employee bargaining procedures.

Meetings should be held within working hours and convened on (at least) a monthly or bi-monthly basis. Some schemes rotate the chair of the joint consultation committee annually between management and employee representatives. All levels of employee and major sections within the firm should be represented.

Joint consultation procedures require decisions concerning:

- how it will be done (institutional and organisational arrangements), where and when
- whether consultation is to occur *before* decisions are made or *during* the decision-making process
- the scope of the issues that will be subject to consultation
- whether separate joint consultation bodies will exist for differing occupational categories or divisions within the company.

Institutional and organisational arrangements need to encompass such matters as who will chair meetings, periods of office, numbers and constituencies of employee representatives and their method of election, periods of office, voting procedures (where appropriate), and so on

Failure of joint consultation

Reasons for the collapse of joint consultation procedures are many and varied, and might include:

- unclear objectives
- poor performance by the chairperson
- lack of trust and commitment on the part of the participants
- apathy resulting from the amount of time and effort devoted to discussing minor issues
- deliberately disruptive behaviour by management or union representatives
- breakdowns in communication between union members of a joint consultation committee and the workers they are supposed to represent.

12. Worker directors

These are directors elected to the board directly by all employees, or appointed by existing union officials. They may or may not be excluded from major decisions on capital investment, organisation structure, appointment of key management personnel, and so on. The essential argument for having worker directors is that since many employees devote much of their working lives to a particular firm they are entitled, through elected representatives, to some say in how the firm is run.

Against this is the fact that firms are owned by entrepreneurs and/or shareholders who put their personal capital at risk. Owners of firms may resent the imposition of worker directors who, in part, will control the owners' assets without having been elected by the owners themselves. Specific problems facing worker directors include the following:

(a) Possible reluctance of other board members to disclose confidential information to employees' representatives, in case it is passed on to union negotiators. But if worker directors agree not to reveal sensitive data, they face criticism from union colleagues who expect them to divulge information gained in board meetings. To whom does the worker director owe loyalty, management or the union?

(b) Hostility and social ostracism from other board members, who might conduct secret board meetings to decide key issues without the presence of worker directors.

(c) The fact that special privileges are afforded to worker directors – higher status, preferential treatment, expenses, time off for board meetings, perhaps even higher wages – might cause them to lose contact with the workers who elected them.

(d) Although a company's board of directors is nominally the most powerful body in the enterprise, real power might in fact lie elsewhere.

(e) To the extent that a worker director can influence the board's decisions, he or she will be presenting arguments *as an individual* and not as an employee representative as happens with collective bargaining: there is no question of negotiation occurring during board meetings.

(f) Worker directors may be patronised but effectively ignored.

(g) Company boards take *strategic* decisions the outcomes to which might not be visible for several years, so the employees the worker director represents may not see any tangible short-term benefits to electing worker directors.

(h) Boards of directors have to deal with a wide variety of issues, not just employee relations. Board members other than worker directors will have been selected for their knowledge of and ability to contribute to these wider discussions. Worker directors who have no experience of practical management but who wish nevertheless to express opinions on all matters could impede effective decision-making.

(i) Worker directors may not be able to relate their immediate workplace concerns with the need to adopt an overall perspective on the enterprise. Can worker directors realistically be expected to think strategically?

Perhaps the most immediately useful functions of a worker director are to voice criticism of management's stated intentions and to articulate the workplace point of view. Management is confronted with new and different interpretations of issues. Also, the presence on the board of employee representatives underlines senior management's commitment to employee welfare, and a climate of mutual confidence and co-operation between management and labour may emerge.

Employee representation on company boards is compulsory in Belgium, Germany, Luxembourg and the Netherlands. In France, voluntary arrangements on this matter are possible which, once entered into, can thereafter be enforced by law.

13. Supervisory boards

In Germany, Belgium and the Netherlands there exist legal requirements compelling large companies to have two-tier boards of directors. The lower tier is an 'executive board', comprising managerial employees of the firm responsible for the day-to-day operational management. Above this is a 'supervisory board', which takes strategic decisions in relation to the overall direction of the enterprise. By law, employee representatives must sit on the supervisory boards of companies in these countries. The functions of supervisor boards include:

- the appointment and dismissal of executive managers and the determination of their remunerations
- deciding the overall direction of the enterprise (its products, markets, major new investments, etc.)

- matters concerning mergers and takeovers and how the company is to be financed.

Two-tier boards were first used in Germany in the 1860s, when the German banks began making large financial investments in industry and demanded representation at board-room level in order to protect their interests. The *advantages* claimed for having a separate supervisory board are that:

(a) General policy-making is undertaken objectively and independently without interference from executives with vested interests in outcomes.

(b) Interpersonal rivalries among lower level managers can be ignored.

(c) Employee interests may be considered in the absence of line managers who control workers.

(d) Tough decisions that adversely affect senior line managers can be taken more easily.

Problems with supervisory boards are that:

(a) The people who determine basic strategy might be remote from the day-to-day realities of executive management.

(b) Decision-making is slowed down by the need to go through two separate boards for decisions on certain issues.

(c) Confusions could arise between executive and supervisory boards, with the decisions of each not being properly understood by the other.

14. Worker directors on supervisory boards

The general advantages and disadvantages of having employee representatives on company boards are discussed in **12**. Specific implications of having worker directors on supervisory boards are:

(a) The knowledge and experience of employee representatives can be directly applied to *strategic* decisions without employee representatives having to argue with line managers.

(b) Matters concerning human relations are automatically elevated to the highest level of decision-making within the organisation. Note that since the supervisory board appoints and dismisses senior managers then the latter will be highly sensitive to worker directors' views, and to human relations issues generally.

(c) Arguably, the presence of employee representatives on a supervisory board facilitates the financial stability of the company, because worker directors' concerns for employees' continuity of employment invariably cause them to argue in favour of profit retention and the accumulation of reserves to guard against temporary economic downturns. Also, employee representatives will oppose any merger or takeover that could result in redundancies.

15. Suggestion schemes

Firms introducing suggestion schemes often experience large financial benefits, and employee motivation increases substantially. The problem is deciding who will receive the benefits from suggestions that result in large financial savings. In most countries the patent rights of a new invention are vested in the firm which employs the inventor, and not in the individual concerned. Workers may be discouraged from suggesting improvements unless they are guaranteed a substantial return. Related problems are that:

(a) Once a suggestion is submitted it becomes known to the firm. How can the inventor subsequently prove his/her claim to be the true initiator of the idea?

(b) If a firm offers a reward of a constant percentage of the financial returns from a suggestion, how can the individual employee obtain access to the company's records to check the accuracy of the firm's estimate of the financial benefits obtained?

(c) If a firm rejects an employee's suggestion, what can prevent the firm subsequently taking it up when the employee has left the organisation, and not rewarding the inventor?

Suggestion schemes operate in many companies and are generally popular with both management and employees. The topics typically covered by a scheme include safety at work, use of materials, efficiency and cost saving, organisation of production and administrative procedures, and the invention of new equipment and techniques. Normally the firm will have a committee consisting of representatives of managers and employees to assess the suggestions and recommend whether they should be adopted, perhaps after taking expert advice.

Advantages to suggestion schemes include the financial benefits that accrue both to the firm and to the employee making the suggestion. There will be higher productivity and less defective production, fewer accidents, and enhanced communication between management and the workforce. Use is made of the employees' ingenuity and creativity; job satisfaction should increase.

If it is to succeed in the long term a suggestion scheme must be well publicised within the organisation (photographs of participating workers in company newsletters, formal presentations of awards, etc.), the monetary rewards to individuals need to be substantial, and a convenient yet secure mechanism for submitting suggestions should exist. Occasional 'suggestion campaigns' focusing on specific issues may be necessary in order to maintain interest in the scheme. Unsuccessful contributors must have the reasons for the rejection of their ideas carefully explained to them.

16. Financial participation

Employees can become part-owners of limited companies through being allocated shares in their firms as a supplement to wages. As part-owners, workers may be motivated into greater effort because they now have direct interests in their employer's profitability. Arguments against the issue of shares to workers include the following:

(a) If workers really want to become shareholders in a company they are free to buy shares on the open market. That they choose not to do so is evidence of their unwillingness to be financially associated with the business.

(b) Shares not allocated to employees would, presumably, be sold to outsiders possibly at lower prices. Employee share distribution schemes – to the extent that they are *alternatives* to higher wages – can thus be interpreted as backdoor methods for firms to raise additional long-term capital.

(c) Financial participation is sometimes used as an alternative to participation schemes that involve workers in management decision-making, creating thereby an impression of participation while not in fact allowing employees any influence over matters relating to their working lives.

(d) There is no immediate link between individual effort and reward.

(e) To the extent that workers accumulate benefits over a long period (as occurs in certain share ownership schemes), they stand to lose this money *as well as* their jobs if the company collapses.

17. Conditions for effective participation

If participation schemes are to succeed they need to satisfy at least some of the following conditions:

(a) Participation should cover substantial matters and not just trivial issues.

(b) The system should be cost effective and not absorb too much management or employee time.

(c) Participation should only apply to matters that the organisation and its workers can control. For example, there is no point in management and employee representatives meeting to discuss government policy or the likelihood of new legislation.

(d) Employees should want to participate and contribute wholeheartedly to the exercise.

(e) Management must sincerely want employees to participate in decision making.

(f) Employees need to be competent to offer sensible and useful ideas to management.

(g) Management should make available to employees whatever information is necessary to enable them to form a considered opinion on relevant issues.

(h) All participants should be clear about the scope and objectives of the system.

18. Advantages and disadvantages of participation

The *advantages* of employee participation in organisational decision making include the following:

(a) It mobilises the talents, resources, experience and expertise of the workforce.

(b) Employees develop their decision-making abilities and administrative skills.

(c) Workers become involved with their work and committed to the organisation.

(d) Management is required to justify its actions to employee representatives and thus will think long and hard about the employee welfare implications of managerial policies.

(e) Workers will usually be more willing to abide by decisions they helped formulate than decisions imposed on them from above.

(f) Bad and unworkable decisions are less likely because those who would have to implement them receive opportunities to point out potential difficulties.

(g) The flow of information through the organisation should increase.

(h) Employees should be less afraid of new working methods and the consequences of change (*see* Chapter 17).

(i) Responsible attitudes are encouraged.

Disadvantages

Opponents of employee participation emphasise that employees do not (usually) own organisations. Owners or their representatives have the right to administer their property in whatever ways they think best – without time-wasting interference from workers' representatives. Management, they argue, is a specialised skill acquired through training and experience: workers have insufficient knowledge of administrative procedures to be good managers. Other criticisms are that:

(a) Much managerial information is confidential in nature, involving personal matters relating to individuals. This should not be disclosed to employees' representatives.

(b) Conflicts of interest between management and labour necessarily occur. These are best resolved through collective bargaining: workers cannot simultaneously represent their colleagues and be part of management. Sooner or later workers' representatives must support unpopular managerial decisions, causing them to lose the confidence of the rank and file.

(c) Participation does not alter fundamental financial realities or a firm's future prospects; businesses can still fail despite extensive prior consultation.

(d) Workers sometimes adopt short-term, mercenary approaches to issues which really require long-term solutions.

(e) Participation can be used to mislead workers into believing they exert an influence on management whereas this is not actually the case.

(f) Organisational decision making might become extremely slow.

(g) Employees might not be competent to comprehend the complex issues sometimes involved in managerial decision-making.

(h) Managers and union representatives could become immersed in the *mechanics* of participation (committee procedures, determination of the scope of the subjects to be discussed, etc.) and lose sight of its fundamental purpose.

(i) Arguably, participation interferes with managerial prerogative (*see* 8:**14**): managers should not have to consider employee interests when making important decisions. According to this view, management's job is to manage; the worker's role is to complete whatever tasks are assigned. Employees have unions and staff associations to protect their interests via collective bargaining and this should be all that is required.

(j) Individual employee participation could undermine collective action and hence a union's ability to organise industrial action. It might be better, therefore, systematically to extend the scope of collective bargaining to include matters currently subject to unilateral management decision-making.

(k) Certain forms of participation (quality circles for example) could require extensive changes in a company's communication system, especially where the firm is organised as a tall hierarchy with a long chain of command.

WORKS COUNCILS

Works councils (referred to as works committees in some countries) are an important feature of the continental European business scene, though not in the United Kingdom. The latter situation is likely to change, however, in consequence of **(a)** the European Commissions's encouragement of the works council system, and **(b)** the growing influence of successful continental EU businesses' organisation structures and management methods as an example to be followed by British companies.

19. Works council in EU countries

These are compulsory for certain sizes of firm (normally defined in terms of a minimum number of employees) in Belgium, Denmark, France, Germany, Greece, Luxembourg, the Netherlands, Portugal and Spain. At present they are not a legal requirement in the UK, Italy or the Irish Republic, but the latter two of these countries are actively considering how they can be introduced on a compulsory basis. In countries where they are required, councils are normally legally obliged to *discuss* particular (specified) matters, and entitled to *take decisions* (effectively giving employee representatives a right of veto) on others.

The ranges of issues involved differ substantially from country to country.

Decision-making powers vary from internal works rules (e.g. the operation of grievance procedures) to recruitment methods and whether the firm is to take on part-time or temporary workers. In Germany and the Netherlands, employee representatives on works councils have the legal right to delay certain important management decisions (on company mergers for instance). Examples of issues that are subject to decision-making by works councils are as follows:

- criteria for hiring temporary staff and for selecting workers for redundancy (Belgium)
- profit sharing agreements (France)
- changes in working hours, training agreements, recruitment and disciplinary procedures (Germany)
- operation of job evaluation schemes, appraisal and grievance procedures, working hours (the Netherlands).

Matters subject to *discussion* by works councils in various EU countries include:

- financial plans and company structures
- acquisitions, physical investments and divestments
- working practices and the introduction of new technology
- proposed incentive schemes and wage payment systems
- company sales, profits and prices
- personnel policies (including recruitment methods)
- health and safety at work.

In Belgium, members of the works council are (legally) bound by confidentiality, and can be prohibited from disclosing sensitive information to other employees. Employers can apply to the Belgian Ministry of Labour to withhold certain information from the works council, although in practice this is extremely rare. German and Portuguese works council members are also statutorily bound by rules on confidentiality.

20. Advantages of works councils

Benefits claimed for the practice of having works council in firms include the following:

(a) The existence of a works council compels management to seek consensus with employee representatives on many important issues, hence avoiding conflicts and disruptive industrial action.

(b) Employees assume *obligations* for the operation of the business as well as rights to consultation. Works councils come to execute certain management functions (allocation of overtime, decisions on working methods, determination of promotion criteria, etc.) that otherwise would have to be undertaken by alternative (and perhaps more costly) management committees. Also, discussions between management and labour encourage the latter to propose new ideas, offer alternative solutions to problems and generally adopt constructive and useful perspectives.

(c) Change can be introduced more easily, since a works council provides a useful forum for explaining the needs for and implications of new methods.

(d) Management benefits as it is quickly made aware of any problems relating to intended developments that are likely to provoke hostile opposition from the workforce and hence can alter its plans in order to remove or minimise employee resistance.

Although it is known that employee apathy frequently results in works councils not operating within many companies in countries where employee representation is legally required, the *existence* of legislative procedures itself can create an environment in which managers are extremely sensitive to the need to consult with and win over the workforce, leading perhaps to greatly improved management/labour relations.

21. Criticisms of the works council system

Opponents of works councils argue as follows:

(a) Wages and conditions of employment in firms with active and influential works councils tend to be higher than elsewhere, possibly causing companies operating works councils to lose competitive advantage.

(b) The administrative costs of running a works council (executive time, rooms, secretarial support, etc.) can be substantial.

(c) Employees may adopt short-term perspectives, and might oppose decisions that would benefit the company in the long run but do not offer many rewards to employees in the immediate future. Innovation and enterprise may be discouraged.

(d) Decision-taking can be slow, and many employee representatives will not have the technical knowledge upon which they can base decisions.

(e) Efficiency improvements that involve shedding labour might be impeded.

(f) Councils can easily degenerate into vehicles for plant-level collective bargaining, undermining normal management/union negotiating machinery.

SYSTEMS THEORY AND THE CONTINGENCY SCHOOL

22. Definition of the systems approach

The systems approach views organisational behaviour as the consequence of the interaction of social and technical factors both within the organisation itself *and* between the organisation and its environment. The school emerged from dissatisfaction with the rigid intellectual straitjackets imposed by the classical and human relations approaches, and was reinforced by a number of important empirical studies (notably those of Lawrence and Lorsch, and Trist and Bamforth (*see* 20:**11–12**)).

Every aspect of the organisation is regarded as interrelated and interdependent. Thus, management's task is to:

- identify the key parts of the wider system
- determine the nature and extent of the interdependence of one part (sub-system) with others
- establish procedures for co-ordinating the system in order that it may achieve its organisational goals.

23. Origins and nature of the systems approach

In the 1930s Chester Barnard noted that, in addition to official structures, organisations typically possess powerful informal systems. Within an organisation there is upward and downward communication and unofficial leaders emerge. The organisation is a system inside which several networks of individuals interact, and which itself interacts with the wider social and economic environment. Many other writers have developed the theme of the organisation as a system dependent on interrelations between its component parts and with the outside world.

Systems theory emphasises the significance of interrelations between the various internal components of an organisation, and relations between the organisation and its environment. Firms, for example, exist in 'open' systems (*see* **25** below). They have relations with customers, suppliers, neighbours, and local and national governments. The usefulness of a particular management style might be affected by such relationships. For instance, laws exist to govern the conduct of industrial relations between firms and employees; limited liability companies are required to apply certain rules regarding rights and duties of shareholders; there are laws to protect customers from untruthful advertisements, and so on.

Systems factors

The systems approach enables changes in environmental conditions and their effects on management to be analysed methodically. An example of a systems factor might be an alteration in the individuals to whom an organisation is accountable; the structure and management style of a firm which must account for its actions to only one or two people will probably differ from the approach adopted by a firm that is accountable to a large number of shareholders. Again, a firm that must explain its behaviour to the government is likely to act in particular ways. Managements which are required to justify their actions to employees will have different attitudes from those which are not.

Systems theory emphasises the need for those in control of a system to define its boundaries clearly. Are, for example, customers to be considered an integral part of the organisation, or does the system end at the point of the sale? Often, a system can be accurately described through specifying where its boundaries lie, and many insights into how a particular system operates can be obtained by analysing what happens at the boundaries between the system in question and others.

24. Objectives of systems theory

The aim of systems theory is to bring together and integrate several approaches to and aspects of organisation. Individuals are known to possess attitudes, beliefs and perspectives deriving from a multitude of sources. As employees of organisations, moreover, people continually interact with others and with their wider environments in attempts to fulfil their material and psycho-social needs. The accurate analysis of how individuals pursue these interactions, their causes and their effects on the working of the overall system, is the main goal of systems theory.

25. Closed and open systems

A *closed* system is one that (*i*) is independent of its environment; (*ii*) determines its own destiny; and (*iii*) controls its own internal relationships. The continuing existence of a closed system does not depend on it entering transactions with the outside world.

Open systems, conversely, are in continuous contact with their environments, and the boundaries of such systems are neither rigid nor easily defined. They have the following characteristics:

(a) They transform inputs obtained from the environment into outputs returned to the environment (e.g. a firm transforms labour, materials and capital into goods and services).

(b) They must enter transactions with their environments (e.g. a firm must recruit workers and persuade customers to purchase its goods).

(c) They need to be able to adapt to external change.

Inputs and outputs

Inputs include human resources (i.e. how many workers are available, their skills and ability levels); physical resources, such as plant and equipment, raw materials, land and buildings, machines, tools, etc.; and financial resources, such as cash, loans, trade credit, and other monetary assets.

The process that transforms inputs into outputs involves:

- organisational policies and procedures
- decision-making systems (*see* Chapter 15)
- control mechanisms (*see* Chapter 16)
- the culture of the organisation (*see* Chapter 20).

Outputs might be in the form of physical goods, improved services, enhanced efficiency of the system, higher wages for staff and/or greater profits for shareholders.

Constraints on a system could include technical factors, actual or potential behaviours of competitors, resource limitations (skills shortages, for example), and the wider macroeconomic and political situation of the country in which the organisation is located.

Organisations as open systems

An organisation is a collection of people with a set of objectives and a number of sub-systems, usually including a technical sub-system for producing goods and a psycho-social sub-system for regulating social relationships and helping individuals attain their personal needs. Clearly, organisations are open systems since they: (*i*) operate within a wider society that impinges on their freedom to behave as they would like (through laws, social conventions, etc.); (*ii*) have flexible boundaries separating them from the wider society; (*iii*) undertake exchanges of information and resources with the outside world.

Specific issues of interest to systems theory include:

(a) whether the organisation should recruit its senior managers externally (open systems approach) or promote from within (closed system approach)

(b) where and how to raise finance, e.g. from retained earnings or from outside sources (share issues, for instance)

(c) the extent to which the organisation should use external agents or consultants

(d) attitudes towards after-sales service, provision of product guarantees, customer care facilities, etc.

(e) the degree of the organisation's involvement with trade associations and outside professional bodies.

26. Advantages and criticisms of the systems approach

Advantages of the systems approach include:

(a) It is *holistic* in that all aspects of an organisation's activities are considered.

(b) The effects of changes in one element of a system can be traced through to changes in others.

(c) Environmental influences are explicitly recognised.

(d) Relationships between inputs and outputs are examined.

(e) Models (*see* 1:9) depicting cause and effect within particular systems can be constructed.

The main problem with systems theory is that it suggests few tangible propositions about how exactly managers should behave. It is one thing to think about businesses in systems terms, but quite another to translate these thoughts into concrete action. Systems theory is abstract and lacks immediately discernible applications. Further criticisms of the approach are as follows:

(a) Organisational systems consist of and are run by people. Accordingly, interpersonal relations might be more important than particular input/output structures and organisational forms, which in any case are subject to human control.

(b) Systems theory has little to say about the causes of motivation to work hard within various types of system.

(c) The boundaries of a system might change according to circumstances and over time (changing patterns of distribution, for instance).

(d) Different members of the same system may have entirely different interpretations of its structure and aims.

(e) The actions of a single individual can instantly transform the nature of a system.

(f) Systems theory cannot of itself explain organisational behaviour without taking other considerations into account.

(g) Often, organisational relationships are highly complex. In these cases the application of the systems approach might naively simplify what in fact is an enormously complicated problem. There is a vast range of variables potentially relevant to organisational performance so that the specification of just a few inputs and constraints is bound to be arbitrary to some degree.

(h) Some advocates of the systems approach have used it to justify centralisation of administrative procedures (*see* Chapter 21) in circumstances where this might not be entirely appropriate. The tendency to centralisation follows from the adoption of a holistic perspective: hence the desire to concentrate decision making at the apex of the organisation.

27. The contingency school

This emerged from the systems approach, and drew much support from the empirical studies conducted by Joan Woodward, C. Perrow, and T. Burns and G.M. Stalker (*see* **20:13**). Contingency theorists emphasise the need for flexibility in both organisational design and leadership style, and assert the impossibility of generalising about appropriate management behaviour for differing situations.

Each set of circumstances is regarded as unique. For example, a military exercise might require the coercion of large numbers of unwilling soldiers to perform dangerous, unpopular tasks. A management style relevant to this situation will not be the same as one suitable for managing a business! Similarly, circumstances within particular organisations vary between departments and over time.

The contingency approach is diagnostic rather than prescriptive, suggesting that the role of management is to identify characteristics which define situations and then apply management techniques appropriate to specific circumstances. The obvious problem is the vast range of variables – environmental, social, physical, economic, legal, technical, industrial – potentially relevant to each situation.

Inadequacy of human relations prescriptions

Whereas feelings of contentment, happiness and job satisfaction can improve workers' performances, not all working environments can be made satisfying or even interesting for the staff involved. Some work is necessarily unpleasant but still has to be done. The human relations approach relates operational efficiency to worker satisfaction. Unfortunately, it might not be possible to create pleasant working environments or adjust conditions to meet the social needs of employees. In this case, financial reward is probably the key motivator, and a contingency theorist would recommend payments which directly relate wages and effort, as would an advocate of the scientific management school. Contingency approaches to organisational design are examined in Chapter 21.

28. Problems with the contingency approach

Adoption of the contingency approach releases managers from the rigid straitjackets imposed by other schools. Managers simply dovetail their behaviour to the needs of various situations. However, the contingency approach does involve certain problems:

(a) A manager who behaves in this manner may appear insincere and inconsistent to colleagues and (particularly) to subordinates. One approach is adopted today, and possibly an entirely different approach tomorrow, according to circumstances. Subordinates and others never know what to expect from the manager. Advocates of the contingency approach might object to this assertion on the grounds that management's role is to allocate different managers to the roles and situations for which they are best suited. In practice, however, most managers will necessarily experience a variety of situations and need to occupy several roles in the course of their work.

(b) The individual manager may not be sufficiently skilled or mature to be able to change his or her approach from one situation to the next, especially if the manager has not been trained in the techniques of contingency management.

(c) It may be entirely appropriate to apply certain basic principles regardless of circumstances, particularly where professional ethics and moral issues are concerned.

29. Post-Fordism

The term 'post-Fordism' is sometimes used to describe the changes in working methods necessitated by the shift from standardised mass production associated with classical scientific management techniques and towards customised production using flexible manufacturing, total quality management, and so on (Sorge and Streeck 1988; Warde 1990). 'Fordism' involved the application of the division of labour to its maximum extent, low-cost production for mass consumer markets, and standardised work routines offering employees little discretion over how they completed their duties. The term arose in consequence of the Ford Motor Company's adoption of scientific management (see 3 to 8 above) in the 1920s. Key elements of post-Fordist production systems are as follows:

(a) Labour flexibility, with employees undertaking a wide range of tasks.

(b) Batch production for multiple niche markets. Firms react quickly to changes in customer tastes and preferences.

(c) Widespread use of the latest information technology and manufacturing techniques.

(d) Great need for trained and qualified labour.

(e) A large peripheral workforce (*see* Chapter 22) with little job security.

(f) Extensive use of sub-contracting, as opposed to company takeovers and mergers.

(g) Output that increasingly competes in international markets in terms of quality and product design rather than the price of the item.

(h) Teamwork and the empowerment (*see* 21:**14**) of working groups and of individuals.

(i) Decentralised collective bargaining, performance-related pay and the hiring of large numbers of workers on individual contracts.

(j) Employees themselves deciding how to complete jobs.

(k) Intense concern for quality management.

Several wider economic and political changes are said to have accompanied the move to post-Fordism, notably the privatisation of state-owned enterprises, a reduction in the level of state intervention in industry, less legally enforceable employment protection for workers, and a rise in corporate concern for employee welfare. Post-Fordism production requires different approaches to job design; the recruitment, selection and training of workers; work supervision; and employee reward systems; than for standardised mass production technologies.

Criticisms of post-Fordist theory are that:

(a) It only applies within a limited number of companies. Mass production is still common, while the latest IT and flexible manufacturing systems are simply not available to numerous small businesses.

(b) Governments continue to intervene in private sector economic activity.

(c) Extensive state-sponsored employee welfare and social security programmes are to be found in all economically advanced countries.

THE POSTMODERNIST CRITIQUE

30. Modernism and postmodernism

The term 'modernism' is sometimes used to describe the ways in which modern society is organised and the basic assumptions underlying social relationships. The 'modern' world is said to be characterised by:

- the advance of science and belief that science is capable of solving all problems: medical, social, managerial, etc.
- specialisation, the division of labour, bureaucratic forms of organisation, hierarchies and other management methods derived from the classical school (*see* Chapter 2)
- rationality and a logical approach to the analysis of social issues
- belief that truth can be discovered through the application of scientific method
- conviction that human beings have control of their own destiny
- codification of knowledge
- the creation of distinct functions within organisations (marketing, personnel, financial management, etc.).

'Postmodernism' challenges the viability of the modern world's institutions, practices and presumptions, arguing that:

- Science has failed to improve the human conditions. Social science in particular is pilloried for asking trivial questions and for being more concerned with individuals advancing their personal philosophical opinions than with the pursuit of truth. It is now recognised that the application of science does not necessarily solve social (or many other) problems. Indeed, scientific attempts to deal with social ills can actually make matters worse (use of scientific management techniques in factories for instance – *see* Chapter 2). If the scientific approach were valid it would already have taken care of most social problems, which is clearly not the case. Scientific theories come and go, and frequently involve diametrically opposing suggestions.
- Technological progress typically occurs *via* big periodic leaps, not by small increments. Each giant step is invariably the result of *disproving* previous conventional wisdom.
- All the major ideologies that promised *inevitable* victory (notably Fascism and Marxism) have been discredited.
- The fundamental legitimacy of hierarchical social structures is questionable.
- Attitudes and practices that were once considered revolutionary have now been absorbed into the 'cultural establishment'.
- Mass communications are so influential that the 'real' world is becoming a copy of the images that the communications media have themselves created.

In short, the postmodern world is one in which there are no certainties. Everything is subject to unpredictable change.

The end of history!

A fundamental reason for studying the history of anything is to learn lessons from the past in order to apply them in the future. But the world has altered so comprehensively (so postmodernists allege) that there *is no connection whatsoever* between what has happened in the past and what is likely to happen in the future. Historical trends and tendencies have been broken. Thus, 'history is dead' in the sense that existing assumptions are no longer valid. The sorts of question that used to be asked are now irrelevant: basic concepts need to be redefined; completely fresh thinking is necessary. History is regarded as having a useful function only to the extent that it supplies a stock of myths and stories (*see* **31**) that can be used to illustrate past happenings.

31. Implications of postmodernism

Clearly the postmodern world has enormous implications for business management. Deregulation, advances in information technology, the globalisation of markets, the rise of consumerism and environmentalism, alterations in organisational culture and other transformations of business situations generate the need for firms that are flexible and responsive to change. Practical manifestations of postmodern society include:

- Disillusion with established ways of doing things
- Privatisation of industry
- Image-based marketing
- Realignment of political parties and the redefinition of the political 'right' and 'left'
- Disdain for hierarchies and orthodox authority systems. Authority is assumed to derive from rules and contexts that are increasingly irrelevant in the postmodern world. Hence, authority only needs to be accepted on a piecemeal and temporary basis.
- Belief in the efficacy of small-scale production and in technologies that meet human needs rather than increasing the wealth of large corporations
- Concern for the physical environment
- Involvement of the customer in business decisions
- Integration of theories taken from widely disparate academic fields (literary criticism, astro-physics and management science for example)
- The demise of corporate planning, which is said to be ineffective in turbulent commercial environments (Moult 1990)
- Increasing awareness of the importance of cultural, symbols, myths, stories and rituals in explaining how organisations actually function. Myths are descriptions of events that are wholly imaginary, as opposed to 'stories' which are based on truth. Myths and stories are passed on and illustrate and perpetuate existing perspectives on issues and events. Eventually, as myths and stories are repeated a combination of truth and fiction emerges which, in effect, become 'reality' to the people exposed to them. Myths and stories commonly arise about particular individuals, post successes and failures, crises and other happenings. They are used to relate the present to the past and hence to *explain* and *justify* the current situation. Often, myths concern 'heroes', i.e. role models to which people aspire, but involving people who left the organisation long ago.

Problems with postmodernism

Although the modernistic application of logic, objectivity and rationality to problem solving has its difficulties, it does provide a concrete basis for action. The world would be much worse off had modernism never occurred, and arguably there is at present no *viable* alternative to the modernist perspective. Hence, the postmodernist so-called 'flight from rationality' is allegedly naive and simplistic. In its extreme form, postmodernism claims that there are no such things as objectivity, rationality or valid grounds for choosing any particular theory, and no values against which behaviour should be compared. Everything is subjective, so there are *no* criteria for taking decisions, organising work or selecting and developing projects. Critics suggest that nothing would ever get done if everyone thought in this manner. Further criticisms of the postmodern approach include the following:

(a) Postmodernism follows modernism; but it is unclear when modernism itself started. Did modernism begin with the scientific revolution of the seventeenth century, with the Italian Renaissance of the fourteenth century, with the industrial revolution, or when?

(b) The feudal-modernist-postmodernist evolution alleged to have occurred in Western societies is not paralleled by historical developments in other parts of the world. Hence the modernist/postmodernist debate is perhaps relevant only to Western culture and does not have a *universal* application.

(c) There is much disagreement over whether the postmodern world is an *extension* of the modern world, or a radical departure from it.

Progress test 3

1. Explain the major differences between the classical and human relations approaches to management theory.

2. What were the objectives of the Hawthorne experiments?

3. List the major criticisms of the human relations school.

4. Explain the principal assertions of the structuralist approach.

5. How can management secure the enthusiastic participation of employees in decisions that affect their working lives?

6. What is a worker director? List the main problems a worker director might face.

7. What are the conditions for effective participation?

8. Define the systems approach to organisational theory.

9. State the objectives of the systems school of management theory.

10. Explain the differences between closed and open systems.

11. List the criticisms of the systems approach.

12. What are the relationships between systems theory and the contingency approach?

13. What are the advantages of works councils?

14. Define 'post-Fordism'.

15. List the implications of 'postmodernism' for business management.

Part Two

INDIVIDUALS AND THE ORGANISATION

4

INDIVIDUAL DIFFERENCES

GENERAL CONSIDERATIONS

1. How individuals differ

Physically, humans are very similar – they (normally) have two arms, two legs, five fingers on each hand, five toes on each foot, etc. Differences do exist – anatomical, racial, those relating to strength and vigour, etc. – but these are small compared with the similarities. Fundamental individual differences are more likely to occur in the psychological and social dimensions of the people being considered. Humans vary with respect to their:

- personality
- motivation (*see* Chapter 8)
- behaviour
- perceptions
- attitudes
- mental abilities (*see* Chapter 5).

This chapter explores the sources and organisational implications of such differences. These are important for the management of organisations because were it not for individual differences it would be possible to treat all people in exactly the same manner and know precisely how they are likely to respond. Clearly, this is not the case. Thus, individuals and groups need to be treated differently in order to get the very best out of them. Each person and group will possess a certain degree of motivation and willingness to work independently.

2. Inheritance, instinct and socialisation

To what extent are behavioural tendencies inherited and to what extent are they learned? This question has intrigued social analysts for generations, and it has no straightforward answer.

Without doubt, many physiological features are inherited. If a very tall man marries a very tall woman there is a high probability that the resulting offspring will themselves be tall. But suppose two highly intelligent people marry; will their children be more intelligent than the children of parents who are not very bright, and if so what is the cause of this outcome? (Intelligent parents might educate their children better and encourage them to be interested in academic matters, hence causing them to appear clever even though the offspring themselves have no more innate mental ability than anyone else.) Intelligence is considered further in Chapter 5.

Instinct

An *instinct* is an unlearned and innate disposition which causes a living organism to perceive, act, feel or think in a certain way. It is something with which the organism is born. Certain types of fish (salmon, for example) instinctively return from thousands of miles to the places of their birth; homing pigeons instinctively fly to their owners' lofts. In humans, the urge for sexual gratification is perhaps a good example of an instinctive drive – it develops naturally and of itself without having to be learnt. Instincts are inherited and are passed on within the species from one generation to the next. Are certain aspects of human behaviour (as opposed to drives such as hunger or sexual frustration that trigger behaviour) instinctual? Is there, for example, an instinctual aggressiveness within human beings?

Arguments for the existence of inherited instinctual behaviour in humans

Those who believe in the inheritance of behavioural tendencies might suggest the following (contentious) arguments:

(a) Certain human activities endure through the centuries (e.g. the urge to wage war, to conquer and to dominate) suggesting the existence of inherited instincts in such respects.

(b) Some seemingly irrational human sentiments, such as fear of the dark, jealousy, curiosity or sympathy can be easily explained if one assumes that they have an inherited instinctual base.

(c) Certain parts of the world have always been more prosperous than other (geographically similar) regions, implying that the inhabitants of prosperous areas are somehow innately better than people in the rest of the world and that the innate factors causing the superior performance must therefore have been passed down through the generations.

Arguments against

Analysts opposed to the idea of inherited behaviour patterns might argue as follows:

(a) Behaviour sometimes categorised as instinctive is in fact merely a *biological reaction* to human need (e.g. reactions to hunger, thirst, sexual starvation, etc.). It is obvious that these needs exist; but how they are satisfied are social rather than instinctual phenomena. Thus, for example, society has an economic system for distributing food and other goods, and social institutions (marriage, for example) for handling sexual relations. Otherwise anarchy would prevail, which is clearly not the case.

(b) Although there is much to suggest the existence of instinct in non-human animals, there is no firm scientific and/or empirical evidence to prove that the same is true of humans. Equally, environment and upbringing is *known* to be massively influential on how people behave.

(c) Those who claim that certain people have inherited superior mental abilities are in fact merely attempting to prop up the existing social system, pretending that the individuals who currently control society enjoy privileges because they are innately superior, whereas in fact their wealth is the result of the exploitation of others.

3. Physique

This can be defined as the attributes of the body; its size and shape, its speed and strength of movement, the efficiency of its senses. Physical qualities are basically determined by heredity, though they can be developed or suppressed by upbringing or training. For example, there are inherited tendencies to be short or tall, fast or slow, but a poor diet will cause a person to be shorter than otherwise might have been the case, and appropriate training will enable an athlete to run longer and faster than before.

It is easy to measure most physical characteristics objectively, i.e. measurements of height, weight, eyesight, reaction speed, etc., can be quickly and simply made, independent observers producing identical results. Under modern conditions physical differences are not very important in placing individuals in appropriate jobs. The advance of technology has greatly reduced the number of jobs in which great physical endurance or strength is required, and instrumentation often decreases the need to rely on the senses of touch, hearing, etc.

Eyesight is the most important physical factor in the employment field; in some manual jobs it is necessary for employees to have above-average eyesight or perfect colour vision. In other jobs, co-ordination of limb movements or speed of reaction may be important. Tests are available to measure these qualities.

4 Sexual and racial differences

The difference between men and women lies in the chromosome (i.e. genetic material) structure of human tissue. At the moment of conception, chromosomes contributed by the male complement an equal number of chromosomes present in the female. Humans normally have a total of 46 chromosomes; 23 from each parent. Twenty-two of the 23 pairs concern the general development of the individual (shape, hair and eye colour, etc.), regardless of sex. These are called *autosomes*, as distinct from the 23rd pair (the *gonosomes*) that determines gender and all physical characteristics associated with sex. Women always carry the basic X gonosome. Men transmit X or Y. An XX combination at the moment of conception results in a female baby; an XY combination means a male. Thus a child cannot enter the world without a female X chromosome, but does not have to possess the male Y. Accordingly, there is no YY gender; the most that can occur is the XY composite. Male chromosomes *must* have female chromosomes, but not *vice versa*, implying that female is the core sex.

Is a man basically a woman with extra bits and pieces (caused by evolution and the biological division of labour); or are men and women *fundamentally* different beings, who happen circumstantially to mate? Medical science is not yet able to answer this question, and there are arguments in favour of both propositions. The issue is important for the theory of organisational behaviour, however, because the belief that men and women are quintessentially different can contribute to sexual stereotyping (e.g. that men are tougher, more aggressive and competitive, rational, etc., whereas women are more emotional, interested in people rather than ideas, dependent, etc.), which can lead to discrimination and the absence of equal opportunities at work.

The case for regarding men and women as basically the same includes the following observations:

(a) Gender difference is only one (albeit important) element of human genetic make-up. Genetic messages for characteristics such as eye colour, facial features, hair texture, etc. are common to both sexes.

(b) Men have breasts that serve no useful purpose, implying a common biological ancestry and both sexes deriving from a single hermaphrodite source.

(c) It has been noted that the timings of the menstrual cycles of women forced to live together in close proximity for several years within isolated and self-contained groups (women serving long-term prison sentences, for example) sometimes converge, suggesting that the timing of the menstrual cycle might be partly determined by psycho-physiological factors and not therefore a purely physical phenomenon. Reproductive functions (such as the menstrual cycle), according to this argument, are nothing more than an evolutionary biological convenience enabling half the population to specialise in bearing children while the other half specialises in other fields of activity.

Arguments *against* men and women deriving from a single source are as follows:

(a) Males and females are constructed from different materials. The sex of an individual may be determined from virtually any part of the human body: a fragment of tissue, a piece of bone, a strand of hair, a drop of saliva, a fingernail, etc.

(b) Arguably, men and women have disparate instincts (*see* **2**) that are independent of upbringing, social experience, etc. Examples might be a woman's instinct to nurture and defend her children, or aggression in males.

Racial differences

All humans belong to a single species, *homo sapiens*, and share common inherited characteristics. Hereditary traits vary among individuals. However, when intermarriage occurs within a group which is isolated from others through geographic or other barriers, some of the characteristics become highly concentrated in the members of a local population. Separations of groups that last for many thousands of generations can result in the emergence of races. Racial differentiation is *fluid*, since races are changeable over the centuries as the pool of common human genes is redistributed and refocused in consequence of intermarriage. Also, individual variability of genetic make-up *within* racial groups often outweighs racial similarities. Racial differences, therefore, are a matter of degree rather than of kind.

Communities adapt to their physical environments, so that outsiders come to associate the physical characteristics of certain groups with behaviour relevant to certain environments (for example, Eskimos coping with the arctic climate). Such communities then come to be perceived by others as representing a distinct racial group.

5. Personality

Personality concerns the *whole* person: attitudes, perspectives, beliefs, values, mental and other personal characteristics. It is the totality of all the individual's dispositions and motives to behave in a certain way. The determinants of an individual's personality thus indicate all the factors that affect his or her attitudes, values, competences, etc. These factors will be either biologically based or environmentally based, or arise from the interaction of environmental and biological variables.

Thus, to understand and predict an individual's behaviour requires the diagnosis of his or her personality. Organisational analysts are interested in the study of personality because of the crucial importance of employee attitudes, intelligence, interests, aptitudes and capabilities for determining workplace behaviour and productivity.

FREUDIAN APPROACHES

6. Freudian approaches to the analysis of personality

Physical characteristics such as height, weight, eye colour, etc. are known to result from the chromosomes that people inherit from their parents. A person's physical qualities will affect his or her childhood experiences (e.g. big strong boys may be able to get their own way by bullying their contemporaries; extremely pretty girls may receive favourable treatment from parents and teachers) and to the extent that these experiences determine the individual's personality there is a link between physique and personality. But the relationship is not of itself *caused* by genetic factors.

The psychologist Sigmund Freud (1856–1939) attributed personality to a mixture of early childhood experiences and instinctual drives (e.g. to obtain pleasure and avoid pain – the *pleasure principle* in Freudian terminology) created by an inborn factor, which Freud referred to as the 'id'. A child's first social interactions are with its parents, upon whom the child depends for emotional and biological support. As the child ages, it is increasingly influenced by its experiences of social relationships beyond the home. Interactions with the environment cause the development within the child of: (*i*) an 'ego' that helps the child co-ordinate its perceptions and hence cope with the outside world, and (*ii*) a 'superego' which determines the child's conceptions about right and wrong.

Thus, according to Freud, an individual's personality emerges from a three-cornered struggle between the id (a mass of impulses lacking any direction or predetermined control), the outside environment, and the superego – or 'conscience' as it could be loosely termed. Initially, the child accepts the guidance, attitudes and moral dictates of its parents. As it grows up, the superego gradually replaces this parental role.

Contributions of Freudian psychology

Freud's major contribution to the theory of personality was perhaps his exploration of the role of the unconscious mind in the determination of human behaviour. According to Freud, many aspects of personality and behaviour that cannot be explained rationally result in fact from unconscious motivation (*see* 8:2). Even feelings that the individual cannot explain (phobias, revulsions, etc.) can be neatly analysed using Freudian concepts and terminology. According to Freud, irrational fears and obsessions are frequently the consequence of attitudes and values uncritically and unconsciously assimilated during early childhood. These feelings lurk within the unconscious, yet continue to influence the individual's emotional condition and behaviour.

THE BRAIN

7. Role of the brain

Arguably, the brain is an important determinant of an individual's personality – although this has yet to be conclusively proven. It is known, for instance, that electrical stimulation of various areas of the brains of certain (non-human) animals can alter their behaviour, e.g. by making an aggressive bull passive and docile. However, the impossibility of conducting wide-ranging experiments on the brains of humans has greatly constrained research in this field.

If it is true that certain emotions result from passing electric currents through specific areas of the human brain then it becomes possible to manipulate personality by means of electrical stimulation of the brain (ESB). Note, however, that the effects on feelings and behaviour end when the ESB finishes, so that ESB should really be viewed as being more like the effects of hypnosis (which always wear off eventually) than as a possible cause of permanent alteration in personality.

How the brain operates

The brain consists of ten billion nerve cells that control physical motions, memory, reasoning, creative ability and awareness of surroundings and self. For analytical purposes, the brain can be conceptualised as comprising three units: the hindbrain, the midbrain and the forebrain. Note, however, that these units do *not* occupy specific locations within the skull, because for most activities many parts of the brain interact simultaneously. Scientists have analysed the functions of these units by observing the effects of physical injury to various parts of the brain (through industrial and other accidents, for example) on individual behaviour and physiological functions. The following results have emerged:

(a) The brain is immensely adaptable. If, for example, the section of the brain that normally controls the movement of the left foot is damaged, then another part of the brain will (usually) take over this function.

(b) The hindbrain controls respiration and heartbeat, concentration, and is important for stimulus-response mechanisms.

(c) The midbrain controls movement of the eye muscles.

(d) The forebrain controls eating, drinking and body temperature.

The brain receives chemical messages from the stomach and other parts of the body, which it then converts into feelings of thirst or hunger. A person's sex drive is controlled similarly, although it is fundamentally different in that whereas food and drink are necessary for individual survival, sex is not – people can live (albeit uncomfortably) without sexual relations.

8. Split-brain psychology

There is a contentious (and unproven) hypothesis that the brain possesses 'hemispheres' associated with various personality characteristics. The *left hemisphere* (which is supposed to be located on the right-hand side of the brain) is said to be concerned with logic, order, analysis, organising information, attention to detail, etc. It governs the planning and control of activities.

The *right hemisphere*, conversely (presumed to be situated on the left-hand side of the brain), is said to involve intuition, spirituality, symbolic representation, perceptions of abstract forms, creativity, emotionality, etc. It concerns invention, manipulation of concepts and the comprehension of complex events. Objections to the right/left hemisphere theory include the following:

(a) The prominence of these characteristics frequently varies more with respect to the age of the individual than any known physiological variables.

(b) Most parts of the brain are known to be simultaneously active regardless of the type of task the individual is undertaking.

(c) Chemical and hormonal differences between individuals can explain many of the differences sometimes attributed to the relative strengths in a person's left/right hemispheres.

(d) The parts of the brain that trigger and control certain feelings are known to extend to all corners of the brain. Thus, there is no 'left' or 'right' side of the brain as such: it could be equally well depicted in terms of front and back or top and bottom.

If it is true, the split-brain hypothesis implies the possibility of being able to insert electrodes into people's heads which, when activated, should stimulate or repress certain of the above-mentioned characteristics.

9. Thinking

Thinking is the manipulation of messages received from the outside world. Messages come in the form of words, visual images, physical contact, heat, light, etc. These messages are examined, combined and/or compared with each other. The processes involved in thinking are called the *cognitive* processes.

Concepts

An important aspect of thinking is the formation of concepts. A 'concept' is a conscious linking together of images, objects, stimuli or events. Individuals receive huge numbers of messages, so the brain needs a system for classifying them into groups which can then be dealt with efficiently. For instance, apples, oranges and bananas are all separate and unique items; but the brain will categorise them into a single concept of 'fruit'. Conceptualisation helps the individual to manage data, identify relations among events and objects, and to discover similarities and differences which enable the *comparison* of items of information.

Thinking and language

Words and the rules for relating them together form a 'language'. Use of a language enables people to explore relations between the objects that words represent, and thus permits individuals to think. Hence it becomes possible to manipulate representations of the world; to examine them from various angles and combine them in different ways. Decisions can be taken, and concepts defined.

10. 'Learning' theories of personality

All approaches to personality recognise the importance of parental influences, child-rearing practices and early experiences on the development of individual personality. Certain psychologists go beyond this and assert that learning experiences are the *major* determinant of personality.

The *neo-Freudian* version of the learning approach asserts that individuals learn during childhood how to cope with innate drives and with anxiety and fear and that the responses involved themselves shape an individual's personality. In contrast, the *behaviourist* version of learning theory, closely associated with the work of B.F. Skinner, is based on the principles of operant conditioning (*see* 6:3). Behaviour is regarded as essentially random until it is either rewarded or punished by the environment in which a person operates. The frequency of various types of behaviour then increases or decreases according to the individual's expectations of the consequences. Thus people become conditioned (*see* 6:3–4) and their personalities change as they alter their behaviour to maximise their rewards and avoid punishment.

Social learning theorists, conversely (*see* 6:6), assert that an individual's observations of events, role models and the general environment are the essential determinant of personality. Rewards and punishments play no major part in the process.

JUNGIAN TYPOLOGY

11. Trait theories and the Jungian typology

Trait theories of personality assume that everyone possesses a number of personality traits, but that each person draws upon them to a different extent. Examples of traits are persistence, cheerfulness, aggression, deviousness, extroversion, nervousness, etc. According to the trait approach, a person exhibiting some strong traits is highly likely to possess certain others. Thus, personality consists of a handful of 'trait clusters' and consequently various 'types' of personality based on these clusters may be discerned.

Trait theories have developed along the lines for categorising personality types suggested by Carl Gustav Jung. The Jungian typology involves four pairs of personality dimensions, as follows:

Introvert – extrovert

Extroverts are socially outgoing, freethinking, and interested in working with other people in groups. They communicate easily and are good at understanding outside environments. However, they find it difficult to function without contact with others, are prone to impulsive behaviour and quickly lose patience with routine work.

Introverts are diligent and reflective, independent minded and capable of working alone. Unfortunately, introverts sometimes misunderstand other people's intentions, find it difficult to cope with interruptions and need peace and quiet to complete tasks.

Intuitor – senser

The intuitor is an imaginative problem-solver who feels at home with complex theories and new ideas. On the other hand, the intuitor is soon bored by practical detail and tedious but necessary work.

A senser is practical, patient, careful and systematic. He or she will attend to detail, but in so doing is inclined to lose sight of the situation as a whole. Sensers are quickly frustrated by complicated work, preferring concrete, factual and structured tasks.

Feeling – thinking

A feeling person empathises with others and is more interested in people than objects. The feeling individual is good at persuasion, conciliation and the identification of colleagues' human and personal needs. Nevertheless, such people can be disorganised, illogical, and uncritical of issues and events. They are guided by emotion and do not analyse issues objectively.

The thinker is logical, analytical and objective, but may be insensitive to other people's views and may misunderstand their values. Thinkers prefer to confront rather than conciliate, and can be quite ruthless at times.

Perceiver – judger

Perceivers can see all sides of a problem and are flexible in their approach. They constantly search for fresh information about issues but, in consequence, may be reluctant to commit themselves and are prone not to finish their tasks.

Judgers are decisive, orderly, and stick with their work. They make quick decisions, but tend to be dominated by their own plans. Decisions may be taken hastily, and this type of person might be extremely reluctant to admit mistakes.

Everyone's personality will exhibit both dimensions of each pair to some extent, but typically one dimension of each pair will be stronger than the other. The dominant dimensions will determine the person's outlook and personality.

12. Possible implications of the Jungian typology

It has been argued that people who have the same dominant personality dimensions will get on with each other better than with individuals possessing alternative types of personality. Equally, individuals with different strengths in the dimensions might experience great difficulty in understanding each others' opinions, actions and views. Accordingly, the implications of the Jungian typology are that:

(a) People's personalities should be considered prior to allocating them to groups.

(b) Employees can be trained to become aware of their own personality strengths and weakness, and to try to overcome the latter.

(c) Individuals of one personality type should seek the counsel of people of others before making important decisions (in order to achieve a fair balance of opinion).

(d) Individuals might choose jobs and occupations to which their personality strengths are best suited.

(e) Executives with various personality characteristics might adopt particular management styles when taking decisions. For example, someone strong in intuition and thinking may prefer a direct and forthright approach, defining problems clearly and precisely, and laying down exact and rigid criteria for completing work. A sensing/feeling person, conversely, might be intensely practical in approach yet still be extremely people-oriented in the way he or she achieves results.

(f) Different organisation structures might be suitable for different personality types. A sensing person, for example, may perform best in a bureaucracy (*see* 2:9), with a clear hierarchy and strong central control. An intuitive/feeling type, on the other hand, may be more suited to a loose-knit decentralised organisation with maximum local discretion over how work is performed.

THE JOHARI WINDOW

13. Personality integration and the Johari Window

Personality should not be confused with personal endearment and/or attractiveness. Everyone has a personality just as everyone has a physique – the particular characteristics of someone's personality depends on how that person's drives, emotions, beliefs and mental qualities are integrated within his or her inner self.

Well-integrated individuals have all the elements of their personalities woven together into a consistent whole. They think and behave in a stable manner and (importantly) possess self-images that reasonably correspond to how they are perceived by the outside world. Also their personalities are unlikely to change significantly over time.

The *Johari Window* is a technique for improving perception by reducing individual biases and stereotyping (*see* 14:6). It was developed by Joseph Luft and Harry Ingham (hence the name 'Johari') as a means for analysing two-person interaction. The idea is that everyone is aware of certain aspects of their own personality, behaviour, and attitudes that are also obvious to other people. This awareness is called the 'open' part of the window. Equally, outsiders may observe things about the individual of which he or she is not conscious. This is the 'blind' area of the window. The 'hidden' part of the window comprises the attitudes and feelings that a person keeps to him or herself. Finally, there is an 'unknown' area comprising aspects of the individual about which neither he/she nor others are aware, but which still influence the person's behaviour.

During initial contacts with other people, individuals reveal little about themselves, and the open area is small. As relationships improve, the open area increases. Feedback from others also increases the open area, simultaneously reducing the blind area.

According to the model, managers should be trained to appreciate how other people react to their behaviour and to increase the openness of their relationships. Hence (in general) the greater the amount of self-disclosure and feedback in a manager's relationships with other people, the better the manager will perform.

This involves trusting other people, hopefully reducing thereby the potential for conflict.

PERCEPTION AND COGNITION

14. Perception

Perception is the process through which the individual interprets sensory inputs (sight, sound, smell, taste, feelings of being hot or cold, etc.). Managers need to know about the process of perception for such purposes as:

(a) Ensuring that employees perceive the organisation's objectives in a similar way.

(b) Understanding workers' grievances and complaints.

(c) Being able to empathise with the problems confronting other departments.

(d) Improving communication between managers and subordinates (i.e. making sure they both interpret issues in the same way).

(e) Avoiding inappropriate stereotyping of individuals during recruitment or appraisal procedures. Stereotyping means the creation of mental images of certain categories of people and the expectation that all members of these categories will be exactly the same.

(f) Making judgements on others (during employee appraisals, for instance – *see* 16:**15**).

How things are perceived depends upon the following factors:

(a) Individual experience of similar events and objects (e.g. one sound may be recognised as belonging to a train, another as that of a motor vehicle).

(b) Collateral evidence supporting a particular interpretation (i.e 'putting two and two together to make four').

(c) Preconceptions of how things *ought* to be.

(d) Self-interest, i.e. deliberately interpreting every issue in a manner that leads to the greatest benefit to the person involved.

(e) Immediate circumstances (e.g. a glass of water is perceived differently by someone who is extremely thirsty and by someone who is not).

(f) The perceiver's background, education and personality (*see* **3** above).

(g) The cultural norms (*see* 20:**19**) of the environment in which the individual operates.

Problems related to perception include:

(a) Sometimes, people see only what they want to see and hear only what they want to hear, especially when the messages being received are damaging to a person's career, status or self-image.

(b) Communication breakdowns (*see* 14:**3–5**) can be caused by colleagues perceiving the same issue in entirely different ways.

(c) Emotionally disturbing events may trigger 'perceptual defence mechanisms' that cause the individual not to recognise the true nature of these events. A fact may be ignored totally, or the perception of it might be modified or distorted to make it consistent with existing beliefs. Such mechanisms enable the individual to dismiss unpleasant information and then to justify diverting attention towards other (more agreeable) things.

(d) Bad first impressions can lead to incorrect perceptions of other people.

(e) The individual might 'project' (attribute) his or her own feelings to others; particularly undesirable thoughts and feelings that the person is inwardly ashamed of and not willing to admit. Projection allows the individual to believe that other people actually exhibit the negative characteristics that the individual subconsciously believes himself or herself to possess.

15. Cognition

Perception is an important element of cognition, which is a more general concept than perception *per se*. Cognition is the mental process whereby knowledge is acquired. Thus it involves intuition, imagination, and reasoning as well as the perception of objects, issues or events. It concerns *how* people come by ideas and how perceptions are organised.

Cognitive dissonance

The term *cognitive dissonance* refers to the state of mind of someone whose perceptions of related objects, events or circumstances are out of balance. Perceptions are inconsistent: they do not add up and the individual feels uncomfortable as a result. Normally, cognitions are *consonant*, i.e. one follows from the other. For example, a knowledge that it is raining is consonant with the experience of getting wet. If it were to rain heavily and a person were outside, unprotected and without an umbrella yet still did not get wet then he or she would experience severe cognitive dissonance. The implications of cognitive dissonance are as follows:

(a) Because it is psychologically uncomfortable, the existence of dissonance induces people to change their perceptions and / or behaviour in order to achieve consonance, e.g. stopping smoking in recognition of it being unhealthy.

(b) People might actively avoid information or situations that would increase dissonance. For example, a politically right-wing person will avoid reading left-wing newspapers.

(c) An individual may seek to alter the environment in which he or she functions in order to remove dissonant elements, e.g. choosing new friends who agree with one's political views.

(d) People experiencing cognitive dissonance may actively look for (and perhaps even invent) collateral evidence to support their initial views. A heavy smoker, for instance, may root out tobacco company literature suggesting that nicotine is relaxing and not really damaging to health.

Information processing

Humans continuously register, process and respond to information gathered from the external environment. Information processing is the conversion of data picked up by the senses (sight, sound, etc.) into meaningful perceptions. This helps the individual to *understand* the outside world: how objects and patterns are recognised, how language is comprehended, how ideas are interpreted, and so on. There exists an information processing 'theory' of cognition (Weiner 1948). Information processing theory rests on several critical assumptions, as follows:

(a) Perception is not an immediate and direct response to a stimulus, but rather the consequence of a *series* of discrete processes – each taking up an interval of time (measured in thousandths of a second) during which the information obtained from the environment is transformed in some way. This series of transformations creates a perception of the stimulus.

(b) The total time that elapses from the onset of a stimulus to the occurrence of a response can be split into time intervals of definite durations and a *different* operation is applied to the received information within each interval. Hence it should be possible to delineate and precisely define all the operations that take place between stimulus and response.

(c) There is a continuous flow of information through the process. Each stage is influenced by preceding stages and itself influences subsequent stages.

(d) Capacity limitations within the information processing system lead to selectivity in the items of information prioritised for processing, since not all information can be processed to the same degree in the time available. Researchers concerned with information processing theory devote much effort to identifying the determinants of which items are selected and the mechanisms of selection. To the extent that it is valid, information processing theory implies that perception is linked to memory *via* a series of complex but identifiable processes. Memory and perception are at opposite ends of a continuum. Also, perception is an active process. People do not simply receive, store and respond to information.

ATTITUDES

16. Attitudes

An attitude is a long-term inclination to perceive, interpret and evaluate events and issues in a certain manner. Thus, attitudes involve feelings, beliefs, values and inclinations to behave in a particular way, although attitudes do not always lead to action.

Numerous factors contribute to the formation of attitude at work, including:

- the influence of other members of a group
- the economic, social and political structures of the society in which the individual lives
- personal background and experience
- immediate working conditions
- a traumatic experience, e.g. being dismissed from a job, can alter a person's entire attitude towards employment.

Knowledge of a person's attitude towards one issue frequently enables the accurate prediction of his or her attitudes in other areas. Holding an attitude towards something means that the individual is able to respond to a problem quickly and with little further thought.

Employee attitudes may be measured directly through interviews and/or written questionnaires which ask workers to register their agreement or disagreement with various statements; or indirectly through observing employee behaviour and listening in to their general conversations.

17. Common attitudes (shared values)

It is desirable that employees at all levels within an organisation share common perspectives on the factors that determine its prosperity and prospects. Common attitudes should concern such matters as the fundamental purpose of the organisation (i.e. its mission), how things should be done, when, by whom, and how enthusiastically, etc.

To some extent, these perceptions may be created by management *via* the internal communications network, style of leadership, organisation system and working methods; but they can only be sustained and brought to bear on day-to-day operations by the firm's workers, who need to *feel* they possess a common objective. Staff should experience a sense of affinity with the organisation and *want* to pursue a common cause. This would help employees to interpret day-to-day events and to structure and reinforce their views about the company.

The following factors contribute to the formation of common attitudes:

(a) Employees' awareness of the origins of the business, what it does and how it is organised.

(b) The frequency of personal contacts between senior and junior employees (assuming that significant issues are dealt with at these meetings).

(c) Employees' knowledge of the extent and severity of external competition facing the business.

(d) The degree of homogeneity of employees' backgrounds *vis-à-vis* their ages, educational experiences, general outlooks, etc.

(e) Company recruitment and induction practices, especially if these cause employees to feel they belong to a highly selective group.

18. Instrumental attitudes

Employees who possess an 'instrumental' orientation to work are motivated mostly by pay and job security. Together, these factors enable them to meet their personal needs *outside* their work. An assembly-line worker, for example, might prefer to put up with mundane and boring duties in order to attain high earnings that support a comfortable life at home (e.g. as a houseowner, the possessor of a car and good-quality furniture, as someone able to afford holidays abroad, etc.) rather than doing more satisfying work but for lower wages.

People with instrumental attitudes perceive work as a means to an end and not as an end in itself. The implications of the instrumental orientation are as follows:

(a) A person's job is not part of his or her 'central life interest' (*see* Chapter 7).

(b) The worker is unconcerned with social and/or emotional aspects of employment.

(c) An employee feels no loyalty to the employing organisation beyond its ability to provide a high economic return.

(d) The worker makes a sharp distinction between work life and non-work life. Interpersonal contacts at work do not spill over into the employee's social affairs.

(e) An employee's opinion of management will depend on the latter's ability to provide material rewards.

(f) The worker is interested in joining a trade union primarily for the economic benefits it might bring and is unconcerned with the wider social and political aspects of trade union activity.

(g) There is little relation between job satisfaction and productivity, since the prospect of economic reward is the dominant motivator (*see* 8:4).

(h) Group norms (*see* 12:3) do not influence the employee's behaviour as much as the pursuit of high wages.

Instrumental attitudes are possibly more likely among the following categories of worker: (*i*) those with dependent relatives, especially small children; (*ii*) those in high-wage industries; (*iii*) those who are geographically mobile and, since they do not stay in any one area for very long, who feel little 'solidarity' with the local community.

19. Maturation

This is the process by which the individual's capacity for intellectual reasoning develops over time. Four stages are involved:

1 *The first two years of childhood.* At this stage the child's understanding of the world depends on physical interactions with outside environments. For example, the child learns that certain things cause pain and others cause satisfaction.
2 *Ages two to seven.* The child now learns language and the rudiments of symbolic representation. However, the child continues to evaluate things on their face value.
3 *Ages seven to twelve.* Abilities for logical reasoning begin to emerge, though only to a rudimentary level.
4 *Beyond twelve.* The individual is now capable of reasoning and abstraction. He or she can communicate using symbols, sees things in perspective, and has a full command of language.

> Note that the age at which people pass through these stages is only approximate, and could vary from one person to the next.

20. Aging

The effect of employee maturity on the effectiveness of leadership styles is dealt with in 13:**13**. Otherwise, the age of the worker has the following implications for employing organisations:

(a) It is known that the older the employee and the longer he or she has spent with an organisation the less likely is that person to quit. Hence, the higher the average age of the organisation's workers the greater the long-term difficulties created by attempts to reduce the size of the workforce through 'natural wastage'. A freeze on recruitment means that *younger* people – who leave more frequently – are not replaced, hence increasing still further the average age of remaining employees. This creates staffing crises as and when older cohorts retire.

(b) Older workers (about 40 per cent of the UK labour force is over 45 years of age) present firms with substantial problems regarding the introduction of new technologies. Young entrants will have learnt about up-to-date methods at school and/or college and will readily accept technical change. Older people have to be retrained, at considerable expense to employing organisations.

(c) A company with a 'top-heavy' age structure might be unattractive to young people because of the lack of immediate short-term promotion prospects. Also the firm's wage and benefits bill will usually be higher the greater the proportion of its workforce in the upper age brackets. Older workers with longer service are usually at the top ends of salary bands, and employer's national insurance and superannuation contributions are based on a percentage of the employee's salary.

Other relevant considerations are that: (*i*) accident rates are highest among very young workers (due to lack of experience) and those approaching retirement (through lack of concentration and the slowing-down of reactions); (*ii*) older workers tend to be more satisfied with their jobs and to have a stronger work ethic (*see* 7:**4**). Over the years, older workers will have lowered their expectations of what a job should offer, and they are better adjusted to work routines. Absenteeism and latecoming is generally lower among older employees.

Progress test 4

1. What are the major respects in which individuals differ?

2. What is an instinct?

3. Define 'personality'.

4. What is the 'learning theory' of personality?

5. Describe the functions of the hindbrain and the forebrain.

6. What is the difference between personality and attractiveness?

7. What is the Johari Window?

8. Define 'perception'.

9. Explain the difference between cognition and attitude.

10. Outline the stages in the maturation of a human being.

5

PSYCHOLOGICAL AND ACHIEVEMENT TESTING

TYPES AND PURPOSES OF TESTING

1. Types of psychological test

There are three main types of psychological test: intelligence, personality, and aptitude. Tests can also be used to assess the level of achievement a person has attained in certain competences (word-processing or shorthand, for example). Students of organisational behaviour are particularly concerned with occupational tests administered by employing organisations. These are used for the selection of new entrants and for assessing the promotion potential of existing workers.

Tests need to be *valid* and *reliable*. For a test to be valid it must measure precisely what it is intended to measure. For instance, an intelligence test should measure intelligence and not general knowledge obtained from past schooling.

A reliable test is one that gives consistent results when repeated on different groups of people. Thus, similar proportions of each sample of individuals tested should normally fall within certain score categories; e.g. about 5 per cent having an intelligence quotient (*see* **6** below) exceeding, say, 130.

2. Selection testing

Often, tests are given to job applicants in order to obtain information about their abilities. Such tests are especially common where interviews are not possible, as for example when large numbers of employees are to be engaged within a very short period, and for situations where candidates have no formal qualifications or experience of work, as in the case of recruiting school leavers who have no academic certificates. Advocates of selection testing claim that tests remove subjectivity in selection procedures. An effective test should achieve the following objectives:

(a) It should be cheap to administer (note that a single test can be given to a roomful of perhaps 40 or 50 people at each sitting, and only a couple of people will be needed to organise and invigilate the test).

(b) It should measure precisely what it is intended to measure. An intelligence test should assess intelligence, not learned responses; aptitude tests should indicate candidates' true potentials for undertaking the jobs for which they are being considered, not other occupations.

(c) It should give consistent results when repeated. Only then can the results obtained from a single sitting be accepted as sufficiently reliable for appointment decisions.

(d) It should discriminate between candidates. If the test is working properly, good quality applicants will obtain high marks and poor candidates should consistently fail. If candidates pass the test but then turn out to be incompetent the test has not achieved its purpose.

(e) It should rank the candidates. The best candidate should obtain the top mark, the next best should get the second highest, and so on.

(f) It should be relevant to the job. The characteristics exposed by performance in the test should relate directly to the job specification for the vacant post.

3. Validation of tests

There are four types of validity that a test needs to fulfil:

1 *Content validity.* This concerns the relevance of the questions asked to the quality being measured. Sometimes the extent of the test's content validity is obvious, particularly in achievement tests (*see* 4 below) such as those to measure typing speeds. Otherwise, content validity must be assessed subjectively by the person devising the test or by an outside expert, such as a manager with extensive experience of a particular type of work.
2 *Predictive validity.* Here it is necessary to demonstrate a significant statistical relationship between performance in the test and subsequent levels of ability. Thus, test candidates scoring the highest marks should display the greatest competence in later endeavours, and *vice versa*. Note that the establishment of a test's predictive ability is a long-term project, which could be extremely expensive.
3 *Construct validity.* To prove construct validity it is necessary to compare a person's performance in a test with some other known criterion of his or her ability. For example, a certain individual's overall academic record and past achievements might suggest that he or she is very bright. Accordingly, this person would be expected to do well in an intelligence test. If his or her performance is poor then the test itself should be re-examined critically.
4 *Concurrent validity.* This is dealt with in 5 below.

The copyright of a test is held by the person or organisation that devised it in the first place. Typically, the copyright holder charges a fee to anyone wishing to use the test on other people (job applicants, for example). Often, the sale of tests is restricted to persons who have attended a training course on how the tests should be administered. The copyright owner will insist that the test be given in precisely the manner described in a test manual and sometimes the results have to be returned to the seller in order that they may be interpreted by a qualified person.

Critics of this practice allege, however, that in so doing publishers and psychologists conceal the foundations upon which tests are constructed and the validity of their assumptions, and thus exclude all possibilities for external scrutiny, criticism and academic debate. Besides, people who take such tests but are then not happy with the scores they are awarded cannot challenge the marking criteria and propriety of the test.

4. Achievement tests

These evaluate the tested person's competence in a particular skill. Examples are tests for word-processing or shorthand speeds, driving tests, machining ability tests, etc. The test is directly relevant to the work the successful candidate is to do, but it will necessarily cover only a part of the candidate's eventual duties. A candidate who fails the test is assumed incapable of doing the entire job, which need not be true. A secretary, for example, might fail to achieve a predetermined minimum speed under test conditions, but this does not necessarily mean that the candidate is an inadequate secretary overall.

Also tests are undertaken in specific test conditions. Success in a driving test proves that the candidate did well over the test circuit, yet may not be a good driver elsewhere. Job applicants will feel nervous during a test, and this may cause them to do badly. It is a fact that people who have done a particular type of test previously do better on average than people attempting that type of test for the first time. Thus, candidates who have already taken and failed a similar test will have an advantage, yet these might be precisely the sort of candidates the test was originally intended to weed out. Further problems are that:

(a) Candidates who have passed a test might assume they possess knowledge or ability which in fact they do not have. Supervisors also might conclude that new entrants are fully competent simply because they did well in a single test, conducted in highly specific conditions.

(b) An internal candidate for promotion who is given and fails a test might lose self-confidence and hence underperform in a currently-held job. That person will, moreover, be identified by colleagues as a failure and in consequence the worker's morale might suffer.

(c) Some ethnic and other minority groups consistently do badly in certain types of achievement test because they have not had access to educational and training programmes necessary to equip them with the basic skills expected of test candidates.

(d) High marks obtained in a test do not guarantee that the successful candidate will do well in the vacant post. In particular, high marks do not show *why* the candidate succeeded; low marks do not indicate *why* the candidate failed. Knowledge of the causes of success or failure might be as valuable to management as identification of individuals capable of obtaining high marks.

(e) Achievement tests do not evaluate the whole person, only a small sub-section of his or her characteristics. Note that a formal educational qualification awarded after perhaps several years' study should in principle offer much more information about a person overall.

5. Aptitude tests

The purpose of an aptitude test is to assess a person's promise, e.g. to undertake a certain type of work, whether they are suitable for training, or the extent to which they possess qualities that might be further developed. The sort of aptitude being looked for might be physical, intellectual, perceptive or emotional, and the problem arises of how these potentials might accurately be evaluated. One approach is to test existing workers doing similar jobs to discover the qualities needed for success in that type of work. This is sometimes referred to as *establishing the concurrent validity of the test*. Then, candidates can be examined for evidence of their ability in these respects and their marks compared with those obtained by current employees.

INTELLIGENCE TESTING

6. Intelligence tests

Intelligence is a complex and subjective concept extremely difficult to define. It is concerned with the use of the intellect: understanding, perceiving, thinking, learning and solving problems. It involves self-awareness, critical and organisational faculties, and might manifest itself in physical dexterity, numerical ability, verbal fluency and / or spatial perception. All these attributes are conceptually nebulous and open to a wide variety of interpretations.

Origins of intelligence testing

Early attempts at intelligence testing involved children. Testers sought to identify in children their 'mental age' by having children complete puzzles such as working out the next number in a series, matching shapes and objects (putting square pegs into square holes), mental arithmetic, anagrams and other decoding exercises. Since intelligence seems to stop developing during the late teens, no person is assumed to possess a mental age greater than 15. A child who is able to solve problems which the testers consider should be capable of solution by a child of a certain age is given a mental age of that many years. In other words, the tester assumes that, say, a 12-year-old should be able to accomplish certain tasks, so that anyone just able to complete those tasks is allocated a mental age of 12. Then the child's 'intelligence quotient' (IQ) is defined as:

$$\frac{\text{Mental age}}{\text{Chronological age}} \times 100$$

To compute intelligence quotients for adults, testers give a series of problems to a large number of people and calculate the average score, which then represents average intelligence or IQ = 100. People scoring above or below level 100 in the tests are regarded respectively as above or below average intelligence.

IQ test questions

Questions asked need to be culturally neutral, independent of general knowledge and past training (otherwise people could learn to become intelligent), while answers given should not depend on environmental factors or be related to the circumstances of the test. In reality, however, results are often sensitive to how people feel at the time the test is attempted – whether they are tired, nervous, have the 'flu', or whatever; and quite often candidates do not take the exercise seriously. Intelligence tests should give consistent results when they are repeated and outcomes should be compared with other indicators of ability and records of actual performance.

Success in an intelligence test does not guarantee that a candidate will perform well in a job. The demands of a particular type of work could be much greater or less than the level of intelligence required by an IQ test. Also, candidates who are told they scored highly might wrongly assume that they possess exceptional intellectual ability when this is not in fact the case.

7. How intelligence tests for adults are devised

Questions intended to assess a person's intelligence are drafted and then carefully examined for cultural bias. Any question which involves material that people from certain cultures, classes or educational backgrounds might already know about is removed. Remaining questions are then given to a widespread and random sample of individuals. The average score is computed to represent IQ = 100.

Choice of this sample is crucially important. A major problem that arises here is deciding whether the sample is to contain people of different races, nationalities, social classes, occupational categories and incomes; or whether to compute separate averages for each racial and / or socio-economic group.

A tester who believes in the existence of differences in intelligence between races, social classes, etc. will separate the figures for each category. Conversely, a tester who believes that the distribution of intelligence is essentially the same for all types of people will take a global average. The issue is critical because the scores of tested persons will be compared against the previously computed average for the sample as a whole, and this average will be high or low depending on who is included in the sample.

As a further check on the usefulness of each question in the test, the frequency with which each question is answered correctly will be correlated with the rate of success in other questions. Suppose, for example, there are ten questions intended to be of equal difficulty and that on average candidates score seven out of ten. Consider the first question. We would expect that out of a sample of (say) 100 candidates attempting the paper, about 70 would answer question 1 correctly. If this is not the case there is probably something wrong with the question since, on average, no particular question should stump candidates more than others. This does not apply, of course, if certain questions are designed to be especially difficult; in which case a low success rate should be recorded.

8. The philosophical debate on intelligence testing

Arguments for and against intelligence testing have been debated for many decades. The arguments *against* intelligence tests include the following:

(a) Testing is socially divisive. Certain individuals are arbitrarily labelled as being of mediocre intelligence, possibly on the basis of just a couple of (poorly validated) 20-minute tests. Then people are unfairly allocated to inappropriate social roles and occupations.

(b) Practice at IQ tests can lead to improved performance, especially if people are deliberately taught what to look for in test questions (regularities in shapes, predictable differences in series of numbers and so on). Accordingly, success in IQ tests measures little more than a person's ability to pass IQ tests.

(c) Individual motivation and state of health at the time a test is taken can significantly affect results.

(d) Human qualities other than intelligence – honesty, capacity for hard work, empathy with others, dependability, etc. – are far more important when assessing the worth of an individual. Thus, intelligence is not worth measuring in the first instance.

(e) Socially-privileged people consistently do well in IQ tests, largely because of their longer and more extensive general education. To the extent that intelligence tests are used for occupational selection this means that socially privileged individuals consistently get the higher-paid jobs but are then able to claim they deserve these jobs on account of their innate superior intelligence!

(f) Forcing a person to take an IQ test can instil in that individual a fear of possible humiliation should he or she do badly. This causes a loss of self-confidence, which in turn leads to poor test performance.

The arguments *in favour* of intelligence testing have been stated as follows:

(a) Although practice at IQ tests *might* raise a person's average score, the increase will not be significant if the test has been properly drafted.

(b) Working-class people and members of low-income ethnic minorities sometimes do extremely well in IQ tests, despite underprivileged backgrounds. This could not occur if the tests taken were always culturally biased.

(c) Genetic differences obviously exist with respect to physical characteristics (hair and eye colour, for instance) so why should they not apply to intelligence? Differences in intelligence need to be measured systematically because they affect the ability to solve problems and individual competence generally.

(d) It is better to discriminate between people objectively and fairly in terms of their intelligence rather than on the grounds of their religion, race, social class, nationality or other inappropriate criteria. Intelligence is a good yardstick for allocating jobs, power, income and privilege.

(e) Society needs to identify its most intelligent members so that it can prepare them to exploit science, develop industry, cultivate the arts and create prosperity for the entire community. Those of the greatest ability in each generation must lead and support the rest.

(f) There is little point in educating or training people to a high level if they are not intellectually capable of absorbing the relevant information. Intelligence testing, its advocates argue, indicates each individual's capacity to take in knowledge and how far, intellectually, each person is capable of progressing.

Race and intelligence

In 1969 the US psychologist Arthur Jensen reported that on all known IQ scales black Americans scored an average 15 points lower than white Americans. According to Jensen, 80 per cent of all variation in IQ was due to hereditary factors. Hence he suggested that black people on average had an inherited and therefore uncorrectable lower level of intelligence than whites and thus should be encouraged to pursue only lower-level learning of specific skills, not higher-level learning that required abstract reasoning. Critics of Jensen were quick to point out that:

(a) The IQ tests applied were devised by American whites, for whites and preassumed that test candidates possessed educational backgrounds common only in white communities.

(b) There was much hard evidence demonstrating that improvements in socio-economic conditions in black areas soon led to huge increases in observed average IQ in those areas (Hunt 1969).

(c) Whites in poor areas were also observed to have a lower-than-average IQ.

(d) Studies of black children adopted by white (middle class) parents in the 1930s and 1940s reveal that these children had an average 20 point higher observed IQ than their natural mothers.

(e) Studies of the recorded IQs of identical twins separated at birth and reared apart showed large differences in the observed IQs of the twins in each pair (14 points on average with a range of 30 points) regardless of race. How could this happen if hereditary factors explained IQ more than environment?

PERSONALITY TESTING

9. Personality tests

A definition of 'personality' is given in 4:4. Personality tests seek to identify individual traits such as introversion, extroversion, personal assertiveness, ability to cope with stress, and/or expected future patterns of behaviour (management style, potential for leadership, etc.). Personality covers very many aspects of individual identity – emotions, motivations, needs, interests, attitudes, social relationships – many of which are environmentally or culturally determined. A personality test tries to discover whether the candidate really wants to do certain things, rather than simply whether he or she is technically capable of doing them. Interpretation of results is of course highly subjective. Specific problems are as follows:

(a) Candidates, knowing their personalities are being examined, will attempt to present themselves in ways that create favourable impressions.

(b) Individual attitudes and behaviour can change drastically over time and according to circumstances.

(c) Assessments relate to observed behaviour and expressed opinions at a particular moment. These might be untypical, so average behaviour is largely ignored.

(d) Because of the subjectivity in interpreting results, candidates might be given very different personality descriptions by differing assessors.

10. How personality tests are devised

A psychologist will prepare a list of questions the answers to which he or she believes will reveal crucial aspects of an individual's personality (introversion or extroversion, intuition, dominance or submissiveness, etc.). Note immediately that there exist conflicting schools of thought in psychology, each with its own ideas about:

- what personality is
- whether people possess 'core' personalities that are essentially constant regardless of age, educational experiences or personal trauma (the death of a close relative, for instance)
- what questions need to be asked to discover someone's personality, and how to interpret the answers he or she gives.

Accordingly, different tests and interpretations emerge from differing psychological perspectives (neo-Freudian versus neo-Jungian schools for instance, see 4:**5–11**).

The test is now administered to samples of people whose personalities are already known, and its predictive ability is validated (*see* **3** above). Next, the test is given to a sample of individuals considered representative of the sort of person the test is intended to evaluate and average responses are recorded. These averages are used to define 'normal' reactions to test questions. The replies of other people taking the test are then compared against the average responses. For example, a test that aims to identify senior management potential in job applicants might be administered to a group of existing senior managers and their average responses noted. Then it is assumed that candidates exhibiting similar responses have similar personalities and could therefore be suitable for senior management.

Two major difficulties attach to this procedure:

1 The sample group used to determine 'normal' test responses might in fact be atypical of society generally, resulting in unfair discrimination against certain types of candidate. Obviously, the average responses to questions (which usually require the candidate to express a preference from alternatives or to select a mode of dealing with a problem from a list of options) of certain racial and/or socio-economic groups can reasonably be expected to differ from the average responses of others. White, middle-aged and affluent American senior executives, for instance, would probably respond to test questions in a manner quite different from (say) managers of agricultural establishments in central mainland China.

2 Some candidates may have received formal instructions in how to respond to personality test questions in order to create the most favourable impression.

11. Development of psychometric tests

The term 'psychometric test' is often used to describe any test that seeks to quantify psychological dimensions in individuals. Hence, the term covers all forms of intelligence and personality assessment. Among the earliest attempts at large-scale psychometric testing was the development of the DISC test (versions of which are still used today) from research conducted on soldiers in the US Army in the early 1920s. In its modern format the DISC test seeks to identify in job applicants the extent of the existence of four aspects of their personality: dominance, influence (or 'inducement'), submission (or 'steadiness') and compliance. Candidates are required to select between various words and phrases (e.g. persuasive, gentle, innovative) which they believe describe aspects of their personality most and least accurately. Results are plotted on to a star-shaped graph, which purports to indicate the test subject's self-image, actual personality and ability to cope with pressure.

Further pioneering developments in psychometric testing included the following:

(a) *The Myers-Briggs type indicator*, i.e. a personality test based on Jung's fourfold categorisation of individual tendencies (introvert/extrovert, objective, intuitive, etc.; *see* **4:11**). Test subjects are required to complete a checklist questionnaire that asks them to express their preferences in relation to various issues and situations.

(b) *The Alice Heim (AH) test*, an intelligence test attempting to avoid ambiguity in the interpretation of test subjects' responses through asking respondents a high proportion of non-verbal questions (e.g. predicting the next number in a series or identifying relationships between symbols). Verbal questions involved the arrangement of words in order, not the interpretation of sentences.

All tests attempt to be 'culture fair' through eliminating the effects of all cultural variables wherever possible. In general, culturally fair tests focus on and are dominated by 'performance' tasks, such as assembling objects, drawing pictures, relating shapes, etc.

(c) *Catell's 16 PF test.* This personality test assumes the existence within people of 16 clusters of behaviour or 'factors'. The factors relate: to (1) whether the person is easy-going or reserved and formal; (2) intelligence; (3) emotional stability; (4) excitability; (5) assertiveness; (6) whether the subject is cheerful or depressed; (7) conscientiousness; (8) extroversion or introversion; (9) self-sufficiency; (10) vigour; (11) whether the person is cultured or uncultured; (12) trustfulness; (13) attitudes to conformity; (14) shrewdness; (15) self-confidence; (16) cognitive ability.

(d) *The California psychological inventory,* i.e. a standardised measure of personality compiled by giving questions to groups of people regarded by their peers as unusual or extreme in certain respects. Average responses to these questions are then taken to represent 'abnormal' answers to similar questions used in personality tests. The word 'inventory' is used to denote the fact that there is no pass/fail cut-off point. Rather, the purpose is to enable individuals to determine for themselves their own personal strengths and weaknesses.

(e) *The Eysenk personality inventory,* which consists of a simple questionnaire requiring 'yes/no' answers to questions intended to measure the degrees of a candidate's introversion/extroversion and stability/neuroticism. These dimensions are then broken down into numerous sub-categories. For example, 'stability' is divided into 'phlegmatic' and 'sanguine'; while 'phlegmatic' segments into: passive, careful, thoughtful, peaceful, controlled, reliable, even-tempered and calm.

This model, the 16 PF test and the Myers-Briggs type indicator are all applications for 'type theories' of personality, which seek to classify individuals into a handful of personality categories. The approach has a long history. For instance, in 400 BC the Greek physician Hippocrates postulated the existence of just four types of temperament: optimistic, melancholic, irritable, and apathetic.

Progress test 5

1. In what circumstances is an organisation most likely to use selection tests when hiring employees?

2. What are the four types of validity that a test needs to fulfil?

3. Explain three difficulties involved with achievement tests and two with aptitude tests.

4. Define the term 'intelligence quotient'.

5. Why has intelligence testing been described as socially divisive?

6. What are the main problems attached to personality testing?

7. What are the arguments in favour of intelligence testing?

6

LEARNING AND THE ACQUISITION OF SKILLS

1. Definition of learning

To learn means to absorb knowledge, acquire skills and / or assume fresh attitudes. Learning results in *permanent* changes in ability or behaviour. Managers need to know about the principles of learning because of their importance for:

(a) the training of employees

(b) their applications to 'learning by doing' within the organisation

(c) developing job rotation and other staff development schemes.

Unfortunately, not everything is understood about the learning process, although certain methods of teaching and training are known to facilitate learning. Many techniques derive from the 'behaviourist' school of learning theory. (Note that behaviourist learning models should not be confused with the 'behaviourist' approach to management as a whole.)

THE BEHAVIOURIST APPROACH

2. Nature of the behaviourist model

The model regards learning as a straightforward relationship between four variables: drive; stimulus; response; and reinforcement.

Drives may be primary and innate (e.g. hunger or thirst); or secondary and acquired through learning (e.g. the desire for occupational status). *Stimuli* are triggers that initiate responses – they *cause* things to happen (e.g. hearing a doorbell causes the householder to answer the door). A *response* is the result of a stimulus. Responses can become automatic (e.g. the motorist who automatically changes into a higher gear as he or she increases speed), and much work-related training is designed to inculcate particular responses to stimuli. *Reinforcements* are occurrences that strengthen responses, especially if they happen immediately after an event. Examples of reinforcements are praise (a positive reinforcement), criticism (negative reinforcement), gestures of affection, or expressions of confidence in someone's performance.

3. Development of the behaviourist approach

The classic experiment relating stimulus to response was conducted by the Russian psychologist Ivan Pavlov in the 1880s with a number of dogs. Pavlov noted that a hungry dog presented with the stimulus of food would salivate in response. The food is the 'unconditioned' stimulus and the saliva is the unconditioned response (i.e. no action is necessary to get the dog to salivate). Reinforcement was provided by allowing the dog to eat the food.

Next, Pavlov rang a bell every time the dog was shown food: eventually the dog's mouth would water whenever the bell was rung even though no food was offered – the dog had been *conditioned* to respond to the sound of the bell. This became known as the stimulus-response (S-R) model, the essential propositions of which are as follows:

(a) Stimuli elicit responses; therefore learning occurs when a clear connection between a given stimulus and a certain response can be discerned.

(b) If a secondary stimulus (e.g. the bell in the Pavlovian example) is removed, then the conditioned response (e.g. the dog salivering) will weaken and eventually become extinct.

(c) Human as well as other animal behaviour is the result of conditioning, and changes in behaviour are the consequence of further conditioning.

The implication of Pavlov's experiments, for human learning is that since people naturally *associate* ideas and events that are experienced together then learning can be enhanced through relating the thing to be learned with something else which is already known or acceptable to the learner.

Operant conditioning

This theme was developed by the American psychologist B.F. Skinner, who introduced the concept of 'operant' conditioning. Skinner experimented with birds and animals, concluding that certain types of behaviour can be induced through offering rewards that are only available for *correct* behaviour. Skinner argued that behaviour is a function of its *consequences*. For example, a hungry animal placed in a maze will eventually find its way to a deposit of food and, if the experiment is repeated, that same animal will (after one or two early blunders) thereafter automatically take the correct route towards the food.

Skinner accepted that the S-R model explained all instinctive behaviour elicited by stimuli, but noted that it could not explain behaviours not directly connected to stimuli. (Behaviour not connected with identifiable stimuli is called *operant behaviour*.) Rather, people became conditioned through associating certain outcomes with certain modes of behaviour, e.g. working hard leading to high wages, entering a restaurant and satisfying hunger, etc. Accordingly, Skinner's model is called the response-stimulus (R-S) approach. For instance, entering a restaurant is the *response* to the stimulus of hunger. The individual gets to know that by going into a restaurant he or she will be able to obtain food.

Classical vs operant conditioning

Operant (also known as 'instrumental') conditioning differs from 'classical' Pavlovian conditioning in that it applies to learning which *results* from certain types of behaviour and is not concerned merely with the identification of *causes* of behaviour. Thus, the subject is not necessarily given a direct stimulus, but rather might behave in a random fashion until he or she discovers by chance that certain behaviour has beneficial consequences.

According to Skinner, any behaviour that is rewarded will tend to be repeated. Thus, for example, a pigeon that has to shift a lever in order to release a piece of food will, by trial and error, eventually discover how this may be achieved. After the correct behaviour has been rewarded a few times, the pigeon will have learned the procedure required to obtain the food and will thereafter follow this procedure on every occasion – it does not require a direct stimulus (noises, electric shocks, etc.) to cause the pigeon to act in this way. Hence, a general theory of animal (including human) behaviour may be defined.

Skinner concluded that positive reinforcement (reward) generally encouraged effective learning much more than negative reinforcement (punishment). This led Skinner to advocate similar approaches to the training of humans. Thus, he suggested, trainees should receive positive reinforcements each and every time they make correct responses. Complex subjects and problems should be broken down into very small component parts and the correct response to each part should be shown to the trainee in sequence. Hence, instead of learning inefficiently through trial and error, the trainee should receive a preprogrammed series of precise instructions, with clearly identifiable rewards for correct responses. Machines, Skinner argued, were far more effective for providing instruction presented in this manner than were human teachers!

4. Operant conditioning and training

Operant learning theory has the following implications for occupational training:

(a) Motivation to succeed on a training programme can be provided by the *benefit* available from the training, e.g. the prospect of a secure job, an increased standard of living and/or higher occupational status.

(b) Trainees' motivation during a course must be kept up by regular rewards.

(c) Appropriate responses to clearly defined stimuli must be plainly spelt out (i.e. the instructor should tell trainees exactly what they must do in various situations).

(d) Trainees should have 'knowledge of results', meaning they should know how well they are doing; and wherever possible should be given intermediate objectives. Whole tasks should be divided into parts, and students offered plenty of opportunity to practise and repeat operations. Learners who know they are improving will be better motivated than those who are left in the dark.

5. Criticisms of the behaviourist model

Behaviourists have been criticised for the following reasons:

(a) Many of their results derive from experiments on (non-human) animals, especially cats, rats and pigeons. Animal experiments are convenient for researchers because:

(*i*) animals are available in large numbers

(*ii*) things are done to animals that would be illegal if done to humans

(*iii*) animals will not (or should not) have preconceived ideas about what sorts of behaviour is expected of them

(*iv*) animals cannot complain, and there is no need to obtain their consent prior to conducting an experiment.

Note, however, that while the results derived from animal experiments may be extremely useful in analysing the psychology of cats, rats, pigeons and other birds and animals, they need not imply anything whatsoever about human behaviour. Animals possess motivations quite different from those of people, and researchers cannot ask animals how they feel or *why* they behaved in a particular way.

(b) Learning is viewed as a *responsive* process, with learners taking no part in determining what should be learned or the methods to be used.

(c) The model ignores critical questions regarding *who* should design curricula and syllabuses for training courses (a curriculum is a listing of all the subjects to be studied, a syllabus is a detailed work programme for a particular subject).

(d) Behaviourism has little to say about the development of insight and the growth of understanding. Moreover, it cannot easily explain how people 'learn how to learn'.

(e) The behaviourist model is not appropriate for the transmission of basic intellectual concepts concerning space, time, logic and philosophical issues where relations between cause and effect are nebulous.

LEARNING

6. Further approaches to learning

Several theories of learning have been advanced in opposition to the behaviourist approach. Among the more important are the following.

Action learning

This regards learning as a participative process in which learners become actively engaged with their environments. Learning is regarded as a form of general intellectual development that cannot always be related to stimulus and response. How, for example, does one learn about time, space and other fundamental logical concepts?

According to this model, learning occurs as people structure and restructure their perceptions in consequence of their experiences of attempting to manipulate external environments. The mind is regarded as working in a manner analogous to the digestive system, constantly assimilating and accommodating new material.

Cognitive approaches

Here, learning is seen as a process whereby individuals come to make sense of their experiences. People learn by continuously re-evaluating their experiences, hence constantly increasing their ability to understand the environments in which they exist. Thus, learners need to be constantly and actively *involved* with learning materials. Learning processes cannot be dismembered into simple stimulus/response components as the behaviourists suggest. The learner must perceive learning materials as valuable, and worth the effort needed to master the subject involved.

Cognitions (perceptual understandings) derive from complex interactions of thoughts, emotions, observations and experiences. Once established, cognitions create expectations that determine behaviour. Cognition is discussed in 4:**15**.

Social aspects of learning

The 'social learning' approach assumes that everyone is born with an intellect which from the first day of life attempts to make sense of the outside world. If people do not learn it is because the learning process has *itself* been mismanaged. The individual, moreover, interacts with and learns from social as well as material environments.

Much of the social learning of humans is based on the observation of other people, e.g. children imitating their parents. *Role learning* is an important aspect of social learning. It means that the individual learns to behave, feel and perceive the world in the same way as other people who occupy a similar role. This involves the individual developing an understanding of the attitudes of occupants of the role, brought about through direct tuition by existing role occupants and by the objective demands of various role situations.

7. Principles of learning

The theories described in previous sections collectively suggest the following general principles of learning:

(a) People learn more and learn faster the more they *want* to learn. Accordingly, learners need to recognise their personal deficiencies and to perceive the material presented as a means to remedy them.

(b) Learning programmes should proceed steadily, and not exceed the intellectual capacity of the trainee.

(c) Learners' progress should be regularly monitored as they move through a programme; learners themselves should be able to assess how well they are getting on.

(d) Educational/training methods should be as varied and interesting as possible with the maximum amount of student/trainee involvement at all times.

(e) Each learner should be given clear targets.

(f) Rapid and effective learning should be reinforced, e.g. through the allocation of high grades for assessed work.

(g) Upon completing a course of instruction, the learner should be able to transfer abilities learned in relation to one task to the completion of similar tasks. For instance, someone who has learned word-processing using one software package will soon be able to master others. Learning can be transferred in either or both of two ways: through common elements in various activities (e.g. using the telephone, typing, dealing with customers), and/or through the transfer of the basic *principles* of what has been learned. An example of the latter is the motor mechanic who learns the general theory of the internal combustion engine prior to any practical work. Such a mechanic is then equipped to repair *any* type of motor vehicle regardless of its age, condition or make. Unfortunately, 'negative transfer' of learning sometimes takes place, i.e. the learner has great difficulty in picking up something new because of previously-acquired habits of thought or working methods. Consider, for instance, the two-finger typist who takes a touch-typing course and makes much slower progress than classmates on account of his or her existing in-built typing reflexes.

(h) Learners need plenty of time to absorb material. Rest periods are especially important here.

(i) Learners absorb and understand more material if they feel relaxed and are not frightened by the learning situation (e.g. the fear of making a bad impression on an instructor).

Barriers to learning might include the following:

(a) Conflicts between working methods, attitudes and behaviour recommended during formal training and those that fit in with the structure and culture of the employing organisation. For example, trainees from bureaucratic and hierarchical companies will know that survival in such a situation depends critically on following the rules and deference to authority. Telling these trainees that they ought to be innovative and creative and to challenge current methods is unlikely to alter their perspectives or behaviour.

(b) Suspicion of the motives of the people delivering the training, fearing perhaps that the outcome will result in employees having to do more work for the same amount of pay.

(c) Existence of stereotypical images in trainees' minds, e.g. mental resistance to learning the details of equal opportunities legislation consequent to racist/sexist preassumptions.

(d) Fears that the patterns of behaviour recommended by instructors will lead to bad personal relationships with colleagues (Salamon and Butler 1990).

Verbal learning

Learning through listening to spoken words is a primary learning method, especially in workplace situations. A number of factors influence how effectively verbal materials are learned:

(a) *Meaningfulness of words.* Verbal communications using words that quickly suggest a single or multiple associations with objects or events well-known to the listener have more meaning than others. The more meaningful the words the faster the learning.

(b) *Similarity.* Words and phrases may be similar in terms of their sound, meaning, or category of associations.

(c) *Frequency of transmission.* Frequent repetition of messages increases the ease with which they are learned and remembered.

(d) *Degree of abstraction.* Concrete words are better remembered than abstract concepts, e.g. 'apple' as opposed to 'fruit', presumably because of the association(s) provoked by a concrete message.

(e) *Type and amount of past learning experienced by the listener.* Education level and the subjects an individual has studied will affect the person's current liability to learn from verbal messages.

8. Learning in parts

Learning is sometimes (but not always) facilitated if the material to be learned is broken into units each of which is learned separately. This is called *distributive learning* and consists of a series of self-contained learning experiences, one after another. The things learned in early units are then practised in parallel with the acquisition of new knowledge and/or skills. Accordingly, material is split into segments in such a way that the learner can: (*i*) learn the first section; (*ii*) practise the first section; (*iii*) learn the second; (*iv*) practise the second section and the first; and so on. This enables the learner gradually to build up an inventory of acquired skills.

Part learning (as opposed to 'whole' learning, whereby all aspects of a topic or procedure are learned together) is useful where voluminous and/or complex material is involved. On the other hand, learners do not see the material in an overall context and thus may become bored.

9. Memory

For learning to occur the information that has been learned must be stored in some manner, i.e. it must be remembered. Note (importantly) that a trainee's failure to demonstrate knowledge of something that he or she should have learned could be the result not so much of the person's inability to learn, but rather of his or her not being able to retrieve what was learned. The latter could be due to:

(a) Decay of learned information, i.e. not using it for a long period so that less is remembered over time. Memories rarely disappear in their entirity, however, and may be recovered decades after an event even though the memories have lain dormant during the interim period.

(b) Interference with information about a certain topic stored in a person's memory by information concerning other matters, e.g. contradictions between material learned in earlier periods with that learned later on, or confusions among information relating to different topics. The latter might be experienced by a student who spends the day and evening before a chemistry examination revising (say) history. Thoughts relating to history may inhibit the student's recall of material relevant to chemistry during the chemistry examination.

(c) Memory 'blocks'. People sometimes know that they have the answer to a question but (frustratingly) cannot bring it to mind. The answer is 'on the tip of the tongue', yet remains elusive. Little is known about the physiological causes of this phenomenon.

(d) Repression, i.e. the stifling of painful memories in order to avoid the feelings of anxiety associated with them. Certain memories might be so deeply suppressed that psychotherapy and/or drugs are needed to facilitate their recovery.

Forgetfulness

A number of events and situations are known to encourage forgetfulness. These include:

(a) inability to practise

(b) lack of repetition of important points during the learning process

(c) an individual's refusal to recognise the validity of a point because it contradicts his or her internal value system, or is seen as distasteful in some way

(d) conflicts between new information and what has been learned in the past

(e) previously acquired bad habits where learning is concerned.

Information that is unusual or particularly interesting is less likely to be forgotten (even if it is unimportant) than information that is mundane. These highlighted items are said to have been 'sharpened' in the learner's mind, the remainder having been 'levelled', i.e. remembered only in very general terms.

10. Dual memory theory

This postulates that individuals can transfer large amounts of information from short-term memory to long-term memory through combining small units of information into larger blocs. This is only possible, however, if the learner *understands* each small unit and is thus able to place units into a meaningful context. Examples are remembering telephone numbers by splitting them into sub-units of three or four digits, or learning a song or poem 'line by line' (each line containing just a few words).

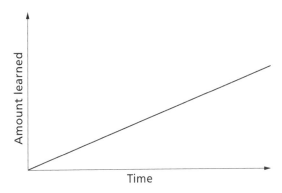

Fig. 6.1 Learning curve for an easy task

Memory is greatly assisted by understanding. Memorisation of information that is not understood is extremely difficult. This fact has many implications for learning, especially learning by parts (*see* **8** above).

11. Learning curves

These measure a person's rate of progress through a learning session (or course or entire programme). Figure 6.1 shows a typical learning curve for an easy task. All aspects of the job are learned quickly and the amount of fresh information absorbed or technical skill acquired soon ceases. Figure 6.2 shows the curve for learning a difficult task, competence in which takes much longer and is only achieved gradually. Sometimes people attain far higher rates of increase of learning towards the end of a course – when they have mastered core concepts and competences – than at the beginning of the programme when they find the material extremely difficult. This is illustrated in Figure 6.3.

Often learners develop quickly at first, but then learn nothing more for a time although eventually they again begin to make progress. Figure 6.4 sketches the phenomenon, showing a 'learning plateau' in the middle of the course. Plateaux result from loss of motivation, from trainees being overloaded with information

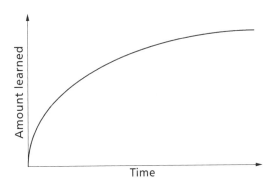

Fig. 6.2 Learning curve for a difficult task

87

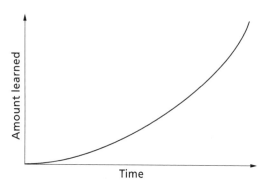

Fig. 6.3 Learning curve towards the end of course

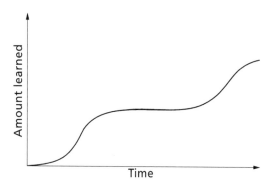

Fig. 6.4 'Learning plateau' in middle of course

which they need time to digest, lack of opportunity to practise, the need for rest and relaxation, or failure to recognise the importance of certain aspects of the training. There could be several plateaux during a particular course.

Typically, learning is fastest in the early training period, slowing down as the level of work becomes more difficult (*see* Figure 6.5).

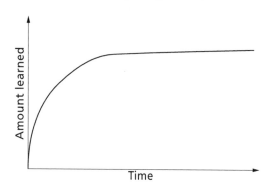

Fig. 6.5 Learning curve fastest in early training period, then levelling as work becomes more difficult

SKILL AND TRAINING

12. Definition

A skill is the capacity to perform a task competently, and need not be based on knowledge. For instance, a skilful machine operator may have no knowledge of the structure or technology of the machine he or she is operating, but rather has learned a *co-ordinated sequence* of actions for efficiently operating the machine.

Skills differ from 'tasks' or 'functions' in that whereas a skill is a pattern of behaviour, a function is an activity (e.g. selecting staff, organising decision making, appraising the performances of others) normally requiring several (possibly disparate) skills. Thus, although we sometimes refer to 'interviewing skills', interviewing is really a function requiring a number of skills – communication skills, listening, analysis and interpretation of information, etc.

Employment skills may be categorised as follows:

(a) *Technical skills* that involve working with physical objects or processes

(b) *Interpersonal skills* needed to operate as a member of a team, to lead others and to communicate effectively

(c) *Decision-taking skills* and techniques for solving problems

(d) *Information processing* related to the discovery and dissemination of information.

13. Education, training and skill

Education is not the same as training. The former is valued for its own sake; the latter for its practical uses. Education seeks to develop within the individual an awareness of cause and effect and the ability to appraise and criticise information; it need not be instrumental in attaining practical objectives. Thus, the educated person is (or should be) capable of: (*i*) understanding the wider contexts of particular tasks; (*ii*) appreciating the implications of various pieces of knowledge and the foundations upon which they are based; (*iii*) constructive criticism and independent thought.

Training, on the other hand, is utilitarian and intended to improve the skills that individuals use in their daily lives. Note, however, that training is not the same as 'teaching', since the latter concerns a range of activities, e.g. influencing, motivating and conditioning, as well as 'instruction' per se.

LEARNING AND ORGANISATIONS

14. The learning organisation

The term 'learning organisation' is sometimes applied to companies operating in turbulent environments that require transformations in working methods and which – in order to facilitate the introduction of new systems – train and develop their employees on a continuous basis. Hence the very essence of the business – its products, markets, processes and orientations – is likely to alter totally from period to period. Learning organisations discover the key characteristics of their environments and are thus better able to plan ahead. The learning organisation will attempt to identify interactions between the firm's sub-systems that facilitate or inhibit the management of change and is better able to cope with environmental and other change because it can accommodate unpredictability. It is not encumbered with rigid and out-of-date plans and procedures.

Nature of organisational learning

To learn means to absorb knowledge, acquire skills and/or assume fresh attitudes. Learning results in permanent changes in ability or behaviour, as opposed to short-term changes which are soon reversed. Organisational learning means all the processes whereby freshly discovered solutions to administrative problems pass into the firm's 'managerial memory', hence becoming integral parts of the organisation's mechanism for reacting to future events. A consequence is that decision-making procedures are continuously modified and adapted in the light of experience.

15. Single loop and double loop learning

According to Chris Argyris, organisations can be extremely bad at learning, unless the learning is simple and routine. Hence an organisation quickly loses the benefits of experience and reverts to its old bad habits. 'Single loop' learning, according to Argyris, is the learning necessary for an employee to be able to apply existing methods to the completion of a job. This is contrasted with 'double loop' learning that challenges and redefines the basic requirements of the job and how it should be undertaken. Single loop learning typically involves the setting of standards and the investigation of deviations from targets. Double loop learning means questioning whether the standards and objectives are appropriate in the first instance.

Implementing DLL

DLL inevitably occurs within organisations as they experience crises, fail to attain targets, and experience environmental change. Learning about mistakes in these situations however is costly and inefficient: decisions are taken too late to be effective, and all the benefits of forward planning are lost. Rather the organisation needs to:

(a) Educate its managers in the methods of learning by doing.

(b) Formulate its objectives and standards in such a way that they can be evaluated on a continuous basis and the basic assumptions that underlie them can be empirically tested.

(c) Seek to learn in advance of environmental turbulence or, if this is not possible, adapt its behaviour systematically through trial and error as situations develop. The first loop in the double loop system is the discovery of facts, acting upon them and evaluating the consequences. Knowledge gained is formal, systematic and explicit. The second loop involves the development of skills and 'know-how' resulting from the first loop and hence a change in fundamental perspectives on the matter under consideration. This feeds back into the interpretation of the facts embodied in the first loop and the actions taken thereafter. Hence, both behaviour and understanding of events and environments will change.

Training, employee relations and staff development

Companies operating in fast-changing environments require regular transformations in working methods and (in order to facilitate the introduction of new systems) must train and develop their employees on a continuous basis. Note however that a learning organisation is far more than a firm which spends large amounts on training. Rather, it requires the unqualified acceptance of change at all levels within the business, including basic grade operatives. Implications of the learning organisation for training, employee relations and staff development are as follows:

(a) Current policies should be open to question and challenged by all grades of employee. Indeed, management should welcome and actively support such questioning.

(b) Individuals should not necessarily be penalised for experimenting on their own initiative and making mistakes.

(c) There is a need for heavy emphasis on employee communication, with management diffusing information on current environmental trends throughout the organisation.

(d) Employee appraisal and reward systems need not be linked to the attainment of existing goals but rather to finding new and profitable fields of activity.

(e) Workers must possess an understanding of customer requirements.

(f) Employees need to 'learn how to learn'; taking their example from top management.

> Note how an organisation is, at base, a group of individuals, so that the manner whereby groups within it learn is affected by social, interpersonal and other intangible factors as well as information systems and other formal learning facilities.

Problems of implementation

Creating a learning organisation is difficult, for a number of reasons:

(a) Employees at all levels within the organisation must want to learn. Thus, the establishment of a learning organisation is a bottom-up process that may not fit in with the culture of a pre-existing bureaucratic and hierarchical system.

(b) Inadequate information gathering and internal communication systems.

(c) Organisational politics that might impede widespread acceptance of the idea.

Progress test 6

1. What is the difference between a stimulus and a drive?

2. Explain the difference between classical conditioning and operant conditioning.

3. List the main criticisms of the behaviourist approach to learning.

4. List the principles of learning collectively implied by the various learning theories.

5. Define the term 'learning in parts'.

6. What causes forgetfulness?

7. What is a learning plateau?

8. What is skill? What is the difference between skill and knowledge?

9. Explain the term 'learning organisation'.

10. What is double loop learning?

7

INDIVIDUAL ORIENTATION TO WORK

1. Nature of work

Does there exist within humans a natural instinct to work? To the extent that work is a natural activity, employees may be left to themselves and relied upon to work hard without close supervision. If, conversely, the average person naturally dislikes work then coercion to induce employees to work energetically will be required, with much supervision, application of the division of labour, rewards and penalties, and so on.

Some kinds of work provide opportunities for creative activity. Managers, for example, can exercise initiative and so might derive great personal satisfaction from their jobs. Those fortunate enough to exercise a craft, or who work in a profession, often find that their work itself is a source of enjoyment. For many people, however, work is a drudge. It is not enjoyable, nor is it satisfying, it is just something that has to be done.

2. Attitudes towards work

Certain societies denigrate work. In ancient Greece, for example, work was undertaken mostly by slaves! Other societies have integrated the work ethic into the fabric of community life. Whatever the attitude is – whether humans are regarded as living to work or working to live – it will be embodied in the child-rearing practices, educational system, arts and general culture of the society concerned.

Work provides income, social status and a means whereby individuals can become involved with society. Work usually is to some extent a social activity; few people work entirely alone. The fact that work brings people into contact with others may itself be a powerful motivator in making individuals want to work. Not only does unemployment cause reductions in workers' incomes, but it also severs many of their links with society. It follows that pay is not the only incentive to work; social factors are also relevant.

3. Problems resulting from monotonous work

Long periods spent undertaking routine and uncreative work create a number of possible difficulties for employees, including the following.

Boredom

Boredom may be caused by continuous repetition of a simple task or by the social environment in which tasks are undertaken. Thus, although a task might be interesting, the worker may still feel bored through the social isolation attached to the work. Conversely, a job might be trivial and repetitious yet not create boredom because the worker is able to communicate with others and find distractions. Complicated tasks need concentration. Workers performing complex jobs typically become absorbed in them and do not experience boredom.

Alienation

This occurs when workers inwardly feel that work is not a relevant or important part of their lives; that they do not really belong to the work community. It is associated with feelings of discontent, isolation and futility. Alienated workers perceive themselves as powerless and dominated. Work is seen as unrelated to real life; it becomes simply a means to achieve material ends. Alienation has been observed most often on automated assembly lines where work is extremely repetitive and personal relations with other workers are difficult to establish. Great unhappiness can result from alienation; indeed, it can adversely affect the worker's mental or physical health.

Frustration

Workers might feel frustrated when they are prevented from exercising control over their work and are not able to achieve their self-defined objectives. In practical terms, frustration may be caused by lack of control over working methods or the speed of production, by having to do work which employees perceive as meaningless, through not being involved in decision making, or through workers feeling that their grievances have not been properly heard. A worker will react to frustration either positively – by attempting to overcome the problem that has caused the dissatisfaction – or negatively. Examples of negative reactions are aggression (quarrels with colleagues, hostility towards management); apathy (lateness, absenteeism); unwillingness to assume responsibility; poor-quality work; high propensity for accidents, and high rates of labour turnover.

Consequences of frustration

Frustration can generate great energy within the person. This energy may be directed in various ways, depending on: (*i*) individual inclination; (*ii*) the nature of the situation; and (*iii*) the extent of the pressure the situation creates. Four characteristics of frustrated behaviour have been identified, as follows:

1 *Aggression*, e.g. when a frustrated person flies into a rage.
2 *Regression*, i.e. abandoning constructive attempts at solving problems and instead behaving in a childish way (e.g. kicking a motor car because it will not start).
3 *Fixation*, i.e. the compulsion blindly to continue doing something that has no objective value (continuation of outdated working methods or refusal to accept proven facts about a situation).
4 *Resignation*, i.e. apathetic attitudes and the abandonment of all attempts to

adapt to and cope with new circumstances (e.g. the unemployed person who eventually stays in bed most of the day instead of looking for work).

Frustration might be reduced through worker participation in decision making, more and better training, improved communications, better job design, and generally by treating employees as responsible individuals.

Making jobs more interesting

Routine jobs can sometimes be made more interesting through the following devices:

(a) task rotation and making individual workers responsible for a greater variety of tasks

(b) creation of coherent working groups with joint consultation on working methods and participative decision making

(c) allowing workers to determine their own pace of work

(d) decentralisation of production

(e) provision of suitable incentives.

4. The work ethic

The term 'work ethic' describes the proposition that work is a moral obligation and that work should occupy a central position in a person's life. Hard work is seen as a desirable activity in itself, for a number of reasons:

(a) It fosters proper personal attitudes and characteristics: industriousness, diligence, perseverance, aesthetism, etc.

(b) It enables the individual to contribute to the economic development and welfare of society as a whole.

(c) A hard-working community is said to be a stable and content community.

(d) Work enhances an individual's feelings of self-confidence and self-esteem.

(e) The range and quality of products available to the public is increased in consequence of employees taking pride in the standard and quantity of their work.

Whether a work ethic exists within a community, and if so its strength, depends on factors such as parental attitudes, child-rearing practices, societal role models (e.g. if high-status public figures do no work), social institutions that help individuals find work, the extent of inherited wealth (which enables inheritees to avoid having to work), and whether society in general expects people to 'make their own way' in life. Individuals possessing a work ethic are likely to experience high levels of job satisfaction and to perform better in their posts.

5. Work and socialisation

From an early age children are socialised into the culture of work and employment. They are prepared for work through vocational education, careers guidance, industrial training and school-to-work transition schemes. Whether the school-leaver looks forward to work eagerly, or approaches it with fear and trepidation, will depend substantially on attitudes towards and perceptions of work within the school-leaver's society.

Children first learn about work through hearing their parents talk about jobs and through observing parents journeying to and from places of employment. In consequence, although young children do not work as such, their play often reflects themes derived from their parents' occupations.

Role of the school

Thereafter, as children grow up they do increasing amounts of school 'work' and, although they have no specific experience of occupations, attitudes generally consistent with the pursuit of occupational success are inculcated in them. Thus, scholastic achievement is rewarded, success in competitive sports is encouraged; parents and teachers regularly exhort young people to excel in work-related activities. Also, aspects of personality specifically relevant to being good at work (intelligence, initiative, ability to concentrate for long periods) are systematically developed. Discipline patterns in school, moreover, are often justified against their value in training young people to fit into patterns of supervision and authority in places of employment.

6. Choice of occupation

In selecting an occupation, adolescents are guided by the advice they receive from teachers and careers officers and by parental role models. Additionally, youngsters are likely to be attracted by jobs associated with characteristics which they perceive themselves to possess. A boy, for example, who sees himself as an outgoing type will probably not want a job that involves spending long periods in social isolation. Hence, different types of work might be favoured at different stages of a person's life, depending on age, family circumstances, etc.

Many factors contribute to a final choice of job: availability, the nature of local industry, the example of older people, and individual personality. Social class (*see* **10** below) is known to be an important determinant of an individual's choice of occupation. Other major factors include:

(a) *Sex*. Most nurses are female; most engineers are men, etc. Although the sex composition of the labour force has altered significantly during the last half century, there are still many occupations where one sex or another predominates.

(b) *Race*. Members of ethnic minorities are hardly ever found in certain occupations.

(c) *Community values*. Localities that are dominated by (say) heavy industry, agriculture, engineering or commerce typically generate their own industrial cultures that encourage local residents to respond favourably to the prospect of certain types of work.

7. Constraints on choice of occupation

Although most people aspire to certain types of employment, their actual choice of a job is frequently the result of a compromise. Occupational 'choices' emerge from a complex combination of environmental and personal factors, and many constraints are involved. The latter might include:

- choice of subjects studied at school
- parental attitudes towards various types of work
- labour market opportunities
- inadequate knowledge of available jobs
- the age of the individual seeking employment.

8. Work and self-identity

During a child's formative years he or she might acquire a self-identity (or self-image) which is carried into work. An individual's self-identity consists of the entire set of perceptions that a person has about himself or herself. These perceptions derive from individual experiences and personalities, and offer the person a means for interpreting his or her place in society. Teenagers, for example, typically perceive their role as different from those of middle-aged or retired people, and behave in accordance with the perceived requirements of the teenage role. How individuals see their social roles usually alters with respect to age, family circumstances, and occupation.

Having taken a job, the employee might then begin to adopt outlooks and patterns of behaviour associated with that particular occupation. Newcomers to an organisation often copy the behaviour of its existing members, and continued exposure to organisational norms might lead them to assume the attitudes already held by the majority of the organisation's members.

Note, moreover, that as employees develop and progress through a chosen career they sometimes acquire new self-images. The self-identity of a supervisor, for example, is usually different from that of a middle-management line executive, who in turn will probably possess an occupational self-image different from that of a very senior director of the same firm. Following a promotion a person will often have to mix with people whose attitudes contrast with those previously held, so that adjustments in attitudes, behaviour and, ultimately, self-perception are required. Promotion brings a higher status, extra income and possibly a whole new way of life.

Work and lifestyle

Certain jobs, e.g. those of coal miners, dockers, shipyard workers or deep-sea fishermen, once provided the basis for an entire way of life. Work and work-related activities dominated the existences of these workers. The social life of a coal miner, for instance, would involve a great deal of interaction with other miners and their families outside working hours, and the social norms of the mining community would greatly affect the individual miner's attitudes, perceptions and behaviour: there is no clear distinction between work and non-work lifestyles in these circumstances – work is the primary determinant of the individual's self-identity.

Retirement from work

Retirement causes the loss of working colleagues, of status, of responsibility, and of a self-identity built up over a long period. For many people work is an anchor; it stabilises their lives, and the loss of work can sometimes lead people to withdraw from all forms of creative activity. It is not uncommon for retired people to become apathetic and unable to divert the energies they used at work to alternative activities. Well-qualified and industrious people typically relate their sense of purpose in life to their work, and its loss can affect the individual dramatically. Adverse symptoms (sometimes referred to as 'retirement syndrome') can include disorientation, failing physical health (not necessarily related to aging), and deteriorating social relations.

Preparation for retirement

Organisations can assist individuals prepare for retirement through offering the following:

(a) Financial advice on the best investments for protecting savings against the effects of inflation.

(b) Counselling to encourage a positive attitude towards retirement, emphasising the leisure and part-time employment opportunities available to retired persons.

(c) Advice on relocation. Many people move house when they retire – foolishly, in some cases, because of the disruptions to lifestyle and social relations this can involve and the possible assumption of fresh financial obligations.

9. Socio-economic status

A person's status is his or her ranking in a social system (e.g. a large company). Within an organisation, the status of any one of its individual members will be related to that individual's occupation, remuneration, rights, privileges, obligations and to the degree of deference (or otherwise) with which he or she is treated or expected to be treated by other members.

Status may be *ascribed* or *achieved*. Ascribed status is independent of personal ability. An example of this is someone who has been appointed to a senior-management position in a business simply because he or she is a child of the firm's owner. Achieved status, conversely, results from education, skill, effort and other personal qualities. Either category of status implies a fundamental *inequality* of individuals within the organisation.

Inequalities due to achieved status may be attributable to the division of work in a business, or to differences in function, or differences in authority or responsibility. Inequalities resulting from ascribed status typically relate to the social class of the people involved.

10. Social class

Among the major determinants of class are family background and occupation (although the former frequently determines the latter), type of education received (comprehensive or private, grammar school, city technology college, or whatever), income and inherited wealth. In certain countries a person's social class is largely defined by economic variables: income, wealth, job prospects, housing standards, etc. Elsewhere (especially in Britain), the determinants of class are extremely complicated, with a wide range of social and cultural variables affecting a person's class position. Thus, for example, a British person might have a very high income yet still feel and behave as a member of the working class! The survival of strong class systems in certain countries results perhaps from the continuation over many centuries of historical distinctions between landowners, tradespeople and labourers, and the absence of radical influences forcing social change (e.g. occupation by a foreign power and/or total economic collapse) that have occurred in other states.

Social class can affect an employee's attitudes towards and behaviour at work in a number of ways: (i) higher and middle class people tend to identify with their employers more than working class individuals do; (ii) working class people are more likely to join trade unions; (iii) the occupational expectations of higher and middle class persons are usually greater than those of members of the working class; (iv) middle class people frequently hold jobs with better working conditions and terms of employment – superannuation, more sick pay, longer holidays, fringe benefits, etc.

Critics of the class system argue that:

(a) It is inefficient, holding back the innate talents and enthusiasm of those at the lower end of the structure.

(b) Hereditary transmission of power and privilege is undesirable in a democratic society.

(c) It is resistant to change and encourages the acceptance of outdated and irrelevant attitudes and values.

(d) Restricting access to top jobs to a small part of the population inevitably means that some low calibre people will occupy senior positions.

(e) To the extent that society is controlled by members of a small privileged upper class, society will inevitably be run for the economic benefit of these people.

Arguments in favour of the class system are as follows:

(a) Class-based societies are inherently stable. They exhibit little social disruption compared to more egalitarian societies.

(b) Resources can be deliberately channelled towards people at the top end of the system, hence creating a highly qualified, literate, articulate and competent ruling elite which is then released from the need to spend time on mundane activities. The latter may be undertaken by people of lower class who have been specially trained and conditioned to undertake these duties.

(c) Social classes cut right across regional and industry boundaries and thus help unite the nation.

11. Occupations and family role

Most research in this area has assumed that the male is the dominant breadwinner. In this context the following propositions have emerged:

(a) The greater a man's commitment to a career, the less committed to family life he is likely to be.

(b) Women identify with their husbands' occupations in one or other of three ways: (*i*) *collaboratively*, whereby the woman becomes actively involved in her partner's work (farmers' wives, for example); (*ii*) *supportively*, e.g. the wives of politicians or senior business executives; (*iii*) *peripherally*, whereby the wife is in no way concerned with the husband's occupation (wives of assembly line car workers, for instance).

(c) Men for whom work is their central life interest tend to dominate in family relationships and not to separate their work and family responsibilities (*see* **12** below). Men for whom home and family are the predominant life interest are inclined to have low occupational aspirations.

(d) Working women who are economically independent of their husbands do not necessarily increase their participation in home decision making that affects the family.

12. Theories of work and leisure

There are various approaches to the theory of work and leisure. One suggests that employees usually try to make clearcut psychological distinctions between their work and non-work existences: different attitudes and decision-making procedures and criteria are then applied in each existence. In other words, employees are assumed capable of 'switching off' immediately after they finish work and adopting entirely different perspectives.

Another view asserts that work and leisure are inseparably intertwined: attitudes derived from work automatically and necessarily spill over into leisure activities. The fact that certain hours of each day attract the payment of wages whereas the rest do not is of no consequence.

S.R. Parker analysed the differences in approach in terms of three possible patterns whereby individuals might relate work and leisure:

1 *Extension*. Here the person extends his or her work attitudes into leisure periods. Hence there is no clear demarcation between work and leisure. Normally, work is the central life interest of this type of individual.

2 *Neutrality*. A worker exhibiting this pattern recognises some (but not many)

distinctions between work and leisure. Home and family are this person's central life interest.

3 *Opposition*. This involves an explicit dichotomy between work and leisure activities which are not regarded as being connected in any way. Again, the family is the central life interest of this person.

13. Empirical findings on work and leisure

The following relationships have been discovered between work and leisure:

(a) Persons of high occupational status are more likely to participate in voluntary associations. However, high-status people whose work requires them to work alone for long periods have low degrees of involvement in voluntary non-work activities.

(b) There is no clear relationship between occupational level and the extent of active participation in local political activity.

(c) As the average length of the official working week is reduced the amount of overtime working increases, leaving the actual number of hours worked each week approximately the same.

Progress test 7

1. What are the main influences on the formation of attitudes towards work?

2. List the major problems that result from monotonous work.

3. Describe the processes through which individuals choose to enter particular occupations.

4. Define 'self-identity'. How does a person's occupation affect his or her self-identity?

5. Distinguish between social status and social class.

6. Explain the relationships that empirical research has found to exist between work and leisure.

8

MOTIVATION, INCENTIVES AND JOB DESIGN

MOTIVATION

1. Definition

An employee's motivation to work consists of all the drives, forces and influences – conscious or unconscious – that cause the employee to want to achieve certain aims. Managers need to know about the factors that create motivation in order to be able to induce employees to work harder, faster, more efficiently and with greater enthusiasm. Employees are motivated in part by the need to earn a living and partly by human needs for job satisfaction, security of tenure, the respect of colleagues, and so on. The organisation's reward systems (pay, fringe benefits, job security, promotion opportunities, etc.) may be applied to the first motive and job design to the latter. Much research has sought to discover the sources of motivation at work, but the theory of motivation is tentative and no definite conclusions can be advanced.

Motivation theory has developed in two directions: there are 'content theories' which focus on why certain goals are more important to some people than to others, and 'process theories' that seek to explain *why* individuals behave in a particular way. Thus, content theories ask the question 'What are the needs a person will seek to satisfy and how do these affect motivation?', whereas process theories examine the thought processes that people experience prior to taking action. Details of content and process theories are given in **6–17** below.

2. Early approaches to motivation

Social philosophers such as Jeremy Bentham and John Stuart Mill defined motivation in hedonistic terms. Humans, they asserted, are driven by the desire to obtain pleasure and avoid pain. As the science of psychology developed, this approach gave way to the view that innate instinctual differences in humans caused individuals to be motivated in different ways. It was believed that people were born with unique predispositions towards various motivating influences.

Sigmund Freud (*see* 4:5) suggested that a person's motivations could be greatly influenced by his or her unconscious mind. Individuals, he argued, are frequently unaware of their true desires and the forces which cause them to behave in particular ways. Often, repressed sexual motives were the actual cause of behaviour. B.F. Skinner's theory of operant conditioning (*see* 6:**3**) implied that motivation emerges from the interplay of stimulus and response. For example, poverty causes the search for work and, once the individual obtains employment, to work hard in order to maximise income. Immediate rewards (high wages) are obtained for correct behaviour (working energetically). Effort is regarded as the product of drive (*see* 6:**2**) and learned behaviour. Modern theories focus on the relationship between motivation and human need. The latter is regarded as central to the motivation process.

Biological approaches to motivation

In the early years of the twentieth century Clark Hull suggested that humans possess certain biological drives – gained over the centuries through the Darwinian process of natural selection – which largely explain individual predispositions towards certain actions. Initially Hull considered just the primary drives of hunger, thirst, sex, and pain avoidance. Deprivation of a physiological need would produce a drive to initiate behaviour aimed at satisfying the need, e.g. lack of water creates thirst and hence the search for liquid refreshment. Variability in actions taken depended on differences in the intensity of the drive, which itself depended on the degree of deprivation. Need satisfaction reinforced the behaviour patterns that led to fulfilment, so that these behaviour patterns would become habitual. 'Secondary reinforcers' were defined as factors that, while not of themselves satisfying primary needs, would nevertheless help obtain things that did indeed satisfy primary requirements. Money is an example of a secondary reinforcer. The concept of secondary reinforcement enabled Hull to attempt explanations of complex aspects of human behaviour. Consider for instance the motivation to achieve. In infancy a person's needs for food are satisfied by his or her mother, who also provides most of the infant's social contact. Hence the child learns to associate the reduction of hunger with maternal attention and approval, which becomes a secondary reinforcer. Over time the child thus becomes motivated to perform activities that have the mother's approval, e.g achieving success at school. Eventually the quest for success might assume a permanent role in the person's motivational system.

Problems with the biological approach to motivation include the following:

(a) The theory is extremely difficult to test empirically. How for example can the extent of habitual behaviour be measured? Most experiments in the field have been conducted on rats. This has generated large amounts of information on rat psychology, but may have little to do with human motivation.

(b) Unlearned drives are not restricted to hunger, thirst, sex and the avoidance of pain.

(c) Biological approaches fail to explain many forms of human behaviour.

(d) Arguably the theory is very naive in its assertion that complex behavioural processes can be understood by examining just a handful of variables.

(e) Altruistic motives are ignored.

Tolman's cognitive model of motivation

In the 1930s Edward C. Tolman suggested that human knowledge and understanding were more important for motivation than biological drives. Tolman
was a leading precursor of late twentieth century motivation theories in that he
approached motivation *via* the concepts of *expectation* (i.e. a person's estimate of
the probability that a certain action will have a particular result), and the value
to the individual of the expected outcome to his or her behaviour. Hence,
whether or not an act is performed was said to depend on the outcome expected
and the perceived worth of the outcome. It follows that motivation is more
concerned with incentives than with drives. The latter might determine how a
person acts, but not necessarily whether he or she *wants* to act in that manner.

3. Needs and motivation

All contemporary theories of motivation involve the concept of human need to
some degree, because attempts to satisfy needs seem to determine substantially
when and how human activity occurs. The most basic needs are physiological:
food, drink, sleep and shelter. Thereafter, most people experience needs for
affection and contact with others; they like to feel wanted by and useful to the
community in which they live and work. Higher-level needs include demands
for social status and personal development.

Employment satisfies many needs – wages pay for food and clothing, and
jobs bring people into contact with fellow employees. Working environments
and company personnel policies can help individuals fulfil their needs, or can
be sources of workers' dissatisfaction. The need for security is fundamental;
people seek assurance that basic requirements will always be met no matter what
the circumstances. A job supplies security through tenure arrangements, sick
pay and pension schemes, redundancy payments, and so on. Similarly, the need
for status, self-esteem and personal enhancement might be satisfied through
promotion systems, participation in decision making, training and the provision
of fringe benefits.

Achievement needs

According to David McClelland (1961), the need to achieve is a primary motivating factor. Other important needs, he suggested, are the needs for power and
affiliation. Achievement-oriented people were said to (*i*) prefer tasks for which
they had sole responsibility, (*ii*) avoid risk, and (*iii*) monitor continuously the
effects of their actions. 'Need achievers', as McClelland called them, worked
extremely hard and constantly sought to improve their performances. Power
seekers, conversely, were motivated by the prospect of controlling subordinates.
Affiliators wanted pleasant relationships with colleagues and to help other
individuals. McClelland used the term nAff to characterise an individual's need
for friendly relations with others. People with a high nAff had strong desires for
approval by peers and in consequence tended to adopt conformist attitudes
when working in groups. The work of David McClelland is discussed further in
5 below.

Arguably, individuals with high achievement needs often make good entrepreneurs running their own businesses, or managers of self-contained units within large companies. Note however that need achievers are not *necessarily* effective managers. They are concerned with their personal advancement, but may not be capable of encouraging others to succeed (a vital management skill). It could be that the best executives are those with a high need for affiliation.

4. Motivation and wages

According to F.W. Taylor (*see* 2:**1**), the primary motive for hard work is high wages. Therefore, the role of management is to organise work as efficiently as possible, so that high wages can be earned. This, Taylor argued, meant stringent application of the division of labour, work measurement and method study. The human relations school, conversely (*see* Chapter 3), asserts that social factors – particularly inter- and intra-group relations – are (at least) equally important in motivating workers.

Arguments *in favour* of money being the dominant motivator are listed below:

(a) High wages provide access to physical goods, services and lifestyles greatly valued by the majority of employees.

(b) High incomes indicate occupational competence and are a mark of success. This itself constitutes an important motivating factor.

(c) Money can *simultaneously* satisfy many needs. Thus, for example, it could be used to purchase expensive luxury goods that meet esteem needs (*see* **6** below), or to finance a personal hobby thereby helping satisfy a need for self-actualisation. People may say they do not value monetary rewards *per se*, but they still want the things that can be purchased with money.

(d) Comparison of a person's wage with the wages of others enables the individual to relate his or her job to others within the organisation and within industry generally.

The arguments *against* wages being a primary motivator are as follows:

(a) Workers may fear that once the high performance targets attached to large pay packets have been met, these targets will be regarded by management as the norm so that no further pay increases can then be expected. Accordingly, employees might prefer a less intensive pace of work, albeit on lower incomes.

(b) The definition of 'good pay' is itself subjective. A certain level of wage might be seen as excellent by one person, but as paltry by another.

(c) Workers might assume that an offer of higher pay implies job losses among the labour force, including perhaps their own jobs.

(d) Employees often wish to assert their independence from management and may do this through the formation of tightly-knit and socially coherent work groups which influence workers' behaviour more forcefully than the prospect of higher wages.

Whether it is a primary motivator or not, money is a convenient way of measuring the worth of a job and of indicating the standards expected of the worker (by way of bonus schemes, for example). Also, pay rises awarded for excellent performance can greatly increase a worker's commitment and general morale.

Money is perhaps a better motivator in the short term rather than in the longer term. Note in particular that increasing amounts of money might be needed to achieve equal increments in employee satisfaction (for example, an extremely large pay rise may be necessary to increase the motivation of someone who is already on a high salary).

5. The work of D.C. McClelland

According to David McClelland, the need to achieve (labelled by McClelland as nAch) is an important motivating factor for many individuals. Other key motivators were the needs for power (nPow) and for affiliation (nAff). McClelland defined the achievement motive as a predisposition to compete against a self-defined standard of excellence. A person with high nAch would work hard to try and achieve standards whenever these were available, and would create his or her own standards if none existed. 'Achievers' have the characteristics that they:

- might not put a great deal of effort into activities (*i*) with little chance of success (because there is little possibility of achieving anything), or (*ii*) that are very easy to complete (since no sense of achievement will follow). Hence high nAch people are likely to work best when there is an intermediate probability of succeeding.
- experience feelings of anxiety when confronted with the prospect of failure
- prefer tasks for which they have sole responsibility
- continuously monitor the effects of their actions
- want to do better than others, solve problems, and find better ways of doing things
- commonly succeed as entrepreneurs or as managers of self-contained units within large organisations.

'Affiliators' have strong needs to be involved with others, to have pleasant interpersonal relationships and to help their colleagues. People with high nAff experience strong desires for approval by peers and in consequence tend to adopt conformist attitudes when working in groups. They avoid conflict and are keen to participate in social activities. Power seekers, conversely, are motivated by the prospect of controlling others. They want to influence people and be responsible for them. Hence they will try to change other people's attitudes or behaviour, and gain control over information and resources.

CONTENT THEORIES OF MOTIVATION

6. Content theories and the work of A.H. Maslow

The major content theorists are A.H. Maslow, C.P. Alderfer, F. Herzberg and D. McGregor. Content theories of motivation seek to determine the individual's choice of goals and hence why certain things are more important to some people than others. Perhaps the most influential of all the proponents of this approach has been A.H. Maslow, who suggested that individuals are motivated by five levels of need. When the first level has been satisfied the individual will attempt to satisfy second level needs, then move to third, fourth, and finally fifth levels. The five categories of need in the order in which (according to Maslow) a person will seek to satisfy them are as follows:

1 *Physiological.* These must be satisfied for a person to survive. They include food, shelter, clothing, heat and light. Income from employment allows people to satisfy such basic needs.

2 *Security.* Once physiological needs have been met the individual will, Maslow argued, seek security at home, tenure at work, and protection against reduced living standards. Purchase of life, house and medical insurance, and collective activities through trade unions are examples of attempts to achieve security.

3 *Social.* Most people desire affection; they want to belong to a community, and to feel wanted. Hence, social groups, religious, cultural, sporting and recreational organisations are formed. At work, people create activity groups, trade unions and information communications systems.

4 *Esteem.* Esteem needs include needs for recognition, authority and influence over others. Also relevant are desires to acquire possessions and internal demands for self-respect. Such needs could be met through the occupation of highly-ranked jobs, together with the provision of status symbols: large expensive company cars, wall-to-wall carpeting, etc.

5 *Self-actualisation.* The highest level of need in the Maslow hierarchy concerns creative activity and the search for personal fulfilment. Having satisfied all other needs, the individual will want to accomplish everything he or she is capable of achieving; to develop individual skills, talents and aptitudes. Few people ever reach this final stage.

7. Problems with Maslow's approach

Maslow's framework offers a convenient taxonomy of human needs, and he is much quoted in management studies literature. There are, however, a number of problems associated with his approach:

(a) Some needs might not exist in certain people. What is considered important by one person could be regarded as trivial by another. Social environments influence individual perceptions; much depends on the traditions, cultures and lifestyles of the societies in which people live.

(b) Assuming that all the needs suggested by Maslow are in fact present, they might not be ranked in the order outlined. Needs can exist simultaneously and horizontally as well as sequentially and vertically.

(c) Maslow had little to say about sources of need. The fact is that many basic needs are actually learned responses with cultural, not physiological, origins. Behaviour can be conditioned; wants may be created. Equally, current perceived needs can be suppressed by social pressures.

(d) The theory states that individuals will seek to attain higher-level needs only when lower needs have been satisfied. Many people, however, are acutely conscious of higher needs even though their fundamental physiological needs have not been fully met. In a consumer society, the poor may yearn for status symbols even though they are unable to satisfy their immediate requirements.

8. C.P. Alderfer and ERG theory

Alderfer restructured Maslow's theory into three groups of basic need: existence; relatedness; and growth. (ERG is the acronym for these three words.)

Existence needs correspond to the physiological and security needs of the Maslow system. *Relatedness* needs include the needs for affection, and for personal relationships as a whole. *Growth* needs involve self-actualisation and the desire to take decisions and exert effort and control.

The three levels are said to occur as a hierarchy (as in Maslow's theory) so that individuals are assumed to wish to satisfy them sequentially. However, ERG theory suggests that if a person cannot achieve the next highest level, then the one below it will assume far greater importance in that individual's mind. Thus, for example, an employee who is not allowed to take significant decisions at work might concentrate instead on building up good interpersonal relationships with colleagues.

9. The complex man model

Maslow's theory implies that humans naturally seek personal fulfilment. This, in association with theory Y (*see* 13:8), has been termed the 'self-actualising man' approach to employee behaviour, which differs from the 'economic man' view of human nature associated with scientific management (*see* Chapter 2) and the 'social man' view of Elton Mayo (*see* 13:7). All these approaches have been criticised as excessively general and oversimplistic. The 'complex man' approach (first suggested by E.H. Schein) has thus been offered as a more realistic alternative. The assumptions underlying the complex man model are as follows:

(a) No single management style can succeed in improving the performance of all workers; different employees respond to any particular management style (autocratic, democratic, etc. – *see* 7:3–6) in different ways.

(b) The motives of any given individual are extremely complex and liable to change over time and with respect to the circumstances of situations – especially those surrounding his or her job or employing organisation.

(c) Experience causes people to acquire new motives.

(d) A high level of satisfaction does not *necessarily* lead to increased productivity. The belief that individuals are essentially unpredictable and subjective, and that each person responds to a unique set of complex motivators, is known as the 'phenomenological' view of human behaviour – implying that behaviour cannot be explained through scientific analysis and observation. This contradicts the behaviourist model (which asserts that individual actions are determined by environmental stimulus-response factors) and the 'rational' view, which sees behaviour as the outcome of logical thought and objective reasoning.

10. F. Herzberg and the two-factor model

According to Herzberg, two separate sets of factors influence human behaviour – on the one hand people need to avoid pain and obtain the basic necessities of life; on the other hand they need to develop their personal capacities and potentials. Herzberg asked professionally-qualified employees (engineers and accountants) what events at work had increased or reduced their satisfaction. Factors generating dissatisfaction were: inadequate pay; bad personal relations with colleagues; poor supervision; unpleasant physical working conditions; and the absence of fringe benefits. These are called hygiene or maintenance factors (from the analogy that hygiene does not improve health, but does prevent illness): when catered for they do not actually increase a worker's job satisfaction, but their deficiency creates dissatisfaction.

Note that hygiene factors relate to the conditions of work rather than to work itself, thus an improvement in a hygiene factor will not be noticed for very long. For example, a worker who is feeling cold may complain and as a result the firm's heating is turned up, but the worker will quickly become acclimatised to the higher temperature and forget how cold it was in the first place. Improvements prevent dissatisfaction, but do not increase satisfaction in the long run.

The factors responsible for creating satisfaction (motivating factors, in Herzberg's language) were:

- sense of achievement on completing work
- recognition from others within the organisation
- responsibility assumed
- varied work, involving an assortment of interesting tasks
- prospects for promotion.

Motivators encouraged better-quality work, hygiene factors did not: a worker might resign because a hygiene element was inadequate, yet would not work harder because the factor was satisfactory. Likewise, the absence of suitable motivators would not cause employees to resign, but an increase in the strengths of motivating factors would significantly improve effort and performance.

Herzberg's model

Herzberg was concerned with the attitudes towards work of qualified professional and managerial staff, and not with shop-floor workers who might be much more concerned with prospects of immediate financial reward. And managers themselves respond to different factors in different ways.

Perhaps the most controversial of all Herzberg's conclusions was that pay and fringe benefits were classified as hygiene, not motivating, factors. Bearing in mind Herzberg's research methodology – questionnaires and interviews with managerial staff – it is reasonable to suspect that many employees stated that money was not an important motivator whereas in actual fact it was. Nevertheless, it would be wrong to overestimate the influence of the financial element.

The value of Herzberg's work lies in his pointing out the importance of job satisfaction in employee motivation, though it must be said that relegation of pay to the role of hygiene factor is probably a major oversimplification.

Implications of the model

Herzberg's approach is called the two-factor theory because it involves two factors: hygiene and motivation. Hygiene relates to *extrinsic* rewards, i.e. those which result from work but are not inherently a part of it. Examples of extrinsic rewards are money, security and fringe benefits. *Intrinsic* rewards, conversely, relate to the nature of the work itself: feelings of achievement, fulfilment and personal autonomy. These constitute the primary motivators.

A major implication of Herzberg's two-factor model is that managements should seek to 'enrich' the work of their employees so as to maximise the incidence of motivators in each person's job. This involves: (*i*) restructuring work in order to increase its consequence and variety; and (*ii*) extending the individual employee's control over his or her work situation. The processes of job enrichment are discussed in **27** below.

11. Douglas McGregor

According to McGregor, theory Y managers (*see* 13:**8**) would seek to motivate their subordinates through the goals of achievement, self-esteem and (possibly) the prospect of self-actualisation. Theory X managers, on the other hand, would limit subordinates' abilities to exercise discretion and use incentive schemes and penalties as primary inducements for increased effort. Theory X and theory Y are discussed in Chapter 13.

PROCESS AND EXPECTANCY THEORIES

12. Process theories

The major process theorists are V.H. Vroom, L.W. Porter and E.E. Lawler, whose work is collectively referred to as 'expectancy theory'. Equity theory (*see* **13** below) also belongs in the process category. Process theories seek to predict individual motivation by identifying the processes that determine the patterns of behaviour a person will follow when pursuing desired objectives.

13. Equity theory

This asserts that employees' own assessments of whether they are being fairly treated is a major factor influencing motivation. According to the theory, individuals regularly compare (perhaps unconsciously) the returns they are experiencing with the rewards given to other employees, in relation to the effort they contribute to their jobs. If a worker believes his or her returns correspond to those of other employees (proportionate to the effort involved) then a state of 'distributive justice' is said to occur, and the worker will be content. Otherwise, 'cognitive dissonance' (*see* 4:**15**) exists, meaning that the individual adopts a state of mind whereby he or she perceives the reward/effort ratio to be out of balance compared to the ratios of other workers. Removal of dissonance (through a pay rise or some other form of recognition, for example) will be greatly appreciated by the worker concerned.

The argument, put simply, is that if, having compared the inputs to their jobs with the outputs experienced, the workers involved then perceive they are not paid enough, they will reduce their effort, and *vice versa*.

There are three major problems with equity theory: (*i*) an individual's perceptions of equity will be subjective and thus extremely difficult to measure; (*ii*) inputs to and outputs from a job might not be accurately identified by workers; (*iii*) many other factors (e.g. group pressure and influence) are bound to affect a person's motivation.

14. Expectancy theory

This asserts that an individual's behaviour will reflect: (*i*) self-selected goals; and (*ii*) what the person has learned or believes will help achieve them. Thus, people are motivated by their *expectations* that certain modes of behaviour will lead to desired events.

Consider, for example, a worker who feels a strong need to achieve promotion and a higher standard of living. This person will be motivated in a currently-held job according to whether he or she believes that excellent performance will be noticed by superiors and that it will lead to promotion and hence significantly higher wages. Accordingly, motivation depends not only on personal needs and objectives, but also on *how* needs can be fulfilled and objectives accomplished. If someone feels that extra effort is unlikely to achieve results then little or no extra effort will be made.

15. Vroom's expectancy theory

V.H. Vroom asserted that an individual's behaviour is affected by:

(a) what the person wants to happen

(b) that person's estimate of the probabilities of various events occurring, including the desired outcome

(c) the strength of a person's belief that a certain outcome will satisfy his or her needs.

111

The theory can be stated in the following formula:

$$\text{Motivation} = \text{Valence} \times \text{Expectation}$$

Here 'valence' means the strength of the person's desire for a particular event or outcome. If someone wants something badly we say that he or she has a high valence for that outcome. Valence may be negative as well as positive. Negative valence means the person hopes that something will *not* happen. Valences (which represent 'preferences' in a loose sense) arise from personal experiences, and internally from within the individual.

The 'expectancy' part of the formula refers to the strength of the belief that certain activities will lead to an outcome. It shows the individual's estimate of the probability that one thing will lead to another. Note how if either valence or expectation is zero then motivation is also zero.

Vroom's model implies that to motivate a person it is necessary to increase the value of outcomes (in order to raise the level of valence), and/or to strengthen the visible connection between particular modes of behaviour and the occurrence of desired events.

Predictions of what will happen in the future are usually based on what has happened in the past. Thus, situations not previously experienced (for example, new working practices, job changes, environmental alterations) will give rise to uncertainty and may in consequence reduce employees' motivation. This is because the individuals concerned have no precedents upon which to base their assessment of the probable consequences of new situations. Hence, management should make clear to employees what precisely it expects from any alterations in policy or working practices that might be introduced.

Implications of the model

Employees should be able to see a connection between effort and reward, and the rewards offered should satisfy workers' needs. Vroom would argue that a complicated, unintelligible bonus scheme is unlikely to increase output even if higher wages are offered as part of the scheme. Similarly, experience of particular jobs gives workers precise knowledge of how output is connected to their activities. In this case expectancies are easily formed; workers know that the quantity and quality of production depends on how they perform their work. This implies that innate satisfaction derived from working hard and actually seeing the results – planned, predicted and brought about by the worker involved – is a primary motivator.

Note that since individuals possess different preferences for outcomes and different perceptions of the relation between effort and reward they will be motivated in different ways. Thus, expectancy theory is an element of the *contingency approach* (*see* 3:21) to management.

16. Porter and Lawler

These authors sought to explain the nature of the relationship between performance and effort. They hypothesise that two factors determine how much effort employees put into their work. The first factor is the extent to which the rewards from an activity are likely to satisfy the individual's needs for security, esteem, independence and personal self-development; the second is the individual's expectation that effort will lead to such rewards. It follows, the authors suggest, that the higher the probability that the reward depends on the exertion of effort then the greater the effort the individual will devote to an activity.

The efficiency of a person's effort depends, they argue, on: (*i*) his or her ability (skills, intelligence, etc.); and (*ii*) that person's interpretation of his or her role in the organisation. Obviously, individuals place different values on expected rewards. Some may be especially concerned with the quality of personal relations, others with money and similar physical recognition of their contributions.

17. Problems with expectancy theory

These include the following:

(a) Individuals might not recognise the importance of certain aspects of performance which significantly contribute to attaining desired objectives. For example, effective salespeople require good communication ability, including verbal communication skills. A salesperson who fails to see the crucial importance of verbal communication in selling will not bother to seek to improve this aspect of his or her behaviour.

(b) The theory assumes that individuals think logically and always act in a rational manner. Experience suggests this might not invariably be the case.

(c) Analysis is restricted to just two basic variables. It is extremely likely that (at least) several factors affect motivation.

(d) It is almost impossible to test the theory empirically (*see* 1:7).

BONDING

18. Bonding the worker to the firm

Motivation in practice seems to involve a mixture of factors relating to incentives, accountability and appraisal (*see* 16:**13–14**), individual perspectives, and the degrees of interest and challenge attached to jobs. Incentives may be positive or negative, the latter possibly including strict supervision and threats of disciplinary action against staff. Positive factors that encourage motivation encompass training and staff development, internal promotion, and (increasingly) the use of *symbols of attachment* of workers to the firm.

Staff uniforms

Staff uniforms are an example of the use of symbols as a means for bonding employees to companies. A staff uniform is at once a fringe benefit (staff do not have to buy clothes for work), a means for ensuring that employees appear neat and tidy in front of customers, an extension of the firm's corporate image, and a device for encouraging workers to identify with the organisation.

Advantages and disadvantages of staff uniforms

The advantages of having employees wear uniforms are said to include the following:

(a) They create a basic equality within the workplace.

(b) Workers assume the *personality* of the organisation and, in consequence, are able to convey powerful and positive non-verbal messages about the firm to the outside world. The physical appearance of staff tells customers much about the character of the company: what it is, does, wishes to be, and how it wants to relate to the external environment.

(c) The enterprise demonstrates its concerns for customer care. Consumers (hopefully) will perceive staff as dressing to please customers rather than themselves.

Problems with staff uniforms mainly relate to the possibility that the solid, reliable and well-established company images that uniforms project may encourage among employees a conformist attitude and lack of initiative. Critics allege, moreover, that uniforms can lead to staff not being prepared to think for themselves and to the adoption of arrogant and officious attitudes towards the public. The latter might occur through:

(a) Employees mentally associating the wearing of staff uniform with rules and procedures, hence creating an organisational culture inclined towards bureaucracy and red tape.

(b) The fact that how employees dress becomes totally determined by management which, in a sense, exercises a form of censorship over how the staff visually communicate with other people during working hours. Wearers of staff uniforms give up their own right to dress and be treated as individuals and may translate this into feelings that others need not be treated as individuals either – including the firm's customers.

(c) Staff being encouraged to act mechanically, as if they were robots and little more than appendages to reception desks or shop counters.

(d) The anonymity that uniforms create, enabling the uniformed employee to hide away behind the standardised modes of communication and behaviour that uniforms psychologically suggest.

19. Organisational behaviour modification (OBM)

This is a model of motivation based on Skinnerian stimulus/response theory (*see* 6:3) applied to business situations. According to the model, management can change employee behaviour by altering the consequences of certain forms of behaviour. This might be achieved through:

- positive reinforcement of desirable behaviour (*via* compliments or pay rises for example)
- 'avoidance learning' whereby a worker alters his or her behaviour in order to avoid unpleasant consequences, such as criticism every time he or she is late for work
- 'extinction', i.e. deliberately not providing reinforcement of certain behaviours so that eventually they lapse
- imposition of penalties (negative consequences).

OBM theory was developed by W. C. Hammer, who in 1974 suggested a six-step procedure for its use, as follows:

1 Relate rewards to performance. Do not reward everyone to the same degree.
2 Always praise desirable behaviour.
3 Advise individuals as to what they can do to obtain reinforcement.
4 Always tell people when they are doing wrong.
5 Issue reprimands in private, never in public.
6 Treat all subordinates even-handedly.

Clearly OBM programmes rely on management being able to identify clearly the performance-related behaviours that are crucial to the success of the firm, and the measurement of these behaviours and of subsequent improvements (or deteriorations). Critics of the technique allege that, while it may work in the short period, its damaging effects on management/worker relations and employee morale will negate its effectiveness in the longer term. Reinforcements such as praise for higher output become stale eventually, especially if they are not accompanied by higher pay.

JOB DESIGN AND JOB SATISFACTION

20. Definition of job satisfaction

Job satisfaction is the extent to which employees favourably perceive their work. High job satisfaction indicates a strong correlation between an employee's *expectations* of the rewards accruing from a job and what the job *actually* provides. Workers who are satisfied in their jobs will be co-operative and well motivated; those who are dissatisfied will be more inclined than others to:

- produce low-quality output
- go on strike
- be absent from work
- invoke grievance procedures
- leave the organisation.

Note, however, that high job satisfaction does not *necessarily* lead to improved performance. A worker may be extremely satisfied with a job, but still perform badly.

115

21. Factors affecting job satisfaction

The main factors affecting job satisfaction are as follows:

(a) *Performance.* Rather than increases in satisfaction improving job performance, the direction of the relation could in fact be the other way round – high performance may *itself* create high job satisfaction. The argument behind this proposition is that the attainment of stiff targets generates a sense of achievement and hence a pleasure in completing the work, especially if high performance results in higher financial and other rewards. Equally, if the rewards accruing to improved performance are regarded as inadequate, the worker will experience job dissatisfaction. In either case, it is the feedback on the consequences of performance that determines satisfaction. This approach is sometimes referred to as the 'performance–satisfaction feedback loop'.

(b) *Age of the employee.* Older workers tend to have lower expectations of what a job should offer and hence are more easily satisfied.

(c) *Interpersonal relations within a working group.* Employees who feel they are an integral part of a tightly-knit group and who support its norms (*see* 12:3) and objectives will probably experience higher job satisfaction than others.

(d) *Quality of supervision.* The style of leadership (*see* 13:3) applied by managers to their subordinates can greatly influence the latter's job satisfaction. It seems that satisfaction is highest when supervisors apply participative 'employee-centred' leadership styles (*see* 13:4–5).

(e) *Job content.* Work that involves varied, interesting and challenging duties is more likely to create job satisfaction.

(f) *Pay and working conditions.* Wages represent an index of the value of a worker's job (*see* 4 above). Working conditions affect the physical comfort of the employee while completing tasks.

(g) *Status of the job.* Employees who occupy higher-level positions in an organisation are on average more satisfied with their jobs.

(h) *Ease of communication within the organisation.* Workers in large organisations sometimes experience low job satisfaction because of interpersonal communication difficulties which create frustration (*see* 7:3) and feelings of inability to influence events that affect their working lives.

22. Job satisfaction surveys

Indications of job dissatisfaction are evident in high rates of staff turnover and absenteeism and in a high incidence of employee grievances. Confronted with such difficulties, management might conduct a survey among its employees to ascertain their feelings towards their jobs. The purposes of job satisfaction surveys are to:

(a) identify the sources of low morale

(b) distinguish differences in satisfaction among various grades of staff and employee groups (young and old workers, males and females, workers in different departments, etc.)

(c) improve communication between management and labour

(d) give employees the opportunity to express their views

(e) assess the impact of the organisation's policies on its employees.

23. The measurement of job satisfaction

Job satisfaction questionnaires are used to find out to what extent employees are satisfied at work. They may take several forms, some of which are described below.

(a) A series of questions covering different aspects of the job and working conditions. Against each question there are usually five possible answers; the employee is asked to indicate the answer he or she agrees with, e.g.

I feel that my job is:

(*i*) extremely boring
(*ii*) rather boring
(*iii*) fairly interesting
(*iv*) interesting
(*v*) extremely interesting.

It is possible to give a numerical score to this type of questionnaire by giving one point to answer (*i*), two points to answer (*ii*) and so on.

(b) A list of factors in job satisfaction which the employee is asked to rank in order of importance. This type of questionnaire is not directly linked to the conditions in which the employee works, or to the nature of the job, but its results may be used as a guide to future company policies.

For example, consider the following factors in a job and put the figure 1 against the factor you think is the most important, 2 against the next most important and so on:

Security
Pleasant colleagues
Pay
Good boss
Efficient organisation
Fringe benefits (pension, sick pay, etc.)
Interesting job
Authority over others
Promotion prospects
Responsibility; freedom from close supervision
Pleasant working conditions

In such surveys pay is usually placed about fifth in rank order, behind such

117

things as promotion prospects, responsibility, interesting job and security. When employees are asked instead to put the factors in the order in which the average person would place them, pay usually comes first.

(c) A free expression questionnaire, in which the employee is asked to write an essay on what is liked or disliked about the job and the employer. Sometimes the employee is interviewed and asked to reply orally instead of in writing.

Advantages of free expression questionnaires are that employees can use their own words instead of those chosen by someone else, and that they can discuss topics which might not have occurred to the investigator. Disadvantages are that:

- Unless employees are quite sure that their remarks will be treated in complete confidence, they will not be frank.
- The analysis of a large number of completed questionnaires of this type is difficult and often subjective.
- Some employees find great difficulty in expressing themselves clearly, particularly in writing.

Comments on job satisfaction questionnaires

Although the results of questionnaires often correspond with actual behaviour, there must always be some doubt regarding their reliability. They are open to objection on the following grounds:

(a) The questions asked may be interpreted in various ways by different people.

(b) The form of the questions may call for a misleadingly definite answer, omitting conditions and qualifications.

(c) An individual's self-perception may lead to replies which are thought to be true, but which do not in fact represent that person's actual behaviour – a form of innocent self-deception.

(d) When responding to questions, people often give the answer they think will be most acceptable, or will show themselves to the best advantage.

The following conclusions regarding job satisfaction seem to be generally accepted, because they are confirmed by large numbers of questionnaires given to a wide variety of employees:

(a) Job satisfaction usually increases with age.

(b) Higher social class and status are related to greater satisfaction but, among those doing the same job, better education is associated with lower satisfaction.

(c) The less secure the job, the less the satisfaction.

(d) There is no firm relationship between job satisfaction and productivity.

Behavioural evidence of job satisfaction

A more reliable way of assessing job satisfaction should be through behaviour at work rather than replies to questions. Unfortunately, the interpretation of much working behaviour is highly subjective, e.g. whether the employees seem 'happy'. The most objective measures seem to be the extent of absence from work and the rate at which employees leave the company. It is logical to assume that if people are satisfied in their jobs they will tend to remain in that employment and have little avoidable time off. Of course, job satisfaction is not the only influence on leaving or absence; for example, suitable alternative jobs may not be easily found, or the employee may lose pay for absence.

Job satisfaction and productivity

Although common sense might lead us to expect that a worker who finds a job satisfying would produce more than one who is not satisfied, many investigations have shown that, generally speaking, productivity and job satisfaction are not related. It is possible for any degree of job satisfaction to be associated with any degree of productivity, i.e. a satisfied worker may have low productivity or a dissatisfied worker may have high productivity, or vice versa. Closer analysis may provide at least a partial explanation of this apparently irrational effect.

The expectation that a satisfied employee will work hard is basically a paternalistic attitude on the part of the employer. It implies either that the employee, grateful for being given a satisfying job, will show gratitude by complying with the employer's wishes, or that because the worker is satisfied he or she is inevitably enthusiastic, conscientious and persistent and therefore produces at a high rate. However, a more realistic assumption is that the employee may not have any feelings of gratitude towards the employer and that the worker's enthusiasm may either show itself in a form unwelcome to the employer, for example an overemphasis on accuracy, or may be tempered by other considerations, for example a wish to adhere to group norms of production. The interests of the employer and the employee do not always coincide.

From the employee's point of view, work brings many kinds of rewards: money, friendship, status and achievement among others. In some circumstances working harder may increase these rewards, in others it may reduce them. Status and achievement, which might be expected to favour higher productivity, are needs which have little appeal to some employees, or are needs which they do not expect to satisfy at work. It is quite possible for employees to work hard in jobs they dislike because they fear dismissal, are attracted by a high level of pay, or simply find hard work the best way of making the time go quickly. On the other hand, many employees, in particular professional and skilled workers and those who have a moral involvement in their jobs, combine high job satisfaction with high productivity, perhaps because they are motivated by loyalty towards a profession, craft or ideal rather than towards an employer. The relationship between productivity and the motivation of employees is extremely complex, and much research remains to be done.

24. Absence from work

Absenteeism is a major source of cost and disruption in British companies. Currently, UK industry is losing 200 million working days each year to deliberate non-attendance. The average worker takes eleven days per year off, and on

119

any given day up to 7 per cent of the workforce of a typical large British company will be absent – four times more than the rate among UK industry's leading international competitors. Losses attributable to absenteeism include reduced production, sick pay, the need for additional overtime to cover for absent workers, hassles resulting from having to reschedule projects, failure to meet deadlines, additional clerical and supervision expenses (telephone calls, administering statutory sick pay, etc.) and so on. Factors contributing to non-attendance include:

(a) *The nature of the job*: physical conditions, boredom, inconvenient working hours, stress, unsatisfactory interpersonal relations, poor supervision.

(b) *Characteristics of the worker*: individual disinclination to work, age and sex (young people and females on average take more time off work than others), length of service (long-serving employees are less prone to absenteeism), a person's state of health, extent of family responsibilities, attitudes and perspectives concerning regular attendance, travelling difficulties.

(c) *Motivating factors*: incentive schemes (bonuses, special awards for consistent attendance), availability of sick pay, extent of piece rate working, effectiveness of managerial exhortations aimed at persuading employees to turn up for work, the firm's readiness to apply disciplinary actions (formal warnings, deductions from pay, and other penalties short of dismissal, etc.).

Note how some of these factors interconnect, e.g. the fact that on average women take more time off than men but that women are also known to predominate in many tedious and low status occupations.

Measures for controlling absenteeism include job design and job rotation intended to make work more interesting, increased employee participation in decision making, explicit consideration of job applicants' attitudes towards absenteeism during employee selection procedures, employee counselling, implementation of flexitime and job sharing arrangements, and careful record keeping to identify individuals and types of work with the highest absenteeism rates.

25. Grievances

Grievances can result from external circumstances – such as an employer imposing detrimental working conditions on employees, or from internal feelings of unhappiness and / or frustration. Externally created grievances may be remedied through altering the environmental circumstances that cause them: restoring a contractual right, improving conditions, increasing a benefit, or whatever. Grievances resulting from workers' hurt feelings might be best resolved through counselling.

Many grievances develop from misunderstandings rather than fundamental conflicts of interest, and a simple statement of facts may be all that is required to resolve the difficulty. Minor complaints can arise from breakdowns in communications, from petty jealousies, interpersonal rivalry, or from interdepartmental disputes. Such problems may usually be settled quite easily through increasing the flow of information within the organisation, by defining the authority and responsibilities of people and departments more carefully, and by generally promoting co-operation between sections.

No organisation is so well managed that its employees never need to complain, and even if a firm consciously seeks to be a good employer, staff may still *feel* that certain complaints are justified even if, objectively, they are not. Well-constructed grievance procedures enable firms to resolve complaints quickly, fairly, and without resort to industrial action on the part of employees. Formal procedures minimise the risk of inconsistent decisions: the employer is seen to be trying to be fair. And, of course, the absence of formal procedures will severely prejudice an employer's case if the grievance eventually results in legal proceedings.

A grievance 'procedure' is an established set of agreed rules for enabling management and the aggrieved employee to settle a complaint. Such rules restrain both sides from behaving irresponsibly, provided both are committed to their application and have confidence in their impartiality. Other advantages of formal procedures are as listed below:

(a) Both sides have a common understanding of how a grievance will be received and processed.

(b) The managers and union representatives who deal with grievances change periodically on account of promotions, resignations, retirements and staff transfers. However, the existence of written rules enables procedures to be applied consistently over time.

(c) Written rules clarify important matters such as who has authority to take decisions in settlement of disputes, the time-scale for registering a grievance, how an appeal should be lodged, etc.

(d) Formal records of grievance hearings avoid subsequent disputes about what was discussed and agreed in the hearing.

(e) Employees have the security of knowing that whenever major problems arise they can air their concerns to the highest levels of management within the firm.

There are, however, arguments in favour of *informal* procedures. Formalisation reduces flexibility, since precedents established through following formal rules must be adhered to in future cases. A mini legal system will build up around the policies, with its own protocol, norms, case law and rules of interpretation. It becomes impossible to 'turn a blind eye' to certain practices regardless of the circumstances in which they occur.

JOB EXTENSION

26. Job design

The process of job design is that of deciding which tasks and responsibilities shall be undertaken by particular employees, and the methods, systems and procedures for completing work. It concerns patterns of accountability and authority, spans of control and interpersonal relations between colleagues. The purpose of job design is to stimulate the worker's interest and involvement, thus motivating the worker to greater efforts. Jobs may be *enlarged* or *enriched*.

27. Job enlargement and job enrichment

Job enlargement means increasing the scope of a job through extending the range of duties and responsibilities it involves. This contradicts the principles of specialisation and the division of labour whereby work is divided into small units, each of which is performed repetitively by an individual worker. The boredom and alienation caused by the division of labour can actually cause efficiency to fall. Thus, job enlargement seeks to motivate workers through reversing the process of specialisation.

Job enrichment involves the allocation of more interesting, challenging, and perhaps difficult duties to workers in order to stimulate their sense of participation and concern for the achievement of objectives. Extra decision-making authority may be assigned to workers; or they might be given duties requiring higher skill levels or be required to have greater contact with customers and/or suppliers. Equally, existing single tasks might be combined into a composite whole; or workers might be made responsible for controlling the quality of their output or be allowed greater discretion over how they achieve objectives.

Job extension

The term 'job extension' is used to embrace both enlargement and enrichment. Its underlying philosophy is, quite simply, that the wider the variety of the tasks undertaken the more the worker realises the significance of the job in the broader organisation and the more contented and productive the worker will become.

Some jobs are more easily extended than others. Assembly lines in automated factories offer few opportunities for interesting work. In this case, higher pay and/or greater worker participation could be primary motivators. (Note also that not everybody wants to assume extra responsibilities.) In situations where job enlargement is not possible, an alternative is to put workers through sequences of different jobs. Any job is boring, but monotony is relieved through regular job rotation. Hence, workers experience many jobs at different stages in the production process, even though the division of labour has been fully applied. Moreover, employee absences can then be covered from an existing pool of trained, experienced employees.

Job rotation

Some of the difficulties the employee finds in job extension can be avoided if *job rotation* is used instead. Employees are trained in several minor skills and exchange jobs with each other at intervals. Greater satisfaction is obtained because the employee has a greater understanding of the work process through experiencing several jobs within it, and the increased versatility of the workers is useful to management when sickness absence is high. It is not necessary to redesign production methods, and rises in pay, if any, are small.

Not all individuals respond favourably to job enlargement, enrichment or rotation. Some do not appear to be motivated very strongly by the higher needs, or do not expect to satisfy them at work. Others resist any attempt to give them decision-making functions; they say that managers are there for that purpose.

28. The quality of working life

Job extension is a critical aspect of any programme intended to improve the 'quality of working life' (QWL) of employees. QWL means the totality of human satisfaction at work. Accordingly, attempts to enhance QWL within an organisation should examine (in addition to job design) such matters as:

- the extent of employee participation in decision making
- working conditions
- the culture of the organisation
- career development programmes
- interpersonal and intergroup relations within the organisation
- leadership styles
- the degrees of stress experienced by employees (*see* Chapter 10).

The concept of total rewards

An employee may receive extrinsic rewards (pay and fringe benefits) or intrinsic rewards (friendship, status and self-fulfilment) from work. The total reward is the employee's *perception* of the total value of all these. For example, individuals differ in the value they attach to achievement as compared with pay, or promotion opportunities as compared with security. For their part, employers recognise that some rewards compensate for the absence of others; a job which requires a strong moral involvement, e.g. social work, is often accompanied by a low level of pay, and a company which traditionally offers its employees almost complete security of tenure may have lower wage rates than a company with a 'hire and fire' reputation.

Employers and employees may have different perceptions of the rewards to be obtained from various jobs. Changes in working conditions regarded by the employer as improvements may not appear to be such to the employees, for example a new open-plan office instead of small separate offices. Sometimes the way in which the decision is reached and the change introduced is more significant than the change itself.

Progress test 8

1. Define motivation.

2. Why do most approaches to motivation emphasise the concept of human need?

3. According to F.W. Taylor, what is the primary motivating factor that causes employees to work hard?

4. List the five levels of Maslow's hierarchy of need.

5. Explain the ERG theory of motivation.

6. What are 'hygiene factors' in the context of motivation theory? Explain the difference between a hygiene factor and a motivator.

7. Explain the role of cognitive dissonance in the equity theory of motivation.

8. According to V.H. Vroom, what are the major influences on motivation?

9. List the main problems associated with expectancy theory.

10. How can job extension be used to improve an employee's motivation to work?

11. Explain the main problems involved in conducting employee job satisfaction surveys.

12. Define the term 'quality of working life'.

9

ROLE THEORY AND TRANSACTIONAL ANALYSIS

ROLES AND BEHAVIOUR

1. Definition of role

A 'role' is a total and self-contained pattern of behaviour typical of a person who occupies a social position. It follows that people occupy many roles during the course of their lives – as husbands or wives, mother or father figures, as 'office boys' (or girls), supervisors, senior managers, etc. Individual interpretations of roles within a group define the pattern of group interrelations, perhaps even the group's entire structure and organisation.

Role theory concerns how individuals behave, how they feel they *ought* to behave and how they believe other people should respond to their actions. The concept of role is crucially important for a person's self-perception of his or her occupational status and of the value of a job in comparison with those of others.

2. Role set

A person's role set comprises all the other people with whom he or she interacts in the context of a particular role. These other people are called the 'role partners' of the person concerned (who is sometimes referred to as the 'focal person' in the relationship). Examples of role sets are the relations between a manager and subordinates, parent and children, teacher and students, and so on.

3. Role behaviour

Actual behaviour in a role may or may not conform to expectations. Behaviour in fact may deviate significantly from expectations or be quite irrelevant to the role. Thus, for example, a manager might be an extremely bad organiser and/or spend much time on non-productive, highly personal activities. Ideally, individual perceptions of 'correct' behaviour will correspond to senior management's views of what the person ought to be doing and thinking about the role. Serious problems can occur when role occupants and others disagree fundamentally about the expectations of a role, i.e. about what is included in the role, about the range of acceptable behaviour, whether a certain behaviour pattern is voluntary or mandatory and (importantly) which role obligations should assume priority.

In setting role priorities, the individual may adopt any one of several means of approach. He or she might select for priority those role behaviours which:

- correspond to that person's perceptions of moral worth
- are expedient
- bring the greatest personal reward and/or avoid personal cost
- avoid controversy or unpleasant relationships with people whom the individual particularly respects.

4. Roles in organisations

A person's organisational role reflects his or her position in the organisation's hierarchy. Each role will imply certain rights and obligations, authority, responsibility, methods of communication, etc. How exactly an individual acts in an organisational role depends critically on his or her 'role perceptions', i.e. feelings about what constitutes 'correct' behaviour in a particular role.

5. Role categories and role expectations

Attached to every role is a set of standards and norms of conduct that the role occupant (and others) expect from holders of the position. A senior manager, for example, might be expected to behave, perhaps even to dress and speak, in a certain way.

The term 'role category' describes a complete class of persons occupying a particular social position ('leader', 'old person', 'mother', 'senior executive', etc.). Role expectations are then attached to the role category.

6. Role expectations and social norms

A social norm is a behavioural expectation common to all group members against which the appropriateness of individual feelings, conduct and performance may be assessed. A role expectation differs from a social norm in that whereas the latter applies to *everyone* in a group, a role expectation is specific to the individual.

People expect they will behave in a certain manner in a particular situation, and typically possess definite expectations concerning the conduct of others. Such expectations are important because they guide individual actions. For example, colleagues who have worked together for several years usually possess efficient, smoothly functioning relationships because they know exactly how their workmates are likely to behave – each person anticipates the other's reactions to various situations and then adapts his or her own behaviour in appropriate ways.

7. Roles and self-perceptions

The individual might assume that his or her role requires certain outward manifestations of behaviour, for example dressing in a certain manner, speaking with a certain accent, etc. Such behaviour provides information to others about how they should act towards the role occupant.

Through experience, individuals form 'role categories' to which people of the various occupational classes they encounter may be allocated. A supervisor, for instance, may be expected to behave in an authoritarian manner, regardless of that person's personality, background or general approach to management affairs. These categorisations simplify social interrelationships, since it is not then necessary to analyse every situation the individual meets. Rather, the person merely assumes that a certain mode of behaviour is to be expected in the other party and uses this preassumption to guide his or her reactions to events.

8. Role modelling

Individuals often behave in a role as they have observed other people to behave in a similar role. Thus, managers frequently treat their subordinates in a manner analogous to how they are themselves treated by their superiors, who act as *role models* for lower grades of staff.

9. Role incompatibility

This occurs when a person's role contains incompatible elements. A common cause of role incompatibility is differences between how the individual perceives his or her role and how other people expect the occupant of the role to behave. For example, a newly-appointed manager may believe that he or she should rightly adopt a firm and somewhat autocratic manner towards subordinates, whereas the latter might anticipate substantial participation in helping the manager arrive at decisions. Another example is when a person is expected by superiors to adopt an (objectively) unethical approach towards an issue, whereas the individual concerned normally adopts high moral principles when following his or her work.

10. Role overload and role underload

Role overload is the consequence of the individual not being able to cope with several roles simultaneously even though all these roles are essential to that person's tasks.

Role underload, conversely, occurs when the individual's employing organisation fails to place upon that person the requirement to fulfil as many roles as he or she can actually manage. This leads to frustration (*see* 7:3) and reduced performance.

11. Role ambiguity

Role ambiguity arises when roles are not adequately defined. It can cause stress, insecurity and loss of self-confidence.

The more explicit and specific the expectations attached to a role, the easier it is for the person to conform to role requirements, since the individual then knows precisely how he or she should act. Role ambiguity is quite common among, for example, newly-appointed heads of department, who are sometimes not entirely clear about how much authority they possess. Other possible sources of role ambiguity are uncertainty about the precise duties and responsibilities attached to a post, and about how an individual's work is to be evaluated.

12. Role conflict

This occurs when a person does not behave in accordance with expectations attached to a role because to do so would place too great a strain on that person. The role occupant may experience difficulties in meeting its expectations, or might encounter expectations which conflict: consider, for instance, the supervisor whose subordinates expect him or her to represent them to senior management but whose own superiors expect him or her to implement all management decisions regardless of their effects on industrial relations.

The person who cannot live up to role expectations may experience feelings of inadequacy, embarrassment and guilt. Role conflict is sometimes referred to as 'role strain'.

13. Dealing with role conflict

Role conflict might be resolved by using the following devices:

(a) Greater participation in decision making by those affected by important organisational decisions.

(b) Better communications within the organisation.

(c) Giving more formal authority to affected individuals.

(d) Narrow spans of control (*see* 21:**10**) and strict application of the principle of unity of command (*see* 21:**3**).

(e) Training of employees in stress management (*see* Chapter 10).

(f) Role bargaining (*see* below).

14. Role bargaining

When an individual cannot possibly fulfil all obligations associated with a role, he or she might seek to redefine the role's boundaries. This could involve either a direct appeal to other parties to alter their expectations, or the role occupant establishing a distinct set of priorities regarding role relationships.

TRANSACTIONAL ANALYSIS

15. Definition of transactional analysis

Transactional analysis (TA) is a means for understanding interpersonal communication and, ultimately, for changing individual behaviour. The theory was developed by E. Berne who asserted that each individual possesses three distinct *ego states*, referred to as the *parent*, the *adult*, and the *child*. All three exist simultaneously within the person, though any one of them may dominate the other two at a particular time.

According to Berne, these ego states are patterns of feelings and behaviour common to all normal people whatever their ages beyond three or four years old. The child ego state develops in early infancy, but its characteristics (feeling, wanting, playing and manipulating) remain within a person through life and will manifest themselves, from time to time, even in a person, say, 50 years old.

The adult ego state is the thinking and reasoning aspect of an individual's personality. It deals with facts and the development of skills. As people mature, they develop a parent ego state which they learn from others. This concerns attitudes towards right and wrong and how to care for oneself and others. Normal individuals are able to activate a chosen ego state at any appropriate moment, and any one may be used in communications.

16. Categories of behaviour

Transactional analysis is a neo-Freudian theory (*see* 4:5) that seeks to categorise social interactions into predetermined categories. J.H. Morrison and J.J. O'Hearne suggest nine such categories for management situations: four relating to parent ego states, four to child and one to the adult.

Parent ego states

Of the four parent ego states, the authors suggest, two are acceptable and two unacceptable. The first of the unacceptable parent ego state categories relates to *hurtful criticism*, i.e. putting down the other person in a manner deliberately intended to highlight his or her deficiencies and/or attempting to make subordinates look bad or feel inferior. The second involves *dependent nurture* whereby the superior intentionally puts the subordinate into a vulnerable and defensive state thus forcing the subordinate to look to the superior for guidance and decisions. An implication that the subordinate has insufficient experience, inadequate academic qualifications or technical skill to undertake certain responsibilities is an example.

Acceptable parent ego states are (*i*) *helpful intervention*, where the superior, by constructive criticism, prevents a subordinate from doing something that will damage that person (or colleagues, or indeed the entire organisation) now or in the future; and (*ii*) *support nurture*, which actively encourages the subordinate to express respect and concern for other people and their values and to care for colleagues.

Child ego states

Similarly, two of the four child ego states have positive aspects and two should be avoided. The first of the acceptable child ego states is *natural enjoyment*, i.e. taking pleasure in the company of others, being companiable, and having free and easy relationships with colleagues. The second might be termed *liberal conformism* and is associated with the practice of deliberately telling other people what they want to hear in order to make relationships easier and more comfortable for everyone involved in a situation. Of the two unacceptable child ego states, one is *excessive conformity*, which is a slavish mentality that actually induces other people to take advantage of, even persecute, the person concerned. The other is *revenge*, whereby the individual deliberately creates disruption, analogous to a child throwing a tantrum.

17. Uses of transactional analysis

Transactional analysis is especially useful for analysing interpersonal communications because it extends to the transmission of non-verbal communications (body language, facial expression, posture, etc.). Also, it helps individuals because the manner of delivery of a verbal message (tone of voice, vocabulary, accent adopted and so on) helps identify a person's ego state at the moment the message is delivered. Note that transactional analysis focuses exclusively on the interactions that occur within a relationship and not the circumstances surrounding the relationship.

18. Strokes

According to transactional analysis each individual confronted with a trying experience requires a certain amount of personal recognition presented in quite specific forms. An act of recognition of someone else's value is called a *stroke*, and may be positive or negative. A simple compliment is an example of a positive stroke.

Negative strokes are intended to be hurtful (criticism of a subordinate's work, for instance), yet certain individuals actually seek to receive negative strokes from others! This is because such people have developed a view of themselves of being inadequate or otherwise undeserving. They then look for external verification of the bad self-image: they want others to confirm the unfavourable view of themselves they have created within their own minds. Moreover, many perfectly normal interactions with other people will be interpreted as negative strokes by these individuals.

Different people demand differing amounts of recognition. Each person is unique in this respect and managers of organisations need to attempt to ascertain the degree of attention required by each of their subordinates.

Conditional strokes

These are rewards to a person for behaving in a manner that the stroke-giver wishes. Thus, a compliment to a subordinate for having remedied a deficiency (frequent latecoming, for instance) about which a manager previously complained is an example of a conditional stroke. Unconditional strokes, on the other hand, are presented to the individual person irrespective of any particular act or mode of behaviour; they are expressions of appreciation of the total worth of the person.

19. Types of transaction

Although many interpersonal communications may be allocated straightaway to appropriate ego state categories, some transactions are not what the participants anticipate. A *complementary* transaction is one where the person who responds to an initiating action (a remark, for example) does so in a manner that the other person expects. A manager who adopts a parent ego state when addressing a subordinate usually expects that person to adopt a (complementary) child ego state in response. Conversely, a *crossed* transaction involves an unexpected and/or undesired reaction: for instance, when the initiating communication is of the parent variety and is met with a patronising and casually dismissive reply. This might occur, for example, during a disciplinary interview when there is a basic disagreement between boss and worker about whether the subordinate has actually done anything wrong.

Ulterior transactions involve more than two ego states simultaneously and are often associated with symptoms of distress. They occur when someone is fundamentally unsure of his or her own position and of how to relate to other people. Berne suggested that communications can be expected to proceed smoothly provided all the transactions are complementary.

20. Life positions

According to transactional analysis, each person tends – as a result of early childhood experiences – to adopt one of four 'life positions'. A person's life position is his or her dominant way of relating to other people. It reflects how an individual feels about himself or herself and as such tends to regulate the content and character of interpersonal transactions. However, life positions other than the dominant position may be exhibited from time to time. The four possible life positions are as follows.

I'm OK, you're OK

This indicates that the person has a healthy and positive attitude towards him/herself and towards others.

I'm OK, you're not OK

Here the individual has a high regard for him/herself but not for the people with whom he or she enters transactions. It is a common life position among authoritarian managers in bureaucratic organisations.

I'm not OK, you're OK

This is a childlike position in which people think of themselves as they did when they were children – parents were OK, but the child was frequently not! It is a position sometimes adopted by subordinates who show excessive deference to their bosses. Hierarchical organisation systems (*see* Chapter 20) can encourage these feelings.

I'm not OK, you're not OK

A person with this life position has problems. He or she has a poor personal opinion both of him or herself and of other people. Long-term unemployment or persistent failure to achieve personal objectives can engender such a mentality, which can result in severe ill health and normally requires that social work counselling and/or medical treatment be given to the person concerned.

Progress test 9

1. What is a role?

2. Give five examples of pairs of role partners.

3. What are the major influences on a person's behaviour in a role?

4. Define the term 'role perception'.

5. What is the difference between a role expectation and a social norm?

6. Explain the consequences of role incompatibility.

7. Define the term 'role underload'.

8. List the sources and effects of role ambiguity.

9. How can role conflicts be resolved?

10. Define transactional analysis.

11. Explain the difference between the child ego state and the parent ego state.

12. What is an unconditional stroke?

13. Explain the 'I'm OK, you're not OK' life position.

10

STRESS AND CONFLICT

STRESS AND ANXIETY

1. Definition of stress

There is no simple definition of stress, as it comprises a wide collection of physical and psychological symptoms that result from difficulties experienced while attempting to adapt to an environment. Stress has good and bad features. It provides the adrenalin necessary to sustain intense effort and to handle several problems at the same time. Equally, however, it has the effect of draining the individual's physical and emotional resources.

2. Causes of stress

The causes of stress lie partly within the individual's personality, but mostly within the environment in which the individual exists. At work, common causes of stress include:

- ambiguity over which tasks should take priority during the working day
- unclear self-identities, confusions over individual roles in management hierarchies
- perceptions by individuals that they are not competent at their jobs
- frustration (*see* 7:**3**) and the feeling that promotion opportunities have been unfairly blocked
- feelings of personal inadequacy and insecurity
- conflicting demands put on people by superiors who impose different, incompatible objectives
- lack of communication with superiors and colleagues
- bad personal relationships with fellow employees, customers, suppliers, or other contacts outside the organisation.

Often, stress results from overwork. The overload may be quantitative (having too much work to do) or qualitative (finding work too difficult). Long working hours often involve a poor diet, lack of proper exercise, inadequate relaxation and deteriorating interpersonal relationships. People whose knowledge, skills, aptitudes and experience are insufficient for satisfactory performance in their jobs are rarely willing to admit that this is so, fearing loss of status and respect from colleagues, perhaps even demotion. Otherwise, the range of things that could cause stress is seemingly endless: deadlines, anxieties about the slow progress of a project, lack of control over situations, inadequate resources, petty rules and restrictions, aggressive colleagues, and so on.

3. Organisational causes of stress

Stress is seemingly endemic to modern organisational life. Nevertheless, certain measures can be taken by organisations to minimise the degrees of stress experienced by their employees. Such measures include:

(a) Careful job design (*see* 8:26), particularly in relation to the extent of the division of labour and workers' abilities to cope with the difficulty of their tasks

(b) Regular appraisal of employees' performances in order to monitor workers' activities and inform them of any problems at an early stage

(c) Target setting, so that individuals know exactly what they are expected to do

(d) Employee participation in the determination of objectives and in other key aspects of their working lives

(e) Combination of the stressful components of several positions into a single high-stress job undertaken by an employee specially trained in stress management

(f) Conscious attempts by the organisation to manage change systematically and effectively (*see* Chapter 17).

4. Reactions to stress

Confronted with threatening situations the human body naturally prepares itself for 'fight or flight'; with several physical and psychological changes occurring within the individual. There is a release of hormones that drains blood from the skin and the digestive system; glucose and fat are released into the bloodstream, and the pace of breathing increases. Continued exposure to a stressful environment causes tiredness, irritability, physical upsets such as headaches and rashes and possibly alterations in personality and behaviour (excessive drinking or outward aggression, for example). However, stress is not a *measurable* reality; its existence is apparent only through its consequences – how it *affects* individuals.

People respond to stress in different ways. Stress is associated with the idea of pressure. Some people actually thrive on pressure, it helps them draw on physical and emotional resources and they actually enjoy tense and challenging situations. Whether stress stimulates or debilitates depends largely on the background to the event and the duration of the experience. A short-term skirmish is quite unlike a protracted war. Initial excitement can easily turn into long-run distress.

5. Type A people and type B people

This categorisation of personality types is the result of medical research into the factors that cause certain sorts of people to be more prone to heart disease than others. Type A people are more likely to have coronaries and other heart problems. They live 'in the fast track' and are always seeking to accomplish too much in too short a time. Such individuals tend to be assertive, restless, and are frequently workaholic.

Type B people, conversely, find it easy to relax. They take their time and realise their limitations. Often, they are contemplative, unassertive and conciliatory towards the outside world.

The dangers confronting type A individuals include the possibilities of 'executive burnout', of becoming overcompetitive, and of becoming hypercritical of other people's efforts. Equally, however, they do achieve targets on time, and are constantly trying to improve their performances. The type B is stable and reliable; but could be sluggish, casually dismissive of important problems, and incapable of dealing with urgent, top-priority matters.

6. Consequences of stress

The existence of stress within an individual has both physical and psychological effects. There is no doubt that stress causes illness, although the precise mechanisms involved are not fully known.

Stress-related illnesses may result directly or indirectly from stress-inducing activities. Coronaries, for example, can result from stress-created restlessness, hyperactivity, impatience and general angst. Equally, illnesses might be caused by excessive smoking, drinking, inadequate diet, lack of sleep, etc., resulting from stress. Less dramatic physical manifestations of stress include high blood pressure, excessive cholesterol levels, abnormal cardiogram readings, weight loss and skin complaints. Moreover, fainting, frequent profuse sweating and severe headaches regularly afflict those who suffer from prolonged and severe stress. Exhaustion, depression and feelings of alienation from the working environment are also common. Many of these physical manifestations are psychosomatic in origin. Among the most frequent psychosomatic illnesses (i.e. those which emanate from emotional tension) are indigestion, cramp, backache and insomnia.

7. Psychological effects

Stress affects a person's abilities to concentrate and relax, creates irritability and generates feelings of malaise and unease. Perceptions are affected – stress-ridden individuals may become irrational, emotionally volatile and excessively suspicious. Psychological and physical factors do of course interact – stress-related worries have unpleasant side effects on physical health.

Perhaps the most immediate consequence of prolonged exposure to stress is a constant feeling of tiredness due to the combination of the draining effect of emotional conflict, overwork, lack of sleep and general anxiety. Employees who experience stress-created fatigue will be dull, clumsy, unable to think clearly or perform work for long periods.

8. Anxiety

Constant and deep feelings of anxiety are among the most serious consequences of long-term exposure to stress. There are two types of anxiety: 'objective' anxiety caused by external stressful events, and 'neurotic' anxiety that arises within the individual.

Objective anxiety can be dealt with by altering the circumstances of the environment in which a person functions. Neurotic anxiety, however, will not be removed by external events. Rather, each person develops a number of 'ego defence mechanisms' to cope with its effects. The major ego defences are as follows.

Repression

This means forcing into the unconscious mind particular thoughts or memories of events or things the individual does not wish to recognise as having happened or existed. However, much mental energy is necessary for keeping these thoughts or memories repressed, and the psychological processes involved can quickly lead to abnormal behaviour.

Regression

Here, the individual behaves as he or she did in an earlier period. Immaturity in behaviour is characteristic of people experiencing this phenomenon.

Sublimation

People who are excessively anxious about certain aspects of their lives (problems at work, for example) may divert their energies away from these difficulties and instead devote themselves totally to other things. This shift of mental activities towards alternative goals is known as sublimation. A major problem here is that the affected person may direct all nervous energies towards the attainment of irrelevant objectives totally unconnected with the real cause of the anxiety. For instance, a supervisor whose production figures are hopelessly inadequate might devote lavish attention to personnel and welfare matters, replacing the need to tackle fundamental production difficulties with the unnecessary concern for trivial issues.

Projection

This occurs when the individual unconsciously attributes to another person a characteristic which in fact is possessed by the individual concerned. For example, someone who because of anxiety feels extremely aggressive may (wrongly) perceive the presence of aggression in someone else.

Anxiety can relate to specific situations, or to generalised angst. 'General anxiety disorder' occurs when the affected individual feels anxious irrespective of the circumstances in which he or she finds him or herself. Symptoms of the disorder may include acute fear with victims believing that they are going insane (although this is very rarely the case).

Normal and abnormal anxiety

Everyone experiences anxiety from time to time. Common examples are worries about getting to work on time, paying overdue bills, not making progress in a career, and so on. These are normal anxieties, to be expected in daily life. However, for people suffering from anxiety disorders these mundane tensions can blow up out of all proportion, even to the extent of altering their lives. Anxiety becomes abnormal, resulting perhaps in phobias, compulsive obsessions (see below) and/or attacks of panic. Abnormal anxiety can ruin the victim's interpersonal relationships and cause him or her to be excluded from social groups.

Phobias

A phobia is a continual and compelling fear of an object or situation. The sufferer realises that the fear is irrational, but still feels threatened. Phobias may be *specific* (e.g. fear of snakes, spiders, flying, injections, etc.) or *social* such as the fear of being the centre of attention, being humiliated, or of behaving in an embarrassing way. People with phobias will steer clear of the objects or situations that cause them distress and, as their phobias develop, will avoid pictures or even saying the names of the dreaded situation or object. Consequently they become handicapped, even operationally disfunctional in relation to certain things.

The converse to a phobia is the 'compulsive obsession', which typically involves continuous repetition of an activity, e.g. washing, counting, checking, or touching specific objects. It might also entail obsessive thoughts that recur almost constantly. Often these obsessions are connected with feelings of being dirty or contaminated.

Phobias and severe anxiety are a widespread problem which, according to the UK charity 'No Panic', possibly affect up to 18 per cent of the population. The most extensive phobic disorder is agoraphobia, which is the fear of being in any situation or place where the victim feels unsafe. It results in the individual experiencing an uncontrollable urge to escape to a safe haven, e.g. the person's home. (Note therefore that agoraphobia is *not* just the fear of open spaces as many people believe.) Symptoms of agoraphobia include nausea, palpitations, vertigo, chest pains and breathing difficulties, intense sweating, fainting, and perceptions by the individual that he or she is going insane. So unpleasant are these symptoms that agoraphobics do everything they can to avoid them, e.g. by staying at home. But the feelings of security and tranquility they experience through remaining indoors only serves to reinforce their dread of venturing outside. Another unfortunate consequence of agoraphobia is that many sufferers can only travel if accompanied by a trusted relative or friend. Hence the victim becomes totally dependent on this support and unable to go anywhere without the helper, which is extremely stressful for the relative or friend concerned.

9. Behaviour changes

Performance at work typically deteriorates when individuals experience protracted exposure to high levels of stress. The direction of a person's response is difficult to predict. Some individuals become antagonistic, others withdraw into themselves. Tension, tiredness and anxiety often lead to outbursts of hostility and aggression. Workers become oversensitive to criticism and increasingly unable to relate to friends and working colleagues. Sleep patterns alter, daytime tiredness ensues.

The general rundown in a person's health can lead to frequent colds, upset stomachs and other minor illnesses. Routine errors become frequent. Stress-prone individuals have more accidents than others. Many people respond by taking tranquillisers (or conversely anti-depressants), smoking heavily (with consequent health problems) or by drinking excessive amounts of alcohol. Marital and other family difficulties are common among stress-ridden people.

10. Depression

Another possible consequence of long-term stress is depression. This means permanent feelings of dejection and apathy, which may of course be caused by factors other than stress. The cause of work-related depression may be either *exogenous*, such as failure to achieve an important objective or disappointment at not gaining promotion, or *endogenous* (within the person) resulting perhaps from innate feelings of hopelessness, personal inadequacy and inability to cope. Depression manifests itself in abnormal sleep patterns, listlessness, lethargy and agitated behaviour. Loss of appetite and libido may also occur.

Depressions are worsened if employees perceive that they have no control over depressing situations. Participation in decision making, provision of training and staff development opportunities, job rotation and involvement of individuals with teams (rather than working in isolation) may therefore alleviate some depressing circumstances.

11. Reducing stress

A number of measures are available to help the individual cope with stress. These include:

(a) Delegation of part of a person's workload (provided of course that subordinates are capable of handling the work delegated to them).

(b) Deciding in advance not to become involved in certain stressful activities, e.g. not attending meetings or avoiding contact with particular individuals.

(c) Predetermining a maximum personal workload and refusing to undertake additional duties beyond the maximum.

(d) Deliberate relaxation.

(e) Physical exercise.

(f) Greater efficiency in the use of management time.

12. Bullying at work

Workplace bullying is increasingly recognised as a major cause of stress. It can result from personality characteristics within the bully, or from external factors which encourage managers to behave in bullying ways. Examples of such factors include:

- 'macho' management cultures within an organisation
- pressures to meet efficiency targets, reduce costs, etc.
- perceptions that departmental objectives can be achieved more quickly through using threats and intimidation
- implementation of downsizing exercises, restructuring, delayering, re-engineering, and so on.

Manifestations of bullying at work are shouting and swearing, physical intimidation; the use of threatening body language; sexual, racial or age-related harassment; and persistent public and/or private criticism or ridicule. Workplace bullying could also involve:

- seeking complaints about the bullied individual from other members of staff
- deriding the value of the victim's contributions to the organisation's work
- giving a person jobs that he or she cannot reasonably be expected to complete satisfactorily, and then claiming that the individual is incompetent
- removing responsibilities from the bullied worker while simultaneously allocating menial tasks
- withholding information or deliberately supplying false information
- sabotaging or impeding the victim's work performance
- applying excessively tight supervision
- increasing the victim's workload and/or setting impossible deadlines.

The mental effects of bullying can include depression; anxiety; loss of concentration, motivation and self-confidence; and feelings of anger and hostility towards colleagues and the employing firm. Physical consequences are similar to those arising from fear and extreme stress: insomnia, fatigue, headaches, skin rashes, ulcers, and so on. Absenteeism is likely to be high in organisations where extensive bullying occurs. And overall organisational efficiency will fall. Possible solutions to the problem are:

- Changes in the organisational culture of the enterprise
- Appointment of a company ombudsperson with whom victims may discuss their experiences in total confidence. The ombudsperson needs to have direct access to the firm's chief executive.
- Creation of formal grievance procedures specifically designed to deal with bullying
- Provision for rapid redeployment of victims to alternative jobs
- Counselling of bullies, followed by disciplinary proceedings if their behaviour does not improve.

CONFLICT

13. Nature of conflict in organisations

Individuals and sections within organisations occasionally come into conflict in consequence of ambiguities in the rules governing their relationships, or through differences of interest, or because one or more parties deliberately breaks agreed procedures. Wherever people must share work and / or resources and certain individuals are ranked higher than others, conflict is likely to occur.

Conflict has positive aspects: it spurs initiative, creates energy and stimulates new ideas. Unfortunately, it can also cause the misdirection of efforts against workmates instead of towards the achievement of the organisation's common goals.

Indications of conflict

Telltale signs of conflict within an employing organisation are:

- frequent and unwarranted arguments among employees
- communication problems
- destructive competition between functions and / or departments
- employees exhibiting inflexible and insensitive attitudes towards other members of staff
- colleagues withholding information from each other
- unfair criticism of certain individuals
- excessively formal interpersonal relationships between employees.

14. Interest groups

An interest group is any collection of people sharing common perspectives, objectives or views. Interest groups could consist of various grades of employees, shareholders, members of a department, professional workers, and so on. Factors conducive to the formation of interest groups include:

(a) certain individuals collectively being able to gain tangible benefits through belonging to an interest group

(b) geographical proximity of members (so that it is easy for them to exchange information)

(c) the emergence of a threat to the incomes or welfare of particular individuals

(d) the existence of hierarchies with pronounced status differentials within the organisation.

15. Causes of conflict within organisations

Conflicts usually fall into one of three categories: conflicts of interest (pay disputes, for instance); conflicts between functions (e.g. arguments concerning who should do what); and conflicts of authority involving managers and their staff. Specific causes of conflict include:

(a) lack of co-ordination between people and departments resulting in differing perceptions of objectives and roles

(b) breakdowns in communication, so that individuals are not fully aware of what they are expected to do

(c) poor teamwork

(d) imprecise definition of goals and expected standards

(e) excessively complicated relationships between functions and sections

(f) autocratic management styles (*see* 13:**4**)

(g) personality differences among employees

(h) severe reductions in organisational resources

(i) injection into the organisation of new people with backgrounds, views and perspectives entirely different from those of the existing staff

(j) disruption of established work groups and administrative routines.

The consequences of conflict between groups might include greater group cohesion (*see* 12:**5**) and the emergence of strong leaders within particular groups. Also, long-term exposure to conflict situations can distort individual perceptions of other people. Stereotyping (*see* 14:**6**) of the individuals with whom a person is in conflict is likely to occur.

16. Frames of reference

These are the influences which structure a person's perceptions and interpretations of events. They involve assumptions about reality, attitudes towards what is possible, and conventions regarding what is considered correct behaviour for those involved in a dispute. The adoption of differing frames of reference by opposing sides can impair the effective resolution of conflicts.

In labour disputes, for example, it has been argued that management and labour look at industrial relations bargaining situations from completely different points of view, in that management tends to assume there are no inherent conflicts of interest in industry, whereas labour perceives the existence of diverse and conflicting demands. Thus, management would regard collective effort towards achievement of common goals by a united, disciplined workforce as the natural state of affairs, and those in command would not be able to comprehend the motives behind challenges to managerial authority.

If people are considered members of a team striving jointly to achieve greater rewards for all with existing managers as team leaders, disruptive behaviour does not make sense. Co-operation is taken for granted; all dissent is viewed as unreasonable, it cannot be understood. If however the firm's profits are regarded as something to be fought over – each side legitimately seeking to maximise its own reward – then industrial action to secure the largest possible share of revenue for the workforce can be explained.

17. Unitary and pluralistic approaches

Realistically, therefore, it is necessary to recognise that some conflicts are inevitable, but that given suitable procedures there is no reason why most of them cannot be satisfactorily resolved. This latter approach is termed 'pluralism'. Organisations are regarded as comprising various interest groups. Management's role is thus to achieve compromise and to balance these interests. Accordingly, effective management is that which enables each group to pursue its aspirations to the maximum possible extent compatible with the welfare of the organisation.

This differs from 'unitarism', which is the philosophy that everyone is 'in the same boat' and will therefore naturally act as a member of a team (*see* **16** above). Hence strikes and other disruptive behaviour are, in the unitarist view, malevolent and just as destructive to those who participate in them as to employing organisations. Industrial action simply does not make sense since *everyone* should be working together for the common good. Conflicts, where they occur, are due to the emergence of factional interests (which a good management would not allow to arise in the first place), to faulty communications and misunderstandings, or to the efforts of trouble-makers. The unitarist approach might be said to have the following implications.

(a) *For workers:*

(*i*) Working practices should be flexible, with individuals prepared to undertake whatever tasks are required in whichever way is the most efficient.
(*ii*) The main role of a trade union is to act as a means of communication between the individual and his or her employing company.
(*iii*) Employees should be willing to negotiate their pay and other terms and conditions of work on an individual basis (rather than through collective bargaining).
(*iv*) Worker participation in workplace management decision-making must be accepted as a normal part of working life, with individuals actively supporting quality circles, productivity improvement programmes, etc.
(*v*) Employees should recognise and accept the right of management to manage.
(*vi*) Workers need to accept personal responsibility for the quality of the firm's output and for achieving total customer satisfaction.

(b) *For companies:*

(*i*) Management policies should seek to unify effort and inspire and motivate the workforce.
(*ii*) Employees should constantly be made aware of the organisation's wider objectives.
(*iii*) Pay systems need to be designed to secure workers' loyalty and commitment to the enterprise.
(*iv*) Wherever possible, heads of department and other line executives (marketing or production managers, for example) should be responsible for personnel management. If the firm has a personnel department then its functions

ought to focus on supporting line managers and providing advice on technical/legal matters.

(*v*) Since conflict is regarded as the result of ignorance or the activities of troublemakers, great care is needed when recruiting workers in order to ensure they have appropriate outlooks, will fit in with the culture of the organisation, and will quickly learn the company's conventions and norms.

(*vi*) Management should discuss and agree personal objectives with everyone in the business and supply individuals with the training, support and resources necessary for them to attain their goals.

The *advantages* of unitarism are that:

(a) It encourages consensus and harmonious employee relations.

(b) Individuals become part of a team.

(c) Managements are obliged to treat their employees with respect and dignity.

(d) It facilitates the integration of functions and activities within the enterprise.

Problems with the unitarist approach include:

(a) It cannot comprehend the motives of individuals who do not regard everyone in the organisation as 'being in the same boat'.

(b) Arguably, it fails to recognise the *inevitability* of conflicts of interest in certain management/employee situations.

(c) It can impair the efficient resolution of disputes.

Benefits and problems of pluralism

Pluralism has been recommended as a more pragmatic and effective alternative to the unitarist philosophy (Fox 1966). The pluralistic approach sees conflicts of interest and disagreements between managers and workers over the distribution of the firm's profits as the normal and inescapable state of affairs. Realistically, therefore, management should accept that conflict will *necessarily* occur, and thus should seek to resolve conflicts by establishing sound procedures for settling disputes.

Pluralism assumes that the best way to achieve consensus and long-term stability in management/worker relations is for management to recognise conflicting interests, to negotiate compromises, and to balance the demands of various groups. This implies the need for grievance procedures, joint-negotiation committees, union-recognition agreements, arbitration arrangements and so on. Trade unions are seen as occupying a key role in the process of resolving conflicts, which are viewed as normal and sometimes healthy in that they release emotions which otherwise would be (harmfully) repressed. Collective bargaining is regarded as a particularly efficient means whereby management and labour can distribute the profits of enterprises in an orderly fashion. Implications of pluralism include:

(a) The firm should have a personnel manager to act as a sort of intermediary between management and labour.

(b) There should be widespread use of independent external arbitrators to resolve industrial disputes.

(c) Negotiating skills have great importance for both employee and management representatives.

Advantages of pluralism include its emphasis on forward planning, orderly and consistent procedures, realistic approaches to dealing with unions, less uncertainty in employee relations processes, and the development of effective arrangements for resolving disputes. Further benefits (to management) are that:

(a) It encourages management and labour to discuss issues frankly and to perceive them from contrasting points of view.

(b) Through institutionalising conflict, it can enhance management's power.

(c) It increases the flow of information from the workforce.

(d) It adopts a hard-headed approach to employee (and management) motivation.

(e) Stability is sought through *compromises* that are acceptable to all the parties to a dispute.

(f) It balances the interests of the various stakeholders (owners, management, workers, etc.) involved in the creation of the firm's wealth.

Criticisms of pluralism

Despite its essential pragmatism, pluralism has a number of disadvantages. Arguably it encourages destructive 'them and us' attitudes and creates bureaucratic and inefficient procedures which stifle initiative and are highly resistant to change. Further problems include:

(a) It has little to offer the small business where there is extensive face-to-face contact between owners and employees.

(b) The establishment of procedures for settling conflicts and grievances could *itself* encourage 'them and us' attitudes which lead to disputes.

(c) It may cause friction between a worker's loyalty to his or her trade union and loyalty to the employing firm. Employees' long-term commitment to attaining the goals of the organisation may be jeopardised.

(d) The committees and other procedural machinery that emerge from pluralistic approaches could eventually become part and parcel of the firm's management system and be used to legitimise existing (and perhaps inappropriate) employee relations practices.

(e) Pluralism assumes a roughly even balance of power between various interest groups. This fails to recognise that in many employee relations situations there is a dominant participant possessing the power to *impose* its will on the other side.

(f) It could undermine management's authority and create an atmosphere conducive to trade union activity, even within environments where this (from management's point of view) might be counter-productive.

(g) It may be naive to expect management not to wish to exercise managerial prerogative to the maximum extent.

(h) Management might pretend to hold pluralistic attitudes so long as this is convenient, but quickly adopt a unitary approach as soon as circumstances change.

18. Conflict resolution

Conflicts between people or sections of equal rank may be resolved through arbitration at the next highest level of authority within the organisation. Otherwise, the following methods might be used to settle disputes:

(a) *Joint negotiating committees.* These meet at predetermined intervals to discuss problems that have arisen since the previous meeting. Members agree not to take any action that might aggravate a situation before the contentious issue is raised at the JNC. Note (importantly) that willingness to negotiate implies a willingness to compromise on a stated position.

(b) *Avoidance of conflict situations.* For instance, by organising work so as to prevent direct confrontations between individuals with a vested interest in outcomes.

(c) *Increasing the flow of information through the organisation.* This might encourage employees to empathise with other people's problems and views.

(d) *Redeployment.* Transferring certain individuals to other departments.

(e) *Better co-ordination of activities.* Training might be needed to enable managers to accomplish this.

(f) *Clarification* of the roles and responsibilities of those in dispute.

Progress test 10

1. Define 'stress'. What are the main causes of stress?

2. How can organisations help employees avoid stress?

3. How do most people react to stress?

4. What are the characteristics of a 'type B' person?

5. List the main psychological effects of stress.

6. Define 'anxiety'.

7. How might an individual's behaviour change in consequence of stress?

8. Define 'depression'.

9. What are the major indications of the existence of conflict within organisations?

10. What is an 'interest group' within an organisation?

11. List the main causes of organisational conflict.

12. Distinguish between unitary and pluralistic frames of reference.

13. List four ways of resolving conflicts within organisations.

11

CAREERS

DEVELOPMENT AND PLANNING

1. Definition of career

A career is a related series of jobs with the following characteristics: (*i*) the series is fairly predictable; (*ii*) jobs undertaken follow a hierarchy of status.

Thus, any occupation – manual or non-manual – that involves a status hierarchy and within which individuals may deliberately seek to move up to higher-level work can be said to offer a 'career'. It follows that careers are commonest in occupations attached to stable institutions (large corporations, for example) with strong organisational structures.

A person's career development may require movement between jobs within the same organisation; or between jobs in the same occupation but in different organisations; or a mixture of the two. The pursuit of a career (as opposed to holding a sequence of *ad hoc* jobs) gives the individual feelings of security and a logical series of intermediate career goals. These can enhance an individual's loyalty to an occupation and / or organisation and might motivate the individual to work extremely hard.

2. Research on career development

Substantial research has been undertaken to determine whether 'inner-directed' or 'other-directed' people have the most successful careers. Inner-directed individuals are creative and individualistic and inclined to do things in their own way. Other-directed people tend towards conformism and are highly responsive to external influences.

Many large organisations are bureaucracies (*see* 2:**9**) within which co-operation and unquestioning subservience to authority are expected as a matter of course. Accordingly, it might be assumed that bureaucratic organisations will always promote those employees who possess characteristics and personal value systems that support the organisation without question or dissent. Research suggests, however, that this is not the case, for several reasons:

(a) Excessively conformist individuals are sometimes incompetent in their jobs.

(b) Inner-directed thinking generates new ideas and fresh perspectives on difficult problems. These contributions are welcomed by most large organisations.

(c) Creative inner-directed people are perhaps more likely than others to 'fight' their way to the top.

(d) Because large bureaucratic organisations often possess extensive resources they sometimes attract better-educated employees, who tend to be intellectually flexible and inner-directed.

(e) Managing a large bureaucracy involves complex work for which creative inner-directed employees are well equipped.

Nevertheless, these findings do not mean that large organisations will tolerate excessive non-conformity, especially at lower levels. Rather, the most successful people appear to be those who are creative and individualistic, but strictly within the culture and expectations of the employing organisation and who do not move too far out of line.

3. Individual career planning

Individuals may plan their own careers in the following ways:

(a) Comprehensive analysis of personal strengths and weaknesses.

(b) Selection of the departments, divisions and specific positions within an organisation that offer the best means of gaining useful experience, or the identification of different organisations providing suitable opportunities for furthering a career.

(c) Establishment of career priorities and the specification of intermediate career goals.

(d) Close observation of the behaviour and attitudes of successful superiors.

(e) Identification of career alternatives. The individual should select the options which build on his or her strengths and minimise the effects of personal weaknesses, while recognising and accepting that plans do not always work out. Accordingly, a person should develop contingency plans upon which to fall back if things go wrong.

(f) Regular monitoring of achievements to date and careful analysis of the reasons for shortcomings.

4. Organisational career planning

Organisations can plan the careers of their employees through the following devices:

(a) Providing individuals with a sequence of work experiences (e.g. through job rotation) that will equip them for higher levels of responsibility.

(b) Career counselling to guide employees towards the best career choices and to advise them of the training they must undertake in order to achieve promotion.

(c) Devising management succession programmes so that career opportunities for suitably qualified individuals actually exist within the organisation.

(d) Putting employees onto appropriate training courses.

(e) Staff exchanges between subsidiaries, divisions and departments – perhaps even between different organisations.

(f) Job design (*see* 8:**26**) and the restructuring of work to enhance individual opportunities for personal development.

5. Reasons for organisational career planning

There are several reasons why organisations should help employees plan their careers:

(a) Individuals need to be encouraged to develop the skills necessary to achieve personal work goals.

(b) Employees will perceive the organisation as caring for their welfare. In consequence, satisfaction and employee morale should increase.

(c) Career planning is essential for the effective implementation of equal opportunity programmes.

(d) Organisations are better co-ordinated when employees' careers have been planned.

6. Advantages of career planning

Conscious planning of a career has a number of advantages both for the individual and for employing organisations:

(a) The person can assess his or her career progress against logically predetermined expectations.

(b) Individuals have tangible long-term objectives at which to aim.

(c) Employees' competence increases steadily over time.

(d) Each person makes a planned contribution towards the achievement of organisational goals.

(e) Career planning can be directly related to performance appraisal and management by objectives schemes.

7. Levinson's career life-cycle hypothesis

The career life-cycle hypothesis is the proposition that managerial careers typically follow clearly defined and predictable patterns with distinct transitions between phases. At the outset of a career, individuals must learn how to 'fit-in' with their chosen occupation; a task that might be difficult if a person's involves duties that were not expected and/or the job was not their Eventually, however, people 'find themselves' and begin to ir pose their own personalities on working methods. They develop self-confidence and become less reliant on existing occupational conventions.

According to the theory the manager next sets personal career goals and devotes increasing amounts of energy to their achievement. This might involve changing companies, geographical relocations, and perhaps the disruption of established friendships and family relationships (divorces are common among those who dedicate themselves entirely to the pursuit of a career). Daniel Levinson suggests that during this period the individual is likely to seek within his or her employing organisation a 'sponsor' to whom to look for moral support, possibly at the expense of existing non-work friendships.

Some managers will be more successful than others, although sooner or later *everyone* must reach a 'career plateau' from which there is little possibility of advancement. The higher up an organisation the individual progresses the fewer promotion opportunities exist, so that even the most able of senior managers will eventually exhaust their potentials. Ideally the manager will now devote total effort to achieving excellence in his or her current job, although negative reactions might occur: apathy, resentment, loss of commitment to the organisation's goals, diminishing effort, and so on.

Those who are happy in their work will experience great pride in the increasing quality of their output. They re-establish old friendships and 'settle down' at home. This can be the most creative and satisfying period of a manager's career. Managers who are frustrated and resentful, on the other hand, will begin to consider early retirement at this point, or they may change career in middle life – perhaps opting out of management altogether.

At the end of a successful managerial career, the individual must accept the inevitability of retirement. Managers should prepare for this systematically both in terms of maintaining living standards and through finding other things to do. Nevertheless, the transition from successful senior manager to retired employee is difficult for many people.

8. Criticisms of Levinson's model

There is little evidence to suggest that individuals do actually rationalise their career intentions and consciously plan ahead as the theory predicts. Frequently people do not really know what they want to do in the future and are thus reluctant to invest large amounts of time and effort in training and personal development. Note that the research underlying the career life-cycle hypothesis is based exclusively on men in US business corporations; and the cultural, economic and ideological environments surrounding US business do not necessarily apply in the rest of the world. Moreover, patterns of work are themselves changing, with increasing numbers of 'flexible' workers who do not follow traditional career development patterns (*see* **4** above).

How do women managers fit into the hypothesised system? Women managers usually assume positions of responsibility when they are older than male colleagues, and those with young children often require quite different management training and promotion schemes. Also, the model has nothing to say about the problems confronting people in dual-career marriages.

Other individuals with career patterns that conflict with the career life-cycle hypothesis include the following:

(a) Professionally qualified people, such as lawyers, general medical practitioners, dentists, etc., who qualify (usually) in their mid-twenties and then practise their profession for the remainder of their 'careers'.

(b) Those who achieve much in one type of work, then become bored after a few years, change to a different occupation and are equally successful; the pattern being repeated throughout the individual's working life.

(c) People with 'high spots' in their careers, and long periods of mediocrity between the peaks (actors, film stars, musicians or management consultants, for example).

It seems therefore that a simpler and more general model may be required. Accordingly, T. Hall restructured Levinson's (and other) work into three career stage categories, as follows:

1 *Exploration.* The employee searches for an identity and occupational role. Several different jobs may be attempted at this stage.
2 *Establishment.* This is a period of settling down and developing a career.
3 *Maintenance.* Here the employee has achieved his or her potential and operates on a career plateau, i.e. where there is little prospect of further promotion. Nearly everyone reaches a career plateau eventually, either through lack of ability or incompetence at internal organisational politics (*see* 4:**11**), or simply because no further openings at higher levels exist.

Dual-career couples

Career planning is especially difficult when both parties to a relationship have interesting and well-paid jobs, since a promotion for one of the partners that necessitates geographical relocation may involve the other partner abandoning his or her own career. Some companies recognise this problem and consciously avoid the geographical transfer of people in such a situation, or they try to find appropriate work for the relocated person's other half, either within the company or elsewhere. Members of dual-career partnerships need to decide at an early stage in their relationship how they will resolve these issues. Whose career is to take precedence, in what circumstances will a promotion opportunity be turned down?

Partners in a dual-career relationship could experience large amounts of stress, caused by:

(a) their feelings of being overloaded by the combined demands of home and work, especially if the couple have young children

(b) the possible emergence of jealousies and resentments as one partner's career stagnates while the other's flourishes

(c) lack of common interests, since both partners will be heavily involved in the details of their own particular line of work.

THE PROFESSIONS

9. Role of professional bodies

Members of professional bodies (accountants, lawyers, architects, etc.) frequently pursue careers that transcend the individual's affiliation to any one employing organisation. The distinguishing characteristics of a 'profession' are as follows:

(a) Members' activities should be based on an established body of knowledge, the acquisition of which requires several years of substantial intellectual training.

(b) Certain ethical 'professional' standards must be maintained and codes of practice applied to members' work.

(c) Entry should be restricted to persons possessing predefined qualifications, experience and/or characteristics and with common training and perspectives.

(d) Members take a professional pride in the quality of their work, which is seen as an end in itself and not merely as a means for earning a living.

10. What professional bodies do

Professional bodies are organisations that seek: (*i*) to maintain or improve members' occupational status; and (*ii*) to enhance members' standards of performance through the provision of training and a system of certification, usually (but not always) involving a series of examinations.

Traditionally, professional workers have performed service roles (accountants, lawyers, etc.) and have worked for many 'clients' rather than a single employer. Today, however, the concept of 'profession' encompasses a variety of categories of employee. Teachers and nurses, for example, typically regard themselves as 'professional' workers, despite being normally employed by a single organisation on terms and conditions similar to those of any other category of staff.

Development of professional bodies

Some professional associations offer complete and self-contained educational programmes (with examinations) and their members' professional status is linked to examination success. Most professional bodies began through attempts to promote an academic or vocational discipline or to further knowledge within a highly specialised area. These turned ultimately into qualifying associations concerned with the maintenance of 'professional' standards. Individuals who had not taken the relevant association's examinations and thus did not enjoy the accreditation of the 'recognised' body in the field would then experience difficulty in practising the profession.

Services to members

The essential functions of a typical professional body are as follows:

(a) Promotion of the study of a subject, and the creation of an organisation for this purpose.

(b) Examining, training and education; the production of syllabuses, teaching materials, and the provision of short courses. This function involves liaison with colleges, publishers and with others in the education field.

(c) Establishment of standards of professional conduct, backed up by disciplinary procedures and the threat of sanctions (up to and including expulsion from the body) against those who break the association's rules.

(d) Distribution of information on new developments, practices and other items of interest to members. Often, this involves the production of a monthly or quarterly journal or news magazine.

(e) Enhancement of the status of the profession through public relations exercises, contributions to debates on topical issues affecting the profession, and generally acting as a pressure group to further members' interest.

Not all professional organisations undertake all these functions. Indeed, some exist primarily because of the exclusivity of membership and the prestige attached to current members (the Royal Academy in England, for example). However, entry to most professions is 'open' for student membership – provided that minimum basic educational criteria are met. Thereafter, associations set their own examinations (or offer exemption against the examinations in equivalent subjects set by comparable bodies) and award their own certificates and diplomas. The value of these qualifications depends on the status of the body in the eyes of potential employers and the general public. Organisation structures suitable for professionally qualified staff are described in 22:**13**.

MANAGEMENT TRAINING AND DEVELOPMENT

11. Management training

This seeks to improve management performance and to ensure the adequacy of a management succession scheme. Advantages include less need to recruit managers from outside the company (note the high cost of recruiting senior managers), motivation of junior executives, and the creation of more flexible and broad-minded managerial employees. Techniques of management training include short courses, job rotation, planned experience via the systematic delegation of increasingly difficult work to subordinates, coaching and group discussions.

Objections to the value of management training are:

(a) Arguably, many aspects of management can only be learned by doing. Thus there is little point in providing 'academic' management training that has little practical application.

(b) Formal management training cannot inculcate entrepreneurial attitudes.

12. Content of management training

Implementation of a management training programme requires the assessment of the abilities of current management staff and the creation of schemes to enhance the potential of each individual. Typically, management training is provided in the following areas:

(a) Background knowledge of the company, its trading environment, products, production methods, markets and personnel

(b) Elements of management theory and practice, administrative procedures, sources and uses of finance, the legal environment, and specialist techniques

(c) Analytical skills, specification of objectives, organisation, delegation and control

(d) Interpersonal skills, communication skills, leadership, and co-ordination and motivation of staff

(e) Creative abilities, problem-solving techniques and capacity to initiate new activities.

Much management training is done on short courses conducted in hotels or purpose-built residential training centres. These are particularly useful when staff from different departments or firms are able to compare and discuss their various experiences. Note, however, that participants might greatly enjoy a residential short course, but not really benefit from attendance. They could enjoy the company of classmates, meet new people and be impressed by the physical environment in which a course takes place, yet not learn anything of practical value.

13. Outdoor management training (OMT)

The justification for this is the assumption that direct parallels exist between the personal qualities necessary for successful corporate management and those cultivated through participation in outdoor pursuits such as rockclimbing, canoeing, sailing or orienteering, since the essential demands of these activities (planning, organising, team-building, dealing with uncertainty, direction and control) are the same as those needed for business management. Accordingly, outdoor exercises are sometimes used to train managers in leadership, target setting, communication, co-ordination and the motivation of subordinate staff.

The advantages of OMT are as follows:

(a) Individuals are forced to recognise the importance of clear expression, trust and co-operation among members of a team.

(b) Participants learn about themselves; their strengths and weaknesses, relationships with others and capacity for command.

(c) OMT teaches accountability, since it is impossible to hide mistakes or 'pull rank' when helping other people climb a rockface or cross desolate moorland.

Critics of OMT allege that it has little relevance for modern management methods, which rely heavily on information processing, model formulation and data-interpretation skills. OMT, they argue, encourages 'gifted-amateur' approaches to management. The time devoted to such exercises might be better spent learning about advanced management techniques.

Progress test 11

1. What is a career?

2. Describe the main results of empirical investigation into the career development of inner-directed people.

3. What can organisations do to help employees plan their careers?

4. List the advantages of career planning.

5. Define the term 'career life cycle'.

6. What are the distinguishing characteristics of a 'professional body'?

7. List the major functions undertaken by professional bodies.

Part Three

ORGANISATION AND MANAGEMENT

12

GROUPS

THE NATURE OF GROUPS

1. Definition

A group is a collection of two or more people who possess a common purpose. Work groups may be created by management to perform specific functions, or can emerge naturally by themselves. The formation of groups at work is at once a natural consequence of the division of labour and an important means of fulfilling individual social needs.

Work groups may be primary or secondary, formal or informal. A primary group consists of members who come into direct face-to-face contact. Secondary groups are larger, less personal, and lack immediate direct contact between members. Examples of primary groups are small departments within a firm, project teams, families, sports teams or other direct-contact recreational associations. Secondary groups might be factories, communities, long assembly lines where workers do not come into contact with each other, or geographical divisions of a firm. These groups will be less solid and cohesive than primary groups, though interactions between members will still occur. Within primary groups, communications are rapid and direct. Membership will often provide social and psychological support during times of stress.

2. Formal and informal groups

Formal groups are deliberately created by management for particular predetermined purposes. Management selects group members, leaders and methods of doing work. A formal group may be defined with respect to a task, function, status within the managerial hierarchy (such as members of the board of directors), or length of service with the firm (long-serving employees might receive privileges not available to others and hence constitute an identifiable group). Formal groups are characterised by a high degree of managerial involvement in co-ordinating, controlling and defining the nature of the activities they undertake. Group structures are clearly defined, and their tasks are carefully delineated.

Informal groups can form without management support. They are established by people who feel they possess a common interest. Members organise themselves and develop a sense of affinity to each other and a common cause. Often, it is an informal group that actually determines how much work is done.

Hopefully, the aims of the informal group that spring up within an organisation will correspond to the objectives of its management, but they might not. Indeed, informal groups could form specifically to oppose the wishes of management. Formal groups are created to meet the needs of an organisation; informal groups arise to satisfy the needs of its individual members. Management must recognise the importance of informal groups for organisational efficiency and their potential for disrupting organisational plans.

3. Group norms

A group norm is a shared perception of how things should be done, or a common attitude, feeling or belief. Norms may relate to working methods, to how much work should be done and how enthusiastically it should be done; quality of output, relations with management (and trade unions); how various people should be addressed and treated; and a whole range of other issues. Group norms are particularly important in determining workers' attitudes towards change, since norms can create or overcome resistance to new methods and ideas.

As norms emerge, individuals will start to behave according to how they feel other group members expect them to behave. Initially, an entrant into an existing group will feel isolated and insecure and hence will actively seek out established norms that will act as a guide to how that person ought to behave. Norms, therefore, facilitate the integration of an individual into a group, and thus will be eagerly accepted by new members.

4. Group formation and development

The main reason for rapid group formation is physical interaction. Accordingly, the greater the extent to which individuals share activities, the more they will interact and the higher the probability that they will form a group. Interaction enables people to discover common interests, likes and dislikes, attitudes, sentiments, etc. Other important factors encouraging group formation include the following:

(a) *Physical proximity.* For example, students who sit near to each other in a classroom are more likely to establish a group than are students who sit in different parts of the room.

(b) *Physical attraction.* Individuals who are attracted to each other physically might form a distinct group.

(c) *Rewards and penalties attached to mixing with certain other people.* Rewards include the gratification of economic and/or social needs; being able to work faster and more efficiently; access to information, etc. Penalties might involve feelings of embarrassment or personal inadequacy; frustration at having to rely on other people; being required to work harder than previously, and so on.

(d) *The need to co-operate with others in order to achieve personal objectives.*

(e) *Emotional support.* This might be provided by other group members in times of crisis. Membership of a group can *validate* a person's perceptions of events and issues.

Group development

Typically, groups develop through four stages (Tuckman 1965), as follows:

1 Members learn about each other, about the nature and purpose of the group and the constraints that limit its activities. Group structures, status hierarchies and patterns of interaction among members are determined. Rules of behaviour are established and individuals tell each other about their perceptions of the group's structure and objectives. This stage is sometimes referred to as the 'orientation' or *'forming'* phase.

2 Disputes and power struggles arise. There is internal group conflict, criticism and open questioning of the group's goals. This is the 'confrontation' or *'storming'* phase.

3 Conflicts are resolved and a division of work and responsibilities among group members is tentatively implemented. Specialisations develop; individual differences are recognised and 'who does what' disputes disappear. Group norms (*see* 3 above) emerge. This is the 'differentiation' or *'norming'* phase.

4 Eventually, group productivity increases, there is much collaboration among members and commitment to the group. Individuals value the contributions of their colleagues and accept their idiosyncrasies. A decision-making system acceptable to all the group's members is established. People get on with their work. This is the 'collaboration' or *'performing'* phase of the process.

Resistance to change

A group is something to lean on when things go wrong. It acts to support and reinforce the individual's view of the outside world. Such benefits greatly encourage conformity to group norms. Membership of a group provides individuals with companionship, social experience, opportunities for self-expression and social intercourse. Against these benefits, however, individuals must be prepared to modify their behaviour to fit in with group norms. The more valuable group membership is perceived as being, the more the individual will want to conform. Feelings of attachment will be greater, and the power of the group to compel obedience to established norms is enhanced. Eventually group behaviour will settle down to a fixed routine: conformity is demanded of new entrants who must demonstrate their willingness to abide by group norms. The group will continue to function despite changes of personnel. It becomes a self-perpetuating identity.

In consequence, groups are often resistant to change. Members become set in their ways and attitudes; they come to believe the group norm is right – no matter what the circumstances – and of course any deviation from the norm would have to be explained and justified by the individual to other members. And if the deviation is not accepted by the group the deviant member is liable to face social ostracism.

5. Group cohesion

This means the degree to which group members are prepared to co-operate, to continue their association with the group and to share common goals and perspectives. Cohesion encourages conformity to group norms and causes groups to be stable in their behaviour. But the increased pressures for conformity can stifle initiative. Several factors contribute to the creation of group cohesion, including:

(a) *Frequency and intimacy of interactions.* The more often people come into contact with each other, and the closer these contacts, the more they will perceive themselves as belonging to a distinct group.

(b) *Nature of the external environment.* The environment in which a group operates consists of a multitude of physical, technological and social circumstances. If individuals see their environment as hostile they will feel great affinity to any group offering protection from external threat.

(c) *Exclusivity of membership.* Cohesion is strengthened where group membership is selective. Then, members feel a sense of achievement in having been admitted.

(d) *Homogeneity of membership.* To the extent that members are alike in terms of background, education, age, outlook, ethnic or social origin, etc. they will be like-minded and share some common perspectives.

(e) *Members' enthusiasm for group objectives.* A group will be more cohesive if its members feel that its activities are relevant to the achievement of desired organisational goals.

(f) *Ease of communication within the group.* If interpersonal communication is difficult it is unlikely that a collective sense of purpose will easily emerge. Note that groups are more prone to internal cohesiveness the less contact they have with outsiders.

(g) *Nature of the task.* Individuals engaged on identical or very similar work are more likely to see themselves as a group than others.

(h) *Nature of the incentive system.* Group bonuses can encourage cohesion. A group that is able to reward or punish its own members can exert great pressure on individuals to conform. Such a group is likely to become extremely cohesive.

6. Effects of cohesion

High cohesion can result in high morale and productivity. Co-ordination of activities is made easier, the group will itself monitor the efficiency of its own activities and members are encouraged to work hard in order to further the group's interests.

Unfortunately, such enthusiasm might be directed against, rather than in support of, the aims of management. Powerful informal groups can arise to oppose management's wishes. High group cohesion need not always be associated with high productivity, low rates of absenteeism and labour turnover, enthusiasm for work and other desirable characteristics, but rather with the reverse. Cohesive groups might conspire to restrict output, perhaps even to disrupt the organisation's work.

Management must attempt, therefore, to relate group and organisational goals, to establish clear links between individual, group and organisational success. Within cohesive groups there is much social interaction, mutual support and interpersonal co-operation. Management needs to harness these qualities to further its own objectives; to work in concert with group sentiment and not against group norms.

GROUP DYNAMICS

The study of group dynamics is the study of the forces that operate within groups. It investigates how power and authority structures, communication systems, and intra-group conflict emerge. Dynamic interactions and relationships within a group create change and redefine the roles (*see* Chapter 9) of its members.

7. Pioneering empirical studies on group behaviour

Contemporary views on the dynamics of group behaviour derive from a number of influential empirical studies conducted (mainly in the USA) in the early and mid-twentieth century. The following were among the most important.

(a) Auguste Mayer's 1903 experiment which purported to establish that individual performance improved dramatically when people knew they were being observed. Mayer gave test subjects a series of sentence completion tasks and mental and written arithmetic puzzles – first alone and then before others – recording a 30 to 50 per cent improvement in the *group* situation, with fewer errors.

(b) The work of F.H. Allport in the 1920s and of S. Wyatt *et al* in the 1930s, which alleged that workers' physical proximities to each other affected the pace and quality of their outputs. Factors affecting the latter included whether people were sitting alongside or facing each other, whether a high-productivity group is placed between two poor ones (in which case its output was said to go down) or *vice versa*.

(c) Experiments conducted by H.C.A. Knight and K. Gordon in the 1920s that claimed to demonstrate that group judgements were far more accurate and evenly balanced than the average of individual assessments. Test subjects were asked to estimate the temperature of a room, the weights of various objects, the number of items in a glass bottle, etc. alone and in groups. Group evaluations were much nearer the correct answers than individual efforts. It seemed that, in groups, people quickly established which members were most competent in such matters, and competence-based leadership/discussion patterns emerged.

The general conclusions arising from these (and many other) early empirical studies can be summarised as follows:

(a) Group behaviour is fundamentally different from that of individuals.

(b) Attitudes and perspectives are affected by working in groups.

(c) Individuals *themselves* take the initiative in forming group organisation structures, leadership roles, etc., following the arbitrary formation of a group.

(d) The opinions of each group member are likely to be modified and 'levelled' to fit in with group requirements.

(e) Efficient divisions of labour within groups tend to occur naturally, without their necessarily having to be imposed from outside.

8. Group structures

A common justification for the creation of a work group is the assumption that 'synergy' will occur in consequence of its formation. Synergy results from arranging the work of a group in such a way that its *collective* output is greater than the aggregate of members' individual contributions. The concept of synergy is sometimes described as 'making two plus two equal five'. Causes of group synergy include:

- cross fertilisation of ideas within a group
- stimulation of innovation, effort and efficiency through group activity
- cost reductions resulting from undertaking several activities simultaneously rather than one after another
- combination of individual knowledge, talents and experiences.

Note, however, that working in groups is not necessarily more efficient than working alone. Frequent disturbances from colleagues and the need to consult before taking action can retard progress and constantly irritate the individual employee. Thus, great care is required when designing a structure for a working group. The following general principles normally apply:

(a) *Group size should be reasonably small.* Groups of more than (say) a dozen people normally require extensive supervision, and internal communications become difficult. Much time must be spent co-ordinating group activities, and decision taking is slow. Large groups encourage the emergence of sub-groups and factions differing in terms of their status, length of service, opinions on social and work issues, etc.

(b) *Joint decision taking should be encouraged.* Participation in decision taking can improve morale and stimulate employee co-operation. It facilitates the free flow of information through the group and the emergence of new ideas.

(c) *Cohesion should be consciously developed.* Cohesion is enhanced if members frequently interact and depend on each other for support and reward. Management should pay attention to all the factors causing cohesion previously discussed and attempt to implement them in practical ways.

(d) *The group leader should be compatible with the characteristics of the group.* Even if management structures a group according to the needs of its tasks (through selection of like-minded, compatible individuals with similar self-identities and outlooks) an inappropriate choice of group leader can cause the group to fail. If the leader appointed by management is ineffective then an informal (yet powerful) alternative leader may emerge.

9. Role of the group leader

A group leader has many roles. The more important of these include:

- providing direction for group activities
- defining problems and objectives
- obtaining information from group members and communicating information to them
- motivating the group
- appraising group performance
- arbitrating disputes between groups members
- offering ideas and opinions and encouraging others to do the same
- representing the group to outside bodies.

An important responsibility is to define *superordinate goals* for the group. Superordinate goals are high-level, broadly defined organisational objectives which all group members should seek to achieve. Examples of superordinate goals are the maintenance and improvement of the quality of a firm's products, or the provision of maximum customer service.

10. Formal versus informal group leaders

Formal group leaders are appointed by management. They are permanent and hence offer stability of leadership and a focus for group identity. Also they can impose formal rules on individual members. Supervisors, for example, might be empowered to select individuals for better-paid tasks, recommend workers for promotion, and might be authorised to suspend or dismiss subordinates who perform inadequately.

In practice, however, unofficial group leaders – quite distinct from those appointed by management – frequently emerge, and these informal leaders might direct and motivate their groups far more effectively than those whom management has chosen for command. Accordingly, although appointed group leaders possess formal *authority*, actual power to control group activities may lie elsewhere.

11. Authority and power

Authority is the right to control. The exercise of authority might involve such matters as:

- determination of subordinates' workloads and specific duties
- taking decisions on behalf of the group

- giving orders
- allocating rewards to subordinates (pay rises and so on)
- imposition of penalties on subordinates, such as suspension or dismissal.

Formal authority is often accompanied by outward displays of status: different clothing (such as managers wearing suits while operatives wear overalls), separate canteens, different modes of speech and behaviour, etc. These may even differ for each of several levels of authority within the managerial hierarchy.

Lower ranks are expected to treat superiors with deference and respect. There is a clear system of command, co-ordination and control.

Power

Power is the ability to initiate group activity and is not the same as authority *per se*. An individual need not be appointed by management to a position of command in order to exercise power. Appointed leaders might be powerful as well as occupy positions of authority. Equally, however, an official leader might not possess real power. The extent of an individual's power can depend on his or her ability to coerce others into obedience through threats of punitive action. Other determinants of power are:

- personal charisma
- group members' willingness to accept the direction of a particular individual
- the extent to which group members identify with the values of that person
- the person's ability to satisfy group members' needs
- whether group members perceive the person to possess expert knowledge about activities on which the group is engaged
- the extent to which members feel that a person's leadership position is legitimate, say because of seniority within the group
- control over information, resources and access to higher levels of authority.

12. The work of French and Raven

In 1959, J.R.P. French and B.H. Raven published a highly influential analysis of the nature and types of social power. According to the authors, there are five sources of power, as follows:

1 *Reward power*. This is based on one person's perception that someone else is able to grant rewards in return for the former's obedience and/or completion of certain tasks. The more attractive the tasks undertaken by the first person (the influencee), the greater the reward power of the other person (the influencer). Examples of reward power are the capacities to give promotions, allocate enjoyable duties to certain individuals, or send employees on training courses.

2 *Coercive power*. Basically this is the opposite of reward power. It involves the influencer's ability to punish the influencee, e.g. through dismissal, withholding pay rises, denial of requests for time off work, etc. The extent of a person's coercive power depends on: (*i*) the range and severity of sanctions available; (*ii*)

the influencee's perception of the probability that sanctions will be applied, which is determined by the past relationship between influencer and influencee (especially whether sanctions have been imposed previously) and by the degree of surveillance of the latter by the former. The more the influencee feels he or she is being watched, the greater the perception that improper behaviour will lead to punishment. Comparable considerations determine the extent of reward power (e.g. the range and attraction of rewards available).

3 *Referent power.* A person who wishes to identify with or be like someone else is said to be subject to the latter's 'referent' power. This could result from the influencer's charisma, or from the influencer having rewarded the influencee so that the influencer becomes attractive to the influenced person. Peers as well as occupational superiors can exert referent power.

4 *Expert power.* This is based on the belief that someone has special knowledge in a particular situation, e.g. through the possession of recognised qualifications, or past experience of similar problems or events. Expert power is normally restricted to the specific subject area of the influencer's expertise. For example, the advice of a medical doctor will almost certainly be followed in relation to matters concerning physical ailments; but not necessarily *vis-à-vis* which political party to support or which stocks and shares to purchase. The strength of an individual's expert power depends on: (*i*) the influencee's perception of the level of the influencer's expertise (especially if the former is totally ignorant of the subject under consideration); and (*ii*) the reliability of the advice of the expert. A series of mistakes will destroy the influencer's credibility.

5 *Legitimate power.* Acceptance by the influencee of the propriety of the power relationship between him or herself and the other party is referred to as 'legitimate' power. It can derive from the influencer's age, social class, position within an organisation, or his or her formal appointment to a position of authority. Examples of people who hold legitimate power are managing directors of companies, elected politicians, police officers, etc. Influencees inwardly *feel* an obligation to accept the other person's directions. The strength of an individual's legitimate power depends on the degree to which the influencer and influencee share common norms, objectives and moral values. Legitimate power is usually limited in scope. For example, a head of department in a commercial organisation will normally be perceived by subordinates as possessing legitimate power over job-related matters, but not in connection with their family and social lives.

13. Responsibility

Formal authority usually carries with it responsibility for decisions taken and, ultimately, for the performance of the group. Members who possess much power but little formal authority are fortunate in that they do not have to take the blame when things go wrong. Appointed leaders have to accept the consequences of their actions. If they make bad decisions they are expected to pay. In consequence, official group leaders are often reluctant to take crucial decisions, either passing difficult problems upwards to higher managerial levels or ignoring them in the hope that other group members (those with power) will quietly sort them out. Responsibility, then, is a constraint on the exercise of authority, and might restrain the exercise of power.

14. Teams

A team is a special sort of group. All teams are groups, but groups do not necessarily behave as teams. The defining characteristic of a team is that its members *voluntarily* co-ordinate their work in order to achieve group objectives. Team members are highly interdependent, and each individual must to some extent interpret the nature of his or her particular role. Teams have leaders who may or may not be appointed by an outside body (higher management, for example), but the authority of the leader of a team – as distinct from any working group – is fully accepted by all its members.

The team leader represents the group to the outside world and is formally answerable for its behaviour. Within a team there will be a high degree of group cohesion, much interaction, mutual support and shared perceptions of issues. Team members will be willing to interchange roles, share workloads and generally help each other out. Typically, each team member will hold other members in high regard, and will experience much satisfaction from belonging to the team. The leader of a team can improve team spirit through:

- representing and defending the team in the outside world, e.g. by fighting for extra resources on their behalf
- clarifying 'territorial divisions' among team members, hence ensuring that all members are fully aware of their individual and collective responsibilities
- encouraging members to suggest new working methods.

Other causes of good team spirit are:

- a fair distribution of work and responsibilities within the group, especially of unpleasant or exceptionally demanding tasks
- well-designed work programmes with realistic completion dates
- compatibility of the personal characteristics of participants.

Symptoms of poor teamwork are easily recognised: absenteeism, latecoming, high staff turnover, bad temper, deprecatory remarks about other team members, and so on. Staff lose confidence in the team's ability to achieve its objectives; comment is interpreted as criticism, the quality of work declines, staff lack effort, and petty grievances arise. Causes of such problems may include bad physical working conditions, wage levels and relativities, terms and conditions of employment (feeling of job insecurity, for example) or poor interpersonal relations within the group. Further problems might relate to the status of the group in the hierarchy of the total organisation.

15. Team building

In the 1970s, R Meredith Belbin and colleagues developed a theory of team building which suggested that certain types of individual do not perform well when working together in the same team. Belbin argued that people have different psychological characteristics which cause them to adopt particular roles at work, and that an appropriate combination of persons assuming various roles is essential for the creation of a well-balanced team. Nine team roles were identified, each of which needed to be fulfilled within a successful team (although they did not have to be present in equal measure). Team members would instinctively adopt specific roles according to their psychological make-ups, defined in terms of their intelligence, extroversion/introversion, dominance, and degree of stability or anxiety. The nine team roles were as follows:

1 *Co-ordinator*. The co-ordinator is a mentally stable individual, extrovert and dominant, and makes an ideal chairperson. He or she is self-confident, mature, a good speaker and listener, and adept at clarifying issues and facilitating group decisions. Unfortunately, other team members may perceive the person as manipulative and as someone who personally avoids completing tasks.

2 *Team worker*. This person is also mentally stable and extrovert, but low in dominance. The team worker is perceptive, able to identify problems, and promotes harmony within the group. However, he or she will avoid confrontation and tends to be indecisive.

3 *Specialist*. The specialist is a dedicated professional who provides technical skills and knowledge. He or she may fall into any personality category.

4 *Plant*. A 'plant' is a major source of a team's ideas and creativity, although the person might not be a good communicator. Plants are imaginative problem solvers: intelligent, introvert and dominant.

5 *Shaper*. This personality type is dynamic, outgoing, extrovert, dominant and highly strung. The shaper is task-orientated, argumentative, and thrives on pressure. He or she will overcome obstacles, albeit at the expense of other team members' feelings.

6 *Completer-finisher*. The completer-finisher is an unassertive introvert who is reluctant to delegate, and inclined to worry unduly. Strengths of this personality type are that such people are painstaking, conscientious and have a permanent sense of urgency.

7 *Implementer*. An implementer is practical, stable and controlled, and capable of turning ideas into action. He or she is disciplined and reliable, but prone to inflexibility and rigid attitudes.

8 *Monitor-evaluator*. This person is a critic rather than a creator: stable, intelligent, introvert, and capable of deep analysis of issues. Such individuals lack warmth, are rarely able to inspire others, yet are usually correct in their assessments.

9 *Resource investigator*. The resource investigator is a relaxed, positive and enthusiastic person who goes outside the group to discover new ideas and information. He or she is a dominant extrovert who inclines towards over-optimism and tends to lose interest in projects once his or her initial enthusiasm has passed.

Problems with the Belbin approach include its subjectivity (there is little empirical evidence concerning the personal characteristics of members of highly successful teams) and the difficulty of appraising *team* as opposed to individual performance. There is little hard evidence that any one mix of team types is any more effective than others (Furnham 1990).

A somewhat similar categorisation of team roles was developed in the 1980s by C Margerison and D McCann (see IRRR 1994). According to these authors there are three aspects of team performance:

1 The extent of the functions that need to be carried out by the team. Margerison and McCann measured this by a 'types of work index' (TWI).

2 Individual preferences concerning the way each person works. Typically, people concentrate on things they enjoy doing and neglect or perform badly tasks they dislike. A 'team management index' (TMI) was constructed to analyse personal preferences.

3 Communications and interactions within the team, as measured by a 'linking skills index' (LSI).

Eight major team roles were identified:

1 The *creator-innovator* who obtains and experiments with new ideas.
2 The *explorer-promoter* who looks for and informs others of fresh opportunities.
3 The *assessor-developer* who tests the applicability of various ideas.
4 The *thruster-organiser* who devises and implements new ways of making things work.
5 The *concluder-producer* who is best at operating existing systems and practices.
6 The *controller-inspector* who checks and audits systems.
7 The *upholder-maintainer* who ensures that standards are upheld.
8 The *reporter-adviser* who gathers and disseminates information.

Additionally all team roles must perform linking activities, in order to co-ordinate and integrate the work of the other eight roles.

Relative needs for the fulfillment of the various roles within a particular team were assessed using the TWI, a 64-item questionnaire. The personal preferences of the individuals who would undertake particular jobs were evaluated *via* the TMI, which categorises people under four headings:

1 Extrovert/introvert.
2 Practical/creative.
3 Analytical/believing. An analytical person uses objective criteria when taking decisions, whereas the other personality type pays more attention to personal beliefs and principles.
4 Structured/flexible. Someone who is 'structured' is well-organised, neat and tidy, and likes to take decisions quickly. A 'flexible' individual prefers to spend time thinking over a problem and will not reach conclusions until all relevant information has been considered.

Comparison of the TWI and TMI supposedly indicates overlaps between job demands and personal preferences. Differences between the two indices might suggest needs for job redesign, training, reallocation of duties or changes in team membership. The LSI diagnoses team members' individual strengths and weaknesses in terms of eleven key linking skills: listening; communicating with others; team development; work allocation; respecting, trusting and understanding colleagues; delegation; maintenance of quality standards; target set-ting; representing the team to outsiders; problem solving and counselling; and participation in team activities. Note the questionable reliability of the three indices used in the analysis, as they are largely based on self-reporting.

Teambuilding in practice

Teambuilding in practice involves a structured attempt to improve the effective-ness of a group in terms of its outputs and/or the quality of internal relations (co-operation, enthusiasm, etc.). This might require encouraging people to become team-centred rather than individualistic; open and communicative rather than reticent; to assume rather than avoid responsibility; and to be creative, trusting and co-operative (Clark 1994).

16. Communication within groups

The basic possibilities for channels of communication within groups are shown below. Experiments conducted to examine the efficiency of communications within these structures suggest the following conclusions:

(a) Matters requiring several comments and opinions are best handled through a circle (Figure 12.1).

(b) The wheel is effective for completing routine tasks, since messages can be transmitted between any pair of members in at most two steps (Figure 12.2).

(c) Complex problems are best dealt with using an all-channel system (Figure 12.3).

(d) The chain is appropriate where instructions need to be implemented quickly and little communication between members on the same level is re-quired (Figure 12.4).

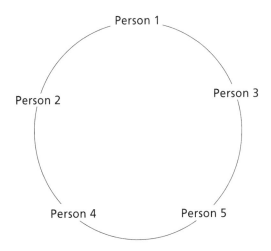

Fig. 12.1 The circle system

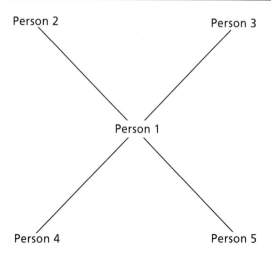

Fig. 12.2 The wheel system

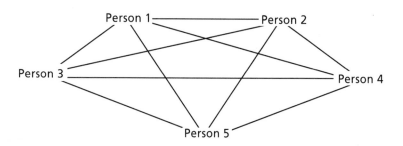

Fig. 12.3 The all-channel system

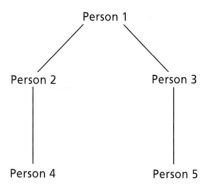

Fig. 12.4 The chain system

17. Intra-group conflict

Conflicts within a group may result from:

- personal disputes
- changing expectations of what might reasonably be demanded from membership of the group
- new technology which demands new working methods and / or divisions of labour among group members
- members perceiving group objectives differently
- breakdowns in communication between group members.

Such conflicts create the need for readjustments in internal group relations, including perhaps the introduction of new group norms. Mary Parker Follett suggested three ways in which internal group conflicts might be resolved:

1 *Domination* of the group by a single person or function within the group. This solution might work if there emerges a strong leader accepted by a majority of members. But it could be destabilising: members who are disadvantaged by the new arrangement may seek to upset the situation in the future.

2 *Compromise*, with each interested party giving something up.

3 *Integration*, where no individual or faction has to make sacrifices. This (ideal) outcome can only occur following discovery of new approaches to the problem or application of new ideas.

18. Intergroup conflict

The causes of conflicts between groups include:

- competition for limited resources
- differing perceptions about the organisation's aims
- loyalty to fellow members of a particular group regardless of external events
- lack of co-ordination of the organisation's activities by senior management
- conflicting goals and frames of reference (*see* 10:**16**)
- attempts by one group to dominate others.

To prevent such conflicts the organisation could:

- frequently shift individuals from one group to another
- create financial incentives to encourage intergroup co-operation
- publicise the organisation's wider goals
- develop project teams and matrix structures (*see* 22:**2**) that cut across existing group boundaries
- regularly exchange the tasks that groups are expected to perform.

(See Chapter 10 for further information on conflict within and between groups.)

19. Competition between groups

The results of a highly influential study of the consequences of creating competition between groups were published by M. Sherif and others in 1961. Two groups of boys were put in competition with each other in a camp situation in such a way that failure to attain group objectives imposed costs on the entire group. The boys were placed into groups at random on their arrival at the camp. For the first two days the two groups had no contact with each other. During this period internal group structures emerged, in-group feelings developed and relationships stabilised. Then, various inter-group competitions were organised and observations on group behaviour were recorded.

Considerable inter-group hostility appeared; manifest in petty acts of vandalism against the other group's property (burning its flag, for instance), name calling, withholding information, and the establishment of social distance between the groups. Further consequences were:

(a) negative stereotyping (*see* 4:**14**) of members of the other group

(b) overestimation by the boys of the ability of the particular group to which they belonged

(c) greater group cohesion (*see* 12:5) and more formality within the internal organisation of groups

(d) task-centred cultures arising within groups, with little concern for individual needs and close personal identification with group objectives. Members ignored their individual differences and focused their attention on attaining common goals.

Further research by Sherif *et al* claimed to demonstrate that the internal dynamics and record of achievement of a group would determine whether:

(a) A successful group would relax and 'rest on its laurels' rather than increase its efforts to perform even better in the future.

(b) An unsuccessful group would become discouraged and apathetic, or intent upon outperforming the other group on the next occasion.

Note that the results derive from a controlled environment with closed competition (i.e. where one group's gain is another group's loss without external interference), predictable outcomes, and easily measurable performance standards.

Progress test 12

1. Explain the differences between formal and informal groups.

2. What is a group norm? Explain the significance of group norms for group cohesion.

3. Why do established groups often resist change?

4. List the causes of group cohesion.

5. Define the term 'group dynamics'.

6. What are the causes of group synergy?

7. Explain the differences between formal and informal group leaders.

8. Distinguish between authority and power.

9. What is a team? How does a team differ from other types of group?

10. What are the major causes of intra-group conflict?

13

LEADERSHIP

THE NATURE AND STYLES OF LEADERSHIP

1. Definition

Leadership is the ability to influence the thoughts and behaviour of others. A leader's position may be formal and result from designated organisational authority (the jobs of appointed supervisors, for example) or informal and depend on the individual's personal ability to exercise power. The distinction between authority and power is discussed in 12:**11**.

Unofficial group leaders frequently emerge in large organisations. Thus 'leadership' is not *necessarily* the same as 'management,' because although managers have authority they might not have total power.

2. Theories of leadership

Several approaches to leadership theory exist. The first (and now largely discarded) is called the 'trait' approach, which asserted that the ability to lead is an innate characteristic (i.e. natural and not having to be learned) possessed by certain individuals. Hence, management's concern when selecting employees for leadership positions was regarded as the need to identify people with appropriate traits. Relevant personality traits might include initiative, decisiveness, self-assurance, assertiveness, intelligence, desire for occupational achievement and desire for financial reward. It has even been argued that a person's dress, stature and physical appearance can affect his or her ability to lead.

Problems with trait theory include the extremely large number of physical and personality traits that potentially affect leadership ability, the difficulty of deciding which traits are especially relevant to a particular leadership situation, and the need to measure these objectively. Other approaches to leadership are examined in **7–14** below. First, however, it is necessary to examine leadership style as a whole.

3. Leadership style

There is a continuum of possible leadership styles extending from complete autocracy at one extreme to total democracy at the other. Different phrases are used to describe various approaches, though all mean essentially the same. F.E. Fiedler, for example, distinguished between 'permissive' and 'directive' modes of behaviour. R. Blake and J. Mouton referred to 'concern for people' as opposed to 'concern for production'. R. Likert described 'job centred' versus 'employee centred' management. Other phrases used to define these concepts have included 'task oriented' (autocratic), and 'people centred' (democratic) styles, 'tight' and 'flexible', 'co-operative' versus 'dictatorial' and so on.

4. Autocratic styles

These involve close supervision of subordinates, with the leader issuing precise and detailed instructions to cover every task undertaken. An autocratic style may be *dictatorial* or *paternalistic*. Dictatorial approaches entail the leader telling subordinates exactly what to do, without comment or discussion. There are rewards and penalties and threats of sanctions for underperformance. Interpersonal relations between the leader and group members are highly formal and there is strict control.

The paternalistic style is similar in that it too imposes close supervision, but the leader genuinely attempts to gain the respect and allegiance of subordinates. Team members who always do as they are told receive special favours, and limited dissent is tolerated – though never condoned.

The *advantages* of the autocratic approach are as follows:

(a) Management takes the initiative in co-ordinating work. It actively seeks better ways to complete assignments. Hence there is a high probability of work being finished on time to a predetermined standard.

(b) Tasks, situations and relationships are clearly defined.

(c) There is fast decision taking, with management at the centre of activities.

(d) Employees receive direct and immediate assistance towards achieving their goals.

However, authoritarianism has a number of *disadvantages*:

(a) Employees' knowledge, skills and experiences are not fully applied to their work.

(b) It suppresses workers' initiative.

(c) Staff cannot develop to their maximum potential.

(d) The absence of the group leader (holidays, illness, etc.) may mean that important work is not completed.

Autocratic approaches may be appropriate for situations where employees have low motivation, show little concern for their work and make no attempt to communicate with colleagues or management. Such environments sometimes occur when work is boring and repetitive, working conditions are unpleasant and wages are low.

5. Democratic styles

Here the leader specifies overall objectives, leaving the subordinate to achieve these as he or she thinks fit. A democratic approach normally involves much communication and consultation between the leader and the group, with group members actively participating in the leader's decisions. An extreme form of this style is the *laissez-faire* approach whereby subordinates are left completely alone to take whatever steps they deem necessary to complete their work. The *advantages* of the democratic approach are that it:

(a) can improve workers' morale through involving them in forward planning, decision taking, and control

(b) increases subordinates' job satisfaction through broadening their responsibilities and making their work more interesting

(c) utilises subordinates' specialist knowledge and skills in achieving objectives

(d) ensures that only reasonable targets are set because the people who must attain them are involved in their formulation.

Disadvantages of the democratic style include the following:

(a) Decision taking may be slow because of the time absorbed by the need to consult subordinates. Disagreements may occur; and it could be that subordinates simply do not wish to become involved in taking decisions.

(b) Lack of positive direction may prevent objectives being attained.

(c) Subordinates might not be capable of working without close supervision.

(d) Encouraging employee participation in minor operational matters while excluding workers from all major decisions may cause great resentment.

6. The managerial grid

Robert Blake and Jane Mouton sought to relate autocratic and permissive leadership styles through a 'management grid' that illustrated contrasting degrees of concern for human relations and for efficiency. The grid is a taxonomy of management styles classified according to the manager's interest in subordinates as people, in comparison with his or her concern for production. Each concern is rated on a scale from one to nine so that a '9,9' manager, for example, is one who possesses both a very high concern for people and a high concern for production.

A '1,9' manager, who has a low concern for production, but who greatly emphasises human relations, will pay careful attention to subordinates' human needs, but will exert little effort to ensure that work is actually done. Such a manager is likeable, enjoys satisfactory relations with subordinates and generates a friendly atmosphere in his or her department. The '9,1' manager arranges work as efficiently as possible, with scant regard for subordinates' feelings. Other potential combinations are '1,1' managers, who make little effort to get work done or develop close personal relationships, and '5,5' managers who balance task performance with human relations considerations. Best of all is the '9,9' manager who achieves higher production from committed, satisfied subordinates.

7. The human relations approach

This suggests that leadership ability depends not so much on innate characteristics but rather on how leaders behave. Thus, managers can *learn* how to adopt modes of behaviour that will make them good leaders. Advocates of the approach argue that leaders should adopt a democratic/participative style, with the leader readily accessible to subordinates and knowing something about their backgrounds and aspirations. Staff are encouraged to initiate activities and suggest new ideas. The role of the leader is to co-ordinate, empathise with subordinates and explore differences of opinion among employees. Solutions should be suggested rather than imposed.

Much of the human relations approach derives from the work of G. Elton Mayo (*see* 3:2) and, more recently, of Douglas McGregor (*see* 8 below). Mayo insisted that the human aspects of management were paramount, particularly where group norms and structures were involved, According to Mayo, individuals look for the satisfaction of *social* needs at work, and the leader who understands this and thereby recognises the power of peer group influences will be more effective than others. This theme was developed by McGregor, who suggested that a leader's style is often determined by his or her assumptions about people and about human nature.

8. Theory X and theory Y

A person's mode of behaviour in a leadership position will depend substantially on that person's perceptions of what people are really like. If, for example, an appointed manager believes that individuals are naturally lazy, then he or she will treat subordinate employees in a certain way – issuing precise orders and exercising tight control over their work.

Douglas McGregor outlined two alternative sets of assumptions about human nature that a manager might adopt. He labelled these 'theory X' and 'theory Y'. Autocratic managers, McGregor asserted, were likely to subscribe to the assumptions of theory X, which (according to McGregor) postulate that:

(a) The average person dislikes work and must therefore be coerced into making the maximum effort, with inducements, sanctions and close supervision over his or her work.

(b) Workers are naturally reluctant to assume responsibility, preferring the security of being controlled by others.

(c) People are happier with clearly defined tasks than broadly defined objectives.

(d) Employees are normally resistant to change, so that change must be imposed on them by higher authority.

Thus, theory X implies that the typical worker lacks ambition, is self-centred and essentially indifferent to organisational needs.

Theory Y, in contrast, proposes that:

(a) Individuals will usually work hard without coercion.

(b) Employees can generally be relied upon to exercise self-direction and self-control.

(c) People seek rather than avoid responsibility.

(d) Most employees possess substantial potential for creative work, no matter how mundane their immediate duties.

9. Implications of theory Y

McGregor suggested that in most circumstances theory Y assumptions were a more accurate description of employee attitudes towards work. Managers subscribing to theory Y will therefore be more efficient.

Work, McGregor argued, is natural to the human species, and those who perform work will normally devote their full attention, effort and interest to its completion. Thus, management's primary concern should be to harness the innate energy and willingness to co-operate of the workforce – managers do not have to coerce and threaten workers to make them work hard; employees are capable of self-control.

To the extent that theory Y assumptions are valid, organisations should be designed to accommodate social and human needs. They should encourage personal initiative and release creative potential. This implies employee participation in decision making (*see* 3:**9**), the joint determination of subordinates' targets by the manager and the worker concerned, and relatively flexible organisational structures that allow for job enrichment (*see* 8:**22**), overlapping responsibilities and the motivation of junior staff.

Self-leadership and self-managed teams

Arguably there is little need for formal leadership in the modern workplace situation, which is increasingly likely to involve working in a team. According to this view, employees are quite capable of motivating themselves to perform unattractive as well as appealing tasks (Manz and Sims 1987) and to determine which group members are best qualified to complete particular duties. Advantages to self-managed teams include lower supervision costs, higher levels of employee interest in the work of the organisation as a whole, and hopefully the optimum use of human resources.

According to S. Kerr and J.M. Jermier, the need for leadership can be mitigated in many workplace situations by a number of factors, as follows:

(a) *Organisational characteristics* such as cohesive work groups that remove the need for supportive leadership, and the formalisation of working procedures (which results in group members not needing to ask a leader how to perform duties).

(b) *Job characteristics*, e.g. routine duties, feedback within a task and/or interesting and satisfying work.

(c) *Employee characteristics.* It is unlikely that workers who are experienced, trained, willing and able will need to be led. Professionally qualified employees are normally capable of looking after themselves.

To the extent that work groups do not need to be led, the particular style of leadership applied by the group's formal supervisor is largely irrelevant, explaining perhaps the very mixed results that have been obtained from many empirical studies in the leadership behaviour field.

LEADERSHIP APPROACHES

10. Advantages and disadvantages of the human relations approach

The advantages of the human relations approach are that it recognises: (*i*) the importance of human factors in the leadership process; and (*ii*) that wider organisational issues (job design, participation, etc.) are relevant to management style. Its major problems are as follows:

(a) The approach perhaps overestimates the enthusiasm for involvement in workplace decision taking among employees.

(b) It is (arguably) altruistic and ignores many realities of work, e.g. that certain tasks are necessarily boring and unpleasant, and that businesses exist in fiercely competitive environments.

(c) Genuine conflicts of interest in industry do exist and might not be solved simply by the adoption of a participative democratic approach.

11. Contingency approaches

These assert that a leader's style should be varied according to the needs of a particular situation because no single approach can ever be fully effective in all circumstances. Hence, leaders must be prepared to adjust their behaviour as circumstances change. Autocratic styles are appropriate when quick and/or unpopular decisions are needed, but the benefits of participation (use of subordinates' expert knowledge, higher morale, exercise of workers' initiative, etc.) are lost. Democratic approaches stimulate subordinates' motivation and sense of involvement; there is consensus on what should be done and general commitment to decisions reached, yet decisions might fail through the lack of experience and expert knowledge of those contributing to them. Moreover, participative decision-taking procedures may be long-winded and inefficient.

Thus, different work situations call for different leadership styles. A relaxed democratic approach is appropriate in some circumstances; an autocratic style in others. Accordingly, advocates of the contingency approach argue that management's role is to match leaders and situations and, to some extent, to control situations. For example, people of similar backgrounds can be allocated to the same work groups so that a relatively homogeneous departmental work-force can be formed. Jobs can be made less varied and more precise, or extended to allow workers greater discretion over how they complete their work. Super-visors exhibiting certain leadership styles should be allocated to groups most likely to respond favourably to them. Leaders should change their styles to correspond with the demands of various situations: a leader might be permissive with one group; authoritarian with another.

Advantages and disadvantages of the contingency approach

The advantages of the contingency approach are as follows:

(a) Managers are released from the ideological straitjackets imposed by other theories. They simply dovetail their behaviour to the requirements of various situations.

(b) Leaders may be matched to the groups most receptive to their styles of command.

(c) It encourages managers to analyse logically the characteristics of various situations.

There are, however, a number of problems attached to the contingency approach, as outlined below:

(a) Leaders who adopt contingency methods may appear to their subordinates as inconsistent and insincere, because they will change their behaviour depend-ing on circumstances. A certain approach is adopted in one situation; different approaches in others.

(b) The individual manager may not be sufficiently skilled to adapt his or her leadership style from one set of circumstances to the next.

(c) There might exist certain fundamental underlying principles that should always be applied regardless of the situation to hand.

Adair's theory of leadership

John Adair suggests that, to be effective, a leader must simultaneously satisfy three sets of interdependent needs, as follows:

(a) *Task needs*, relating to the work that has to be completed. A leader must be seen to strive to achieve group objectives, or he or she will lose the confidence of the group. Failure to satisfy task needs results in (*i*) frustration and disenchant-ment among group members, (*ii*) criticism of the leader, and (*iii*) the eventual collapse of the group. Task needs may be satisfied through planning, allocating duties, giving targets to individuals, setting standards, and the systematic appraisal of members' performances.

(b) *Group needs* connected with team spirit and morale. The group must be held together through effective communication, discipline, and other measures for enhancing team work. Discipline (i.e. the means for ensuring that work is carried out and that rules, norms of behaviour and instructions are obeyed) is improved if there are clear instructions and each group member knows precisely what he or she is required to do. Leaders enforce discipline in order to prevent harm being done to the efforts of the group. Leaders, Adair insists, should set a good example, not break rules themselves, and not exercise favouritism or impose unreasonable obligations on others.

(c) *Individual needs* of group members. A leader should seek to discover what each member wants from the group and how these needs can be satisfied and harmonised with task and group requirements. Examples of measures for meeting individual needs are coaching, counselling, motivating, and staff development.

The three needs interconnect because an action in one area affects others. Hence, leaders must try consciously to relate the satisfaction of individual and/or group needs to the achievement of group tasks. Leadership training, Adair argues, should be directed towards increasing a person's sensitivity to the three sets of needs, particularly through training in how to define objectives, team briefing, organisation of work, practical motivation, planning and control. Adair's is a contingency approach in that it requires leaders to alter the mix of effort devoted to satisfying various needs according to the requirements of the overall situation.

12. The path-goal theory

This is a contingency approach based on the expectancy theory of motivation (*see* 8:**14**). According to the theory the leader is seen by subordinates as the source of rewards. Therefore, a major task of leadership is to clarify to subordinates the paths they must follow to obtain the rewards (goals) the leader makes available to them. Rewards might include higher wages, promotion, social support, encouragement, job security, and respect from supervisors.

Effective leaders will be capable of determining which rewards are perceived as most important by various employees and hence will create reward packages that are particularly attractive (valent) to these people. Leaders should be willing and able to change their style according to: (*i*) the characteristics of subordinates; (*ii*) the nature of their work; (*iii*) the clarity of the organisation's formal authority system (i.e. how easily employees can identify the leader's expectations); and (*iv*) the physical environment in which work is undertaken.

13. The 'maturity of subordinates' approach: the Hersey – Blanchard model

This is a further contingency theory which argues that the major factor affecting the suitability of a particular mode of leadership behaviour is the 'maturity' of subordinates. Maturity in this context means the employee's work experience, ability level and willingness to accept responsibility.

Hersey and Blanchard (who term this model the 'situational' approach to leadership) distinguish two types of employee maturity: 'job maturity', i.e. the worker's skills and knowledge; and 'psychological maturity' relating to the individual's self-image, self-respect and self-confidence. Accordingly, a 'high maturity' subordinate is one who is competent, assertive and self-confident.

Immediately following an employee's entry to the organisation, a relatively directive style of leadership may be most appropriate in order to clarify the subordinate's role and hence avoid feelings of anxiety and confusion within that person. Then, as the relationship between manager and subordinate develops, participation begins to occur and the employee actually seeks additional responsibility. Tight supervision is no longer suitable for the situation.

Eventually the subordinate is capable of working independently so that the need for close direction ceases entirely. A *laissez-faire* approach might now be the most effective leadership style. It follows that four types of leadership behaviour become available:

1 *The telling style*, whereby the leader provides detailed instructions to subordinates. Hersey and Blanchard call this a 'high-task, low-relationship' style and suggest its use on low maturity subordinates.

2 *The selling style*, in which the leader carefully explains the reasons for decisions and seeks to clarify contentious issues. This is a 'high-task, high-relationship' style suitable for subordinates who are enthusiastic but as yet not fully competent to complete work independently.

3 *The participating style*, where the leader shares ideas and tries to involve subordinates actively in the formulation of decisions. This is a 'high-relationship, low-task' approach appropriate for subordinates who are able but currently unwilling.

4 *The delegating style*, whereby the leader gives subordinates full authority to take decisions and implement them. This 'low-task, low-relationship' style should only be used on mature subordinates.

Criticisms of the Hersey–Blanchard model

Problems with this model include:

(a) The concept of 'maturity' is wide ranging and covers a multitude of considerations not incorporated into the model.

(b) Organisational politics and other group influences are largely ignored.

(c) Subordinates might be highly competent yet lack self-confidence; or be extremely assertive but not have sufficient ability to complete their work satisfactorily.

14. Empirical studies of leadership

Empirical tests of the trait hypothesis suggested that energy, height, aggressiveness, enthusiasm and self-confidence could be linked to perceived (though not necessarily to actual) leadership ability. However, everyone possesses these characteristics to at least some extent and the studies could not *explain* leadership. Nor did they agree on which traits were most important.

The failure of the trait approach to discover common elements that could be relied upon to predict leadership success led to a number of important empirical studies which laid the foundations upon which contemporary approaches to leadership continue to be based. Some of the more influential of the studies are outlined below.

Lewin, Lippitt and White

These three researchers studied four boys' clubs in Iowa in the USA. Each club had five members and a leader trained to adopt one of three styles: autocratic, democratic, and *laissez-faire*. Leaders were rotated every six weeks. Democratic approaches were observed to be more productive. The application of the autocratic style caused the boys to become aggressive, discontented, to lack initiative and to feel little concern for the achievement of group objectives. The experiments claimed to have demonstrated direct relationships between leadership style, group atmosphere and individual behaviour.

The Ohio University studies

These studies concluded that staff grievances and labour turnover rates were lowest and job satisfaction highest when leaders adopted employee-centred styles (which the researchers termed 'consideration') rather than a task-centred approach (referred to as 'initiating structure'). However, subordinates rated their leaders as good or bad according to the nature of the situation rather than the style the leader adopted.

Researchers at the University of Michigan also found that the most effective leaders were 'employee centred' (democratic). Such leaders used extensive employee participation in decision taking and set high targets for subordinate groups.

Tannenbaum and Schmidt

Tannenbaum and Schmidt concluded that managers should consider three sets of factors when choosing a leadership style.

The first set related to the background, values and experiences of the manager concerned; including (*i*) attitudes towards employee participation; (*ii*) confidence in subordinates' abilities; and (*iii*) capacity to handle uncertain situations.

The second category involved the characteristics of subordinates (their competence, experience, interests, desire for participation and responsibility, whether they identified with the organisation's goals, etc.).

The third involved the nature of the situation in which leadership occurred (type of task, culture of the organisation, group cohesion, time available for taking decisions, the physical environment, etc.).

Leadership, they argued, involves a continuum of styles (ranging from autocracy to complete participation) from which the manager is obliged to select. There is no presumption that any one approach is superior to the rest. At one extreme of the continuum the leader will simply make decisions and announce them. A little further on, the leader will 'sell' decisions to subordinates (*see* **13** above) by explaining them to followers. Then the leader might consult subordinates about the best decisions. At the final extreme of this side of the continuum the leader will 'join' subordinates in collective decision making, i.e. the leader merely sets the limits within which independent subordinate action may occur. The model is sometimes referred to as the Tannenbaum and Schmidt 'tell-sell-consult-join continuum'.

W.W. Soujanen

This researcher postulated that organisations can be categorised as (*i*) crisis-oriented; (*ii*) routine-oriented; (*iii*) knowledge oriented (those in high-technology industries, for example). On average, the style of leadership that managers adopted within any given organisation would shift as the nature of the organisation changed.

Organisations regularly experiencing crisis situations tended to adopt authoritarian management styles. In 'routine-oriented' organisations (i.e. the normal business firm) there was frequent consultation with employees, but not out-and-out worker participation. The style typical in knowledge-oriented organisations was democratic, with only a minority of workers being treated autocratically.

Rensis Likert

Likert presented a four-fold categorisation of leadership style. System 1 leaders were totally authoritarian; System 2 managers offered subordinates some flexibility over how they completed their work, but only within predetermined limits, and moreover, remained essentially autocratic and remote; System 3 managers would discuss goals with subordinates, who themselves decided how to complete their tasks; System 4 leadership involved group rather than individual decision taking. With System 4, the views of all group members would be considered before a final decision was reached: there was open communication between leader and subordinates, who themselves controlled and appraised their own work.

Likert collected data on productivity, absenteeism, staff turnover, output quality and other efficiency indicators in several industrial and commercial organisations, concluding that employee-centred leadership was generally more efficient. Therefore work group supervisors should be trained in employee-centred leadership styles.

F.E. Fiedler

F.E. Fiedler sought to identify the factors that determine the nature of situations. Three such factors were found to be especially important:

1 Relationships between the leader and the group; in particular the degree of confidence of the group in the leader's abilities;
2 The nature of the tasks undertaken by subordinates: whether the tasks are easy or difficult, routine or varied;
3 How much authority is vested in the leader.

Fiedler described two contrasting leadership styles: people-oriented (associated with considerate, understanding treatment of subordinates) and task-oriented – where the leader is directive and authoritarian.

Each style, he argued, is relevant to particular situations. People-oriented leadership is useful where the work done by subordinates is liked even if the leader is disliked. If the work is disliked and the leader is unpopular, a more authoritarian manner may be appropriate.

15. Transformational leadership

This is the process of transforming employee attitudes in order to increase workers' commitment to the employing organisation. It differs from 'transactional leadership' in that whereas the latter involves nothing more than the efficient organisation of subordinates' work and the provision of the resources and help necessary for subordinates to achieve their goals, transformational leaders have charisma, vision and empathy with subordinates' needs. A charismatic leader is one who is perceived by subordinates as possessing extraordinary powers, characteristics and abilities, and who can inspire loyalty and enthusiasm among those who are led.

Determinants of charisma

Whether a leader is charismatic will depend on the personal qualities of the individual involved, the nature of the situation, the backgrounds and perceptions of subordinates, and the extent to which the leader is able to satisfy subordinates' needs. Other factors include:

- whether the leader and subordinates share a common interest
- the extent of subordinates' trust in the leader's abilities
- subordinates' emotional commitment (if any) to the goals of the organisation
- whether the leader is liked by subordinates
- subordinates' attitudes towards obedience and authority
- the leader's personal conviction in his or her beliefs and abilities
- the leader's persuasive and influencing skills (see 14:9)
- the leader's image of competence, knowledgeability and past success.

The behaviour of a charismatic leader sets an example for subordinates to follow. Typically, his or her approaches to problems are seen by subordinates as being somewhat unconventional, self-sacrificing, risky to the position of the leader concerned, and of substantial value to the entire group.

Techniques of transformational leadership

Transformational leaders raise their subordinates to higher levels of enthusiasm and activity. This might be achieved through:

(a) direct and intimate communication with subordinates

(b) influencing the subordinate's peer group in order to bring pressure to bear on that person

(c) explaining the importance of the subordinate's contribution to the welfare of the organisation

(d) making emotional appeals to subordinates.

Effective transformational leaders, it seems, are those who recognise the need for change, are willing to challenge the status quo, and have a wealth of experience of similar situations.

16. Summary

A great many considerations affect the efficiency of a leadership style. These include:

- the characteristics of both the leader and subordinates
- the nature of the situation
- the culture of the organisation (*see* 20:**18**)
- the leader's perception of subordinates' abilities
- whether the work undertaken is interesting or boring
- the experience and training of the leader
- the physical circumstances of the work
- the quality of interpersonal communications within the firm

Managers who pay attention to these factors will normally improve the effectiveness of their leadership behaviour. Note, however, that to be useful, most of the approaches to leadership previously outlined require that managers be trained in management theory and consciously adopt an appropriate leadership style. In fact, very few practising managers have received leadership training, and even fewer are aware of the broader implications of the style they apply.

Leadership theory

Certain other important questions arise when considering the practical worth of contemporary leadership theory:

(a) Most of the leadership studies which form the basis for current theory were conducted in the USA in the context of US culture, institutions, attitudes and traditions. To what extent can the conclusions emerging from these studies be transplanted to other countries?

(b) The most influential of the pioneering leadership studies were completed in the period 1935–70. Societal attitudes have changed since then, with greater demands for openness, equal opportunities and employee rights. How well do existing theories of leadership fit into current social and economic conditions?

(c) Managerial leadership should involve more than the supervision of workers. It should in addition cause employees to transcend immediate targets and move on to higher levels of performance and efficiency (*see* **15** above). Achieving this requires managements to promulgate an entire philosophy of organisational behaviour and not just to command and control. Conventional leadership theory has little to say about how best to motivate employees to transcend their short-term goals. Japanese management, in contrast (*see* 22:**16**), emphasises the intense and total socialisation of workers into accepting company norms, and the projection of the philosophy and objectives of the organisation to the individual worker.

(d) Technologies are changing drastically and new working patterns and methods are rapidly being introduced. In Britain, for example, there has in recent years been a huge increase in the use of casual and part-time labour that has little commitment to employing firms. The studies upon which leadership theory is based have mostly involved full-time and permanent workers. Is existing leadership theory relevant to the management of 'peripheral' rather than 'core' workers (see 22:6), to networking (see 22:10) and other new organisational forms?

WOMEN IN MANAGEMENT

17. Women and leadership

Leadership studies and theories have in the past focused almost exclusively on the behaviour of male managers. Arguably, however, female managers tend to (and indeed should) apply different approaches to leadership style, possibly favouring persuasive and supportive approaches rather than coercion and autocratic control. How applicable is orthodox leadership theory to the needs of women managers? A number of studies conducted in the USA (see for example Grant 1988, Eagly and Johnson 1990, Eagly and Karan 1991) have suggested that women do in fact tend to adopt more democratic and participative management styles than males, to share power and information and to support and encourage subordinates. As leaders they are allegedly persuasive and influential, charismatic, and make extensive use of interpersonal skills. They are supposedly less directive and controlling than male colleagues, although the investigations concluded that these characteristics declined the greater the extent to which women managers operated within male-dominated environments. It seemed that masculine norms and peer group pressures caused women to abandon their 'feminine' approaches to management and to behave more autocratically. Arguably women managers adopting feminine management styles are better suited to contemporary business conditions than males, since modern management techniques are invariably based on teamwork, flexibility, trust and the free exchange of information.

18. Problems faced by women managers

Women face special problems when pursuing managerial careers, including the following:

(a) The need to balance continuity of employment (and hence the acquisition of managerial skills and experience during the early stages of a career) against requirements to take time out from the workforce for childbearing and initial child rearing. A woman who leaves the workforce for (say) four or five years to have a family is then that many years 'behind' her male contemporaries when she resumes her career. Note how management recruitment and development programmes are typically designed for young college leavers rather than for slightly older women with families.

(b) Possible discriminatory sexual stereotyping by existing male senior managers, who might assume that a woman's role is to look after home and family and not to manage organisations.

(c) Preassumption that family commitments will cause a woman to take more time off work than male colleagues.

(d) Lack of child-care facilities for working mothers.

(e) The existence within organisations of male networks, informal communication systems, and power groups that men can use to help each other and to provide support and understanding when things go wrong.

(f) Lack of female role models for women managers to emulate. Note how the higher the level to which a woman rises within an organisation, the fewer female colleagues of equivalent rank she is likely to have.

19. Recruitment, appraisal and promotion problems

There is evidence to suggest that women managers are more common in certain types of management job (personnel, for instance) than others. Also, females are better represented in the managements of service industries than in manufacturing. This could be due in part to unfair discrimination in recruitment and promotion procedures, and possibly to biases in performance appraisal.

Factors militating against women being recruited to undertake management jobs and/or their achieving promotion might include:

(a) low aspirations among women themselves, leading them not to apply for higher-level positions

(b) perceptions by existing senior managers that women have low aspirations

(c) assumptions (by men) that women are not very good at taking decisions

(d) male prejudices that 'feminine' characteristics of supportiveness, sensitivity, being good at human relations, etc. are inappropriate for people in positions of authority

(e) male selection panels evaluating candidates against masculine values and norms

(f) media portrayal of women as sex objects rather than as thinking and responsible people

(g) possible failure of male superiors to delegate demanding work to female subordinates, hence denying them the experience needed to undertake higher-level duties

(h) male superiors' possible preconceptions that women lack commitment to long-term careers, that money spent on training will be wasted, and that women possess outside interests that will interfere with work

(i) possible perceptions that if a woman is promoted to a senior position her (predominantly) male subordinates will resent being accountable to a woman.

Appraisal difficulties

To the extent that most senior managers are male, performance appraisal means that men appraise women. A possible problem here is that male appraisers who dislike the idea of women managers might (unconsciously) apply inappropriate preassumptions to their assessments of female subordinates' qualities. For example, traits considered desirable in a man might be regarded as undesirable in a woman, e.g. a forceful male subordinate may be classed as 'assertive' (a positive characteristic) whereas a forceful woman might be described as 'bossy'. A man who frequently loses his temper might be seen as a 'demanding taskmaster'; a woman as 'likely to become hysterical'. If moreover a male appraiser considers women to be (say) 'emotional', then he could tend to notice examples of emotional behaviour in female subordinates, while unconsciously ignoring emotional characteristics in males! Other biased preassumptions might be that:

(a) Whereas excellent work completed by male subordinates is due to ability, successes achieved by females are due to chance and/or help given by male colleagues.

(b) The restrained and unobtrusive management styles adopted by some women managers (which are highly effective in many circumstances) indicate lack of initiative and low leadership ability.

Such difficulties could result in women being directed towards careers in areas regarded as more suitable for females. Unfortunately, however, these jobs usually offer fewer opportunities for advancement through line management than do the positions typically occupied by males.

MANAGERIAL IDEOLOGY AND MANAGEMENT STYLE

20. Nature of managerial ideology

The term 'managerial ideology' describes the totality of the ideas, opinions and perspectives of those who exercise formal authority in business situations and which seek to explain and justify that authority. No single managerial ideology is universally held by business executives, since ideology is heavily interconnected with general approaches to management and the latter vary from country to country and time to time. The main managerial ideologies are:

- unitarism, which (together with its opposite, 'pluralism') is discussed in 10:**17**
- social Darwinism, which relies on *laissez-faire* and the idea of the 'survival of the fittest' in competitive employment situations
- paternalism, whereby the employer is assumed to have a moral responsibility for employee welfare
- classical and human relations approaches (*see* Chapters 2 and 3).

Functions of managerial ideology

A manager's ideology will influence his or her sentiments, actions and expectations of how the workforce should behave. Ideologies filter information (downgrading the significance of any facts or occurrences that contradict the predictions of the ideology), and simplify (perhaps naively) complex issues. Possession of a distinct ideology helps the individual to cope with **(a)** uncertainty, **(b)** stress and other psychological demands of work, and **(c)** the strains that arise from ambiguities concerning the legitimacy of a manager's role. The latter is especially important because a manager's perception that his or her position in the social hierarchy is right and proper enables that person to give orders, expect them to be obeyed, and generally to exercise power. Managerial ideologies might be communicated to workers in attempts to inspire the acceptance by employees of management's 'right to manage' without interference from employees. The concept of 'management's right to manage' is referred to as 'managerial prerogative'.

21. Managerial prerogative

Belief in the propriety of managerial prerogative (i.e. management's *moral* right to manage in addition to the fact that management has control over resources and the ability to hire and fire) rests on a number of assumptions, namely that:

(a) Managerial perspectives and activities should focus on serving customers, *not* pleasing employees.

(b) Only management possesses the information, training, skills and resources needed to make effective decisions.

(c) Since management either owns the firm or has been appointed by its owners then management represents the organisation's fundamental interests and aspirations.

(d) Managers are able to take a more objective view of the needs of particular sections and departments than workers and hence can make decisions which maximise the well-being of the *entire* organisation.

(e) Employee representatives frequently lack the professionalism, training and basic education needed to assess the implications of important management decisions.

Workers are expected, therefore, to trust management to make wise decisions and to be impartial and objective. Individual managers' specialist knowledge and competencies should be recognised and respected, and management itself is deemed to know when and in what circumstances it is appropriate to consult with employees.

22. Definition of management style

The term 'management style' has two (related) meanings. One is the demeanour that a manager adopts when dealing with employees; the other is the collective approach of the management of an entire organisation to questions of leadership, worker participation in management decisions, control of employees, and interpersonal relations between managers and basic grade workers. In the former context the particular style chosen will depend on personal inclinations, training and experience and on environmental factors. It will affect managers' relations with their subordinates, group productivity, and patterns of interaction among employees. In the macro-organisational sense, management style helps determine formal structure, line and staff relationships, whether the firm uses project teams, the frequency and character of interactions with workers, and so on.

23. National differences in management style

Significant differences in the management styles predominant within various nations can be identified. In some countries the prevailing style is highly formal and authoritarian, in others it is the reverse. National disparities result from:

(a) *Cultural* factors such as religion, attitudes towards industry and towards management as an occupation, and community views on efficiency, the role of profit, savings and investment. Achievement in business is rewarded more in some societies than elsewhere. Willingness to accept risk also differs markedly between countries.

(b) *Social* factors such as:

(*i*) Whether there exists a *work ethic* in the country. Higher incomes and increasing productivity create possibilities for greater amounts of leisure, yet in some communities managers (and others) choose to work extremely hard and take little time off regardless of their large remunerations.

(*ii*) *Social class systems.* A high degree of class and/or occupational mobility results in individuals from a wide variety of class and income backgrounds reaching the top in management positions. Class systems affect recruitment policies and procedures and promotion and salary grading schemes. Rigid class structures cause an oversupply of trained, educated and competent people in lower-level management jobs, since social barriers prevent their moving up the hierarchy.

(*iii*) *Attitudes towards authority.* Paternalistic management styles and highly formal interpersonal relationships between managers and subordinates are likely in countries where deferential attitudes are valued for their own sake. The psychological distance between managers at different levels affects communication, problem-solving and decision-making systems.

(*iv*) Existence or otherwise of *strong desires to accumulate wealth.*

Progress test 13

1. Define leadership

2. What are the main problems associated with the trait theory of leadership?

3. List the characteristics of autocratic leadership style. What other names have been given to the autocratic approach?

4. List the disadvantages of the democratic style of leadership.

5. What is the leader's role in the human relations approach to leadership theory?

6. Explain the difference between theory Y and theory X.

7. Explain the difference between the human relations and contingency approaches to leadership.

8. Describe the 'path-goal' theory of leadership.

9. What were the major implications of the results of the empirical studies into leadership conducted by F.E. Fiedler?

14

COMMUNICATION

FUNDAMENTALS

1. Definitions

Communication is the transmission of information (a message) and its receipt. It involves the exchange of data, opinion and/or sentiment. C. Shannon and W. Weaver characterised communication as a series of relations between inputs and outputs of information. The Shannon-Weaver model is shown in Figure 14.1.

Within the system there will exist separate mechanisms for: (*i*) encoding messages (e.g. choosing an appropriate form of words prior to transmission); and (*ii*) decoding (interpreting) the information sent. The recipient may or may not provide feedback to the sender of a message. Noise is any form of interference with messages that has the effect of producing extra and distracting information. For example, technical jargon, overlong and obscure sentences or flowery language might so confuse the recipient that the message's original meaning becomes unclear.

The Shannon–Weaver model has been criticised on the grounds that it represents a one-way process, whereas in reality substantial amounts of feedback from the message recipient are likely to be involved. Thus Schramm (1954) suggested the basic model be amended as shown in Figure 14.2.

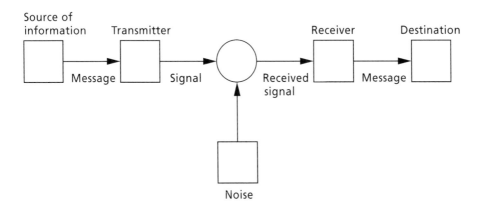

Fig. 14.1 The Shannon-Weaver model of communication

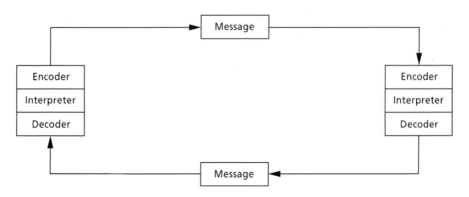

Fig. 14.2 Schramm's amendment to the Shannon-Weaver model

2. Communication systems

A communication system links together the constituent parts of an organisation and provides for the creation, distribution, interpretation and execution of instructions and for feedback on events. Formal communication systems include letters and memoranda, face-to-face verbal communication, meetings, posters, pamphlets, manuals and written reports. Informal communications involve *ad hoc* social contacts, idle gossip, body language (*see* **8** below) and/or other non-verbal cues.

Both the formal system and the informal system need to operate efficiently if an organisation is to be soundly managed, because the co-ordination of work is impossible without effective communication. Good communication, moreover, encourages team spirit, higher performance and greater job satisfaction among employees.

3. Communication problems

Effective communication unites an organisation. Employees become fully aware of management's intentions; management itself remains 'in touch' with happenings at the grass roots. Unfortunately, several factors may hinder communication, including the following:

(a) The distortion of information during transmission can mean that messages sent are not the same as those received.

(b) Individuals might assume that other members of the organisation have been informed of particular issues when in fact they have not.

(c) Incompetence, idleness or indifference might cause people not to pass on important information.

(d) People sometimes communicate less than is necessary to keep interested parties completely aware of current events.

(e) Informal communication systems ('grapevines', *see* below) can spread false information.

4. Grapevines

A 'grapevine' is an unofficial, loose collection of communication passages that circumvent and sometimes even replace orthodox communication procedures. Grapevines are common where employees know each other well and exchange information casually without the knowledge or permission of higher authority. They will be particularly virulent if senior management deliberately withholds information that affects employees' welfare. Hence, rumours concerning possible redundancies, confidential personal matters, gossip or scandal will be quickly and widely dispersed through the grapevine. Although the grapevine is strictly unofficial, people holding key positions within it (namely those who spread the most information) may find that their status in the official system is enhanced because of their grapevine activities.

It seems that the most efficient way of suppressing a grapevine is for management to present clear, accurate and comprehensive information to employees. Yet some managements deliberately allow grapevines to survive because they provide a fast and effective means of distributing news. Also, views which management might not want to broadcast officially can be made known 'on the quiet' through the grapevine.

The obvious disadvantage of the grapevine system is its tendency to distort reality; and it can be used maliciously to initiate unsavoury rumours. Even without deliberate malice, grapevines frequently misrepresent issues because the facts behind situations are exaggerated or otherwise altered at each stage in the dissemination process. There is no mechanism for checking the validity of the information transmitted, or for refuting falsehoods.

BARRIERS TO GOOD COMMUNICATION

5. Communication barriers

Obstacles which prevent the smooth flow of information through organisations are known as communication barriers. Examples are listed below.

Message distortion

Chains of command might be stretched to impractical lengths. Large organisations may contain so many levels between top and bottom that messages take long periods to reach final users, and there is a high probability that message content will be lost or distorted in transit.

Information overload

Individuals might receive so much information that most is disregarded; in large organisations people can easily become immersed in messages. Consequently, decisions about which messages to take seriously and which to ignore become arbitrary. For example, a message received by telephone may be acted upon immediately, whereas one received by letter (which is a much less personal form of communication) might not. Equally, an instruction given by a superior with whom a subordinate enjoys a good working relationship might be obeyed before a more urgent command issued by someone else.

Suitability of messages for a particular audience

Messages might not be suited to the audience for which they are intended. Particular styles of writing and speech might not be understood by certain audiences. Messages, therefore, should be assembled in forms which make them intelligible to recipients.

Semantic imprecision

Vague, meaningless words and sentences fail to convey messages effectively. Indeed, they might alienate and confuse the recipient. Short words and phrases are usually better than long ones; cliches and excessive technical jargon should be avoided.

Note however that 'redundancy' of information – repeating points and providing more information than is strictly necessary – can serve to emphasise important issues. The well-known teaching maxim: 'Tell the students what you are going to tell them; tell them; and then tell them what you have just told them' is highly relevant in this respect. The objective is to ensure that certain individuals receive and understand messages. If this requires regular reiteration of statements (perhaps in slightly differing forms) the extra time spent on communication activities is well justified.

Redundancy, however, does not excuse ambiguity, the consequence of which is to confuse the message recipient. A problem here is the generic nature of so many words in the English language. Often, words have several possible meanings and message recipients have to interpret the intention of the sender of the message in the context in which words are used.

Lack of opportunities for communicating

Long chains of command prevent junior managers meeting their superiors, and middle managers might not pass messages through the system. Also, feelings of embarrassment when communicating with senior managers sometimes cause subordinates to avoid initiating necessary conversations.

Horizontal communication is difficult when departments and individuals are geographically apart; communication may be interrupted, and duplication of effort might occur. Physical separation could even lead to various departments pursuing conflicting objectives.

Information can be distorted during transmission, particularly in conversation. Each time a verbal message is passed on it can lose some of its original meaning, until eventually its initial substance is lost. Written messages can also change as they are interpreted, rewritten in fresh letters or memoranda and sent to other people.

Inability to listen

Communication involves receiving as well as giving advice; feedback on the effects of decisions is essential for effective administration. Some managers are good talkers but poor listeners, hearing only what they want to hear and disregarding all critical or hostile comment.

Membership of a reference group

This can greatly influence a person's interpretation of received communications. A reference group is a group of people with whom the individual identifies (e.g. neighbours, 'management', the working class, a particular religion, an ethnic group, etc.). Messages favourable to the reference group will be received more willingly than others.

ATTRIBUTION AND INTERPRETATION

6. Attribution and the interpretation of information and events

In the psychological context the word 'attribution' means how an individual explains his or her behaviour or that of someone else. Two important aspects of attribution are: (i) *stereotyping*, and (ii) the *halo effect*.

Stereotyping

Stereotyping is the attribution to a person of a number of characteristics assumed typical of the group to which he or she belongs. An example is to presuppose that all Scots are mean, and then to assume that a particular person must be mean just because he or she is Scottish!

Stereotypes are mental pictures of what certain types of people (e.g. ethnic minorities, religious groupings, doctors, accountants, trade unionists, army sergeants, etc.) are thought to be like. Thereby anyone belonging to one of these groups is instantly assumed to possess identical characteristics. Stereotyping is a convenient (though frequently inaccurate) means for categorising the various people that an individual encounters. The problems with stereotypes are that:

- they tend to exaggerate and overgeneralise
- the information upon which they are based may be out of date
- their creation can result in unfair treatment of individuals
- a person might fall into several different stereotypical categories, so that the allocation of that individual to any one of them is an arbitrary decision.

The halo effect

The halo effect occurs when an individual assumes (perhaps wrongly) that because someone exhibits one characteristic then that person necessarily possesses other characteristics as well. This differs from stereotyping in that whereas with stereotyping the other individual is mentally allocated to a particular category of persons and then assumed to possess all the features of that group, with the halo effect the other person's total set of characteristics is perceived on the basis of just one observable trait.

To illustrate the halo effect, consider an employment interview in which a male interviewer assumes that an attractive female candidate for a secretarial position will automatically be good at typing, shorthand, secretarial duties, and so on. Another example would be the assumption that a well-spoken candidate is necessarily intelligent and industrious – which of course need not be true. Note how this phenomenon could work in the opposite direction: an interviewer may consider (wrongly) that weakness in one area implies low calibre overall.

7. Sources of attribution

Attribution results largely from the observation of others. The individual making the attribution will be influenced by:

(a) the nature of the situation observed

(b) what is already known about the people involved in the situation

(c) his or her self-esteem, e.g. individuals often attribute their own successes to hard work, skill and effort while attributing the successes of others to chance

(d) first impressions. The phenomenon of first impressions exerting a disproportionately powerful influence on later interpretations is known as the 'primacy effect'.

8. Interpretation of verbal and non-verbal communication

The following factors influence how messages are interpreted:

(a) *Feedback.* This consists of secondary messages sent by the receiver of information during or after a communication, which may cause the transmitter to change the message *en route.* For example, a glare or hostile utterance on the part of someone listening to another person can cause the speaker to tone down the contents of his or her remarks.

(b) *Body language.* Movements of the body can greatly assist other people in understanding the true meaning of the message that is being sent. Among the more significant elements of body language are:

(*i*) Yawns – a spectacular demonstration of disinterest in an issue
(*ii*) Facial expressions – frowns, smiles, raised eyebrows, and so on, indicating perhaps extreme displeasure with what is being said
(*iii*) Eye contact, to signify interest or hostility
(*iv*) Proxemics (i.e. the physical nearness of one person to another) which sometimes reveals the degree of intimacy of the people communicating
(*v*) Touching (e.g. handshakes, backslapping, and so on) that conveys important messages about the individual's commitment and sincerity.

(c) *Perception.* The transmitter and recipient might perceive particular words or gestures in entirely different ways, depending on the past knowledge and experiences upon which they base their interpretations.

(d) *Paralanguage.* This means the tone of voice, inflection, speed of delivery, deliberate silences, etc. used when speaking. Variation of any one of these can change the meaning of a message:

(*i*)   *Voice tone* may be assertive, aggressive, conciliatory, embarrassed, etc. A change in tone is called inflection, which can greatly increase the recipient's knowledge of how the message should be interpreted.

(*ii*)   *Silence* can itself be an important medium of communication. Pauses may suggest a reluctance to discuss a certain point, or disinterest, or that an issue is of great importance, etc.

(*iii*)   *Speed of delivery*. The pace at which a person speaks can indicate his or her enthusiasm, sincerity, nervousness and general attitude.

PERSUASIVE COMMUNICATION AND ORGANISATIONAL POLITICS

9.   Influence and persuasion

Group leaders sometimes have to *persuade* group members of the correctness of a certain course of action or that they should willingly accept change. Persuasion is necessary when facts do not speak for themselves and when, in consequence, the group leader must express opinions. If the leader's messages are to be believed they must be:

(a)   *Credible* (i.e. be seen to emanate from a reliable source)

(b)   *Consistent* (i.e. fit in to the recipient's existing value system)

(c)   *Logically structured* (i.e. organised in such a way that the most important elements are highlighted and easily remembered).

Moreover, messages should be interesting, and not transmitted so frequently that they irritate the receiver.

Changing the opinions of other people

If, additionally, a message is to change the opinions of others then the recipient should want to accept the change suggested (or at least not oppose it too strongly). This is more likely if either: (*i*) the recipient believes that clear benefits will result from concurring with the sender's views; or (*ii*) non-acceptance of the message will lead to adverse consequences for the recipient.

10.   Techniques of persuasive communication

Persuasive communication typically involves some or all of the following elements:

(a)   a multitude of examples that support and reinforce the transmitter's case

(b)   explanations rather than arguments, thereby presenting issues as facts rather than as opinions

(c) concealment of alternative interpretations of a proposition

(d) frequent statements of points with which recipients are sure to agree, so that recipients get into the habit of agreeing with the transmitter's opinions

(e) systematic progression from the known and agreed to the unknown and controversial.

In general, recipients have to be motivated into the acceptance of propositions by demonstrations of their advantages. The most powerful motivators, it seems, are the desires: (i) to protect one's family; (ii) to acquire possessions; (iii) to exert influence over others.

Persuasive communications are more difficult to convey than others because the communicator is asking message recipients a favour, even if the favour requested is nothing more than emotional support. Senders of messages who are already known and liked by message recipients and who are expected to initiate communications to them as a matter of course are more likely to be able to persuade effectively.

11. Organisational politics

The term 'organisational politics' is used to describe negotiations and settlements within organisations made necessary by the existence of contrasting interests and the differing perceptions of various organisation members. Political activities lead to compromises, toleration, and a stability of relationships which enables the organisation to survive.

Organisational politics typically involves the building of coalitions around issues, persuasion and advocacy, and the skilful deployment of resources and power. Control over information is a key tool in the process. Coalitions rise in consequence of bargaining among various interest groups, and a dominant coalition will emerge. Organisational politics affect which issues assume prominence within the organisation and how they are discussed and interpreted. The manner in which a problem is diagnosed may be determined primarily by the self-interests of influential individuals and coalitions. Hence organisational politics influences how decisions are taken as well as the decisions themselves. Note how certain rules, procedures and interpersonal relationships might develop outside the official management system.

A company's political power system can affect its organisation structure, even to the extent that the latter becomes unsuitable as a means for realising the enterprise's goals. Internal politics helps shape the ideas about organisation structure that are deemed acceptable and, once implemented, the organisation design most favoured by the dominant political group might perpetuate itself indefinitely. Organisational politics can affect planning in the following respects:

(a) disputes over who should undertake corporate planning activities

(b) the status of the planning function in the overall company hierarchy

(c) possible misuse of planning mechanisms by individuals wishing to pursue their own personal objectives

(d) resistance to planning on the grounds that it could pose a threat to vested interests within the firm and/or may expose personal weaknesses

(e) conflicts between various functions (marketing and finance for example) regarding which department's plans are to be paramount

(f) use of a corporate plan as a means for making redundant people who otherwise would be dismissed for underperformance.

Organisational politics are perhaps most likely to develop where:

(a) the organisation faces severe resource constraints, so that individuals and departments are compelled to fight hard for their budget allocations

(b) environments are fast changing and uncertain

(c) there is a lack of leadership at the top of the organisation

(d) the firm does not have clear objectives

(e) key managers have fundamentally different opinions about the basic purpose of the organisation

(f) there is little accountability and inadequate management control.

Organisational politics can damage a company in a number of respects:

(a) Certain individuals may come to act as 'gatekeepers'. An organisational gatekeeper is someone who (*i*) communicates with the outside world on behalf of an organisation (formally or informally), (*ii*) gathers information from external sources and (*iii*) through being able to withhold this information from certain of the organisation's members is able to influence the decisions it makes.

(b) Departments are encouraged to seek to make other sections dependent on them, regardless of whether these inter-relationships benefit the firm as a whole.

(c) Sectional goals might be inconsistent across the organisation and not shared by all individuals and departments.

(d) Managers may become obsessed with ideological struggle, conflict and gaining the upper hand, at the expense of getting on with their work.

(e) Bad decisions might result from the internal political bargaining process.

(f) Interpersonal relationships may deteriorate.

(g) Inaccurate information might be deliberately circulated.

(h) Decision processes can become disorganised and disorderly.

A distinction is sometimes drawn between 'legitimate' and 'illegitimate' organisational politics (Farrell and Peterson 1988; Drory and Romm 1990). The former refers to political activity regarded by organisation members as being 'within the rules', e.g. forming a coalition to block a proposal or circumventing the formal chain of command. 'Illegitimate' organisational politics, conversely, violate established norms of behaviour (whistleblowing or deliberate sabotage of other people's projects for example). 'Whistleblowing' is the practice of an employee reporting to the police or other outside authority the illegal practices or improper actions of the employing organisation. Sometimes, it occurs *via* intermediaries such as newspapers or pressure groups. If discovered the whistleblower is likely to face dismissal, and perhaps even legal action by the ex-employer.

12. Stakeholder theory

This asserts that since organisations are owned and operated by differing interest groups (stakeholders), management's main task is to balance the returns to various group interests. Examples of stakeholders are shareholders, different categories of employee, customers/users of the product, creditors (including banks), unions, and (possibly) local or national government. Managers, therefore, need to be politicians and diplomats. They must establish good relations with each group, develop persuasive skills, create alliances, represent one faction to others, etc.

Stakeholder theory implies the recognition that each interest group possesses certain basic rights. Thus, for example, management should consider workers' interests as well as those of shareholders when taking important decisions.

Stakeholders may or may not hold formal authority although each will have invested something in the organisation, be it work, finance or other resources. Accordingly, every stakeholder will expect a reward from the enterprise and normally will wish to influence how this is determined. Management must:

(a) identify the stakeholders in the organisation

(b) determine the minimum return each stakeholder is willing to accept

(c) seek to influence stakeholders' perceptions of the organisation (e.g. by persuading shareholders that a high dividend is not in a company's best long-term interest or convincing workers that a high wage settlement is not possible during the current year)

(d) identify key individuals in specific stakeholder groups and establish good relations with these people

(e) assess the strength of each stakeholder's influence on the company's behaviour

(f) evaluate various stakeholders' attitudes towards the business's mission, strategies, activities and, where appropriate, the need to implement change

(g) specify which stakeholders support management's current policies and intentions and those which are against, and possible coalitions of opposing groups of stakeholders

(h) assess what will be necessary to 'win over' antagonistic stakeholders. Note how it may be possible to increase the influence of stakeholders who are on management's side and reduce the power of others.

Shareholders are obviously one of the dominant stakeholders in a firm. If a

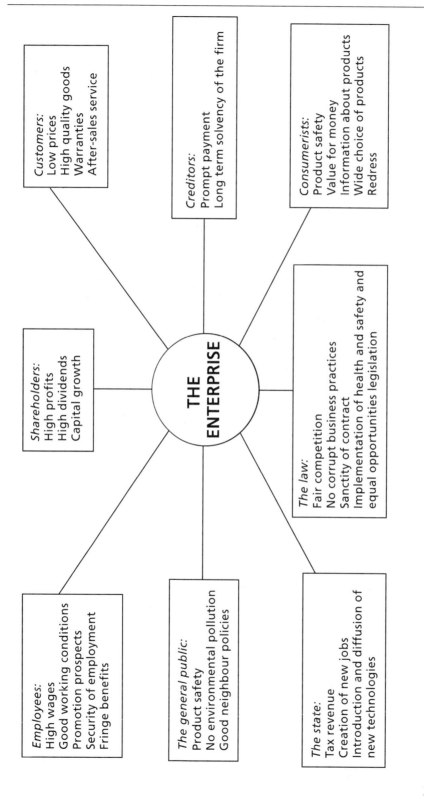

Fig. 14.3 Stakeholders' expectations

majority of a company's shares are concentrated into the hands of just one or two shareholders then the views of these people will exert a major influence on the direction of the business. Wide diffusion of shareholding, conversely, usually means that individual shareholders have little impact on strategy, unless a financial crisis causes them to act *en bloc*.

EMPLOYEE COMMUNICATION

13. Need for employee communication

The need to transmit and receive information is common to all organisations. Management has to pass instructions to the workforce, to explain its policies and objectives, and to tell workers if their jobs are threatened. Specific needs for downwards communication from management to employees relate to such matters as:

- how and when work is to be completed
- employees' duties and obligations
- management's plans and intentions
- changes in organisation structure
- health and safety procedures
- performance standards and company objectives.

Employees need to communicate with management in relation to:

- queries regarding management's instructions and stated intentions
- whether they are able to complete their work effectively, given the resources available
- suggestions for improving working methods and processes
- problems experienced at work.

Sound employee communications are essential for the smooth running of an enterprise for a number of reasons.

(a) Individuals need to be able to behave and take decisions in accordance with company policy. Effective co-ordination of the firm's activities is impossible without good management/employee communications.

(b) Change can only be implemented successfully if the reasons for the change plus its implications for workers are communicated to and accepted by the people likely to be affected.

(c) Employees' basic perceptions of their work and of the company are substantially determined by the quality of its employee communications.

(d) Workers have the chance to respond to communications from management by providing the latter with valuable feedback.

It is important to realise nevertheless that improved communications cannot solve every conceivable employee relations difficulty. Fundamental conflicts of interest need to be resolved by negotiation, not just an increase in the flow of communication. Particularly damaging to the credibility of the employee communication process is management implementing a 'communication blitz' during a crisis situation that requires workers' help and co-operation, followed by complete silence as soon as conditions improve.

14. Costs of bad communication

Inadequate employee communication can impose a number of costs on a company, including:

- bad decision-making consequent to individuals not receiving the correct information
- misunderstandings among sections leading to costly mistakes
- incorrect perceptions of company and personal objectives
- conflicts and industrial disputes resulting from misunderstandings (as opposed to irreconcilable divergences of views)
- lack of employee commitment to the employing organisation
- poorer quality output in consequence of workers not understanding the importance of their role in the quality management process
- employee resistance to change and the possible development of 'them and us' attitudes
- non-implementation of plans and policies
- inconsistent activities and lack of co-ordination.

Note, moreover, that a management's failure to communicate with workers may be interpreted by the latter as management not regarding them as people worthy or capable of receiving and understanding information.

15. One-way and two-way communication

One-way communication (which does not involve any feedback from the recipient) is appropriate for topics that are routine, straightforward and uncontroversial. However, one-way communication is *not* adequate for matters affecting employee welfare or that concern issues about which employees can express useful opinions. Two-way communication (which gives the recipient(s) an opportunity to respond and react) is time-consuming and demands patience and personal skill, but should be used for subjects which are complicated, unexpected, of personal concern to the receivers, or involve matters about which they could make a worthwhile contribution. A better decision may be reached, and it will be accepted more readily.

Autocratic one-way communication is particularly unsuitable for IT-driven computerised workplaces where important decisions have to be taken by lower echelons and where objectives are not attainable without the active *commitment* of employees.

Communication problems

Special problems with management/worker communication in employee relations situations are as follows:

(a) Communicators often have ulterior motives when devising and transmitting messages, which frequently express opinions and attitudes as well as facts. Frequently, the purpose of the communication is to persuade and influence as well as to inform.

(b) Many important items of information are transmitted orally rather than in formal written terms.

(c) Recipients of messages may deliberately choose not to understand them and/or to deny they were ever transmitted in the first instance.

Communication channels

Media for transferring messages include:

- letters and memoranda
- face-to-face oral communication
- telephone conversations
- conferences, committees and meetings
- manuals, employee handbooks, pamphlets
- posters and noticeboards
- house journals.

All these are formal in character, but informal channels are important as well. In particular, the so-called grapevine can be a primary medium for the distribution of information.

16. Employee communication management

People in organisations devote enormous amounts of (expensive) time to communicating with each other, and it is thus essential that communications be conducted in as efficient a manner as possible. Careful attention must be devoted to the questions of *what* and *when* to communicate, *how* to communicate, and *with whom* to communicate, as discussed below. Another important decision is the determination of who is to be mainly responsible for the employee communication function. The possibilities include the personnel department, a public relations manager, line executives, or workplace supervisors. The modern approach is perhaps to shift most of the responsibility for management/worker communications onto first-line managers, who then communicate information to workers on a face-to-face basis.

Policies for employee communication

What to communicate depends on management's communication objectives. Does it want to persuade employees to accept a technical change, relate to unions in a particular manner, identify more closely with the company, or some other aim? Specific managerial objectives regarding communication with employees are likely to include:

- encouraging workers to support the aims of the enterprise
- transmitting instructions clearly and in a manner that maximises the likelihood of their being properly carried out

- receiving prompt and accurate feedback.

How and when to communicate will be determined by the amount of information to be communicated and the media available for the process. Media can be written or oral. Written media include company handbooks and magazines, newsletters and bulletins posted on noticeboards. Oral media comprise team briefings, works councils, and joint consultation. Whichever method is selected it needs to:

- be suitable for and relate to the people receiving the communication
- provide information on important events soon after they have occurred
- be reinforced by management *action*
- be clear and precise
- generate feedback so that communications are genuinely two-way
- inform employees about the matters that concern them most, e.g. planned alterations in company structure or working methods, new payment arrangements or grading systems, overtime requirements, etc.

Typically, an effective system for communicating with employees will involve a mixture of formal and informal channels. Policies for improving the efficiency of management/employee communication include:

- regular communication audits designed to identify communication needs and discover new ways to improve the flow of information
- providing managers with training in communication skills
- developing new systems for canvassing employees' opinions and views.

With whom to communicate

Communication of every piece of information that might be relevant to employees is not feasible, otherwise the firm would devote all its time and energy and resources to transmitting messages, most of which were of little practical use. Thus, choices have to be made.

Correct selection of recipient is also important. An appropriate choice of message recipient will result in an unbroken chain of command. All instructions issued during normal operations will be carried out because those responsible for their implementation will know precisely what they have to do.

TEAM BRIEFINGS

Oral communication can be more effective than written documents, as it is generally more natural and informal. The pace and tone of the communication can be varied in response to audience reactions to the speaker's remarks, and much more ground can be covered in a short period than when using written remarks.

17. Purposes of team briefings

Briefing sessions can occur at periodic intervals (monthly or fortnightly for instance), or on a daily basis (with each session lasting just a few minutes). The *advantages* of the latter approach are that it:

- is a quick and convenient method of communication
- relates immediately to the workplace situation
- creates a bond between the supervisor and other members of the team
- can integrate fresh ideas for improving quality and productivity with more mundane matters concerning work distribution, training plans, company news, etc.

In longer briefing sessions carried out at (say) monthly intervals, the manager conducting the briefing needs to be concerned not only with imparting information but also with inculcating in employees feelings of participation, security and involvement with the firm. Briefing sessions give managers the opportunity to explain company policy and the implications of recent events.

Unfortunately, managers sometimes err in calling these meetings only when crises arise. Rather they should occur regularly and not just when things go wrong. Sessions should be short and offer:

(a) brief reviews of progress to date

(b) the manager's opinions on contemporary problems

(c) outline proposals (with justifications) for future activities.

Suitable topics for briefing sessions include suggested changes in working arrangements, staff transfers and promotions, results of implementation of new methods, details of available welfare and recreational facilities, and examples of how efficiency has been improved in other departments.

Conditions for success

To succeed, briefing groups need to cover *all* levels of the organisation (not just lower grade employees) and to be led by trained and competent people. Restriction of briefing groups to workplace operatives might cause workers to feel that they are being manipulated to make them accept worsening conditions of work. Each session needs to focus on a central theme, should last for no longer than half an hour, and involve no more than 20 people. Employees should be briefed on major company events within two or three days of their occurrence. The information transmitted needs to be relevant to workers' jobs and understandable.

18. Advantages and disadvantages of team briefings

Briefings are normally conducted by line managers (i.e. executives with the authority to take and implement decisions) who thereby disseminate information from the apex of the organisation to its base. Hence, line managers become the major source of information concerning company affairs. This reinforces their authority and helps create a bond between the manager and his or her team. Further *advantages* are that:

(a) Employees develop wider perspectives on the significance of their work.

(b) Briefings help prevent the emergence of grapevines (*see* **4**).

(c) There is face-to-face contact between management and the workforce.

(d) The information transmitted is necessarily kept short, forcing management to highlight the really important issues.

Problems with team briefings are as follows:

(a) Concrete improvements in performance will rarely occur immediately, leading perhaps to a decline in management interest in the idea in the medium term.

(b) There might not be enough interesting items of company information to pass on during a scheduled briefing session, resulting in its cancellation (with consequent disillusion with the entire process) or in managers 'waffling' during the session and filling out the allotted period with meaningless information.

(c) Administration of a briefing group requires the time-consuming preparation of information, short stoppages of work while the briefing is in progress, expenditures on training for group leaders, etc. This might not be cost-effective if apathy prevails during meetings and no concrete benefits emerge from them. Training costs will be substantial, as the training involved needs to encompass public speaking, the organisation and running of meetings, persuasive skills, motivation, listening and counselling.

(d) Line managers are not necessarily good public speakers. Even with training they might be hesitant, nervous and inarticulate. If so then team members will neither hear nor understand what is being said, and will quickly lose interest in the exercise. A line manager might be particularly inept at answering awkward questions.

(e) There is rarely enough time within a briefing session for any genuinely meaningful dialogue or discussion.

(f) Simply because workers are informed of decisions does not mean they will agree with or accept them.

(g) Trade unions might oppose team briefings on the grounds that through establishing direct communications between management and labour they undermine union authority. Also, briefings can be used to circumvent orthodox joint consultation and collective bargaining procedures.

19. Management by walking around

Objective setting, appraisal, accountability systems, etc., are fine for establishing procedures and monitoring progress, but too often they fail to provide the detailed and accurate information on day-to-day operations and most (important) on staff morale necessary for effective control. Management by walking around (MBWA) is a simple solution to the problem of gathering information about actual behaviour within an organisation. The manager looks and listens, talks to employees and becomes personally involved with happenings at the workplace level. More specifically, MBWA concerns:

- reviewing and appraising sources of information
- looking for new and better contacts
- learning how people (senior managers as well as junior employees) *feel* about the organisation and each other
- finding out how the staff perceive customers, and assessing whether they recognise a personal responsibility for customer care.

MBWA brings managers into daily contact with quality and productivity problems. Managers observe at first hand which jobs are easy and which difficult. Further *advantages* of MBWA are that managers cannot avoid recognising employees' difficulties; that it provides valuable feedback on the success of recently introduced equipment and methods; that it demonstrates management's commitment to genuine employee communication; and that it is likely to result in actual changes designed to overcome workers' problems. It is especially useful for obtaining the 'gut reactions' of employees to management's proposals.

Visits should not be at fixed times or dates, or employees might 'prepare' for the visit so that an unrepresentative impression is generated. The system should operate at all levels within the organisation and a variety of managers need to be involved – not just a handful of interested individuals. *Problems* with MBWA include the following:

- Managers might engage in the practice simply to waste time.
- Workers could learn how to manipulate the system in order to present to their bosses favourable but untrue images of their work.
- Visits could become little more than friendly social chit-chats that add nothing to the company's efficiency.
- Managers are taken away from possibly more important duties.
- In a large company a senior manager cannot visit *all* sections on a regular basis.

Progress test 14

1. Define communication.

2. What is the purpose of a communication system?

3. What is a communication grapevine?

4. List the main barriers to communication.

5. What is stereotyping?

6. Explain the major factors that cause a message to be persuasive.

7. What is the halo effect?

8. Define the term 'organisational politics'. List three examples of political activity within organisations.

9. Identify the major stakeholders in a public limited company.

15

DECISION MAKING

1. Decision-making theory

Decision making is the essence of management and all management involves making decisions. The theory of decision making encompasses the steps that individuals and groups should follow when making decisions plus the analysis of the barriers that prevent effective decisions being made. Normally, the higher ranking the manager the more important and wide-ranging the decisions he or she must take.

Strategic decisions

Broad decisions about the direction a firm should follow and its relations with the outside world are known as strategic decisions. They establish organisational objectives and impose frameworks for controlling a firm's activities. Examples of strategic decisions are:

- what products the firm will produce
- how the firm will finance its operations
- whether to aim for the top or bottom end of a market
- pricing policies
- whether to recognise trade unions.

Strategic decisions are taken by the most senior level of management within the organisation.

Tactical decisions

Tactical decision making concerns the *implementation* of strategic decisions. Thus it involves decisions about the acquisition and deployment of resources, allocation of duties, specification of secondary objectives, monitoring performance and reporting back to higher levels of authority. Managerial control of the four basic business functions – finance, marketing, production and personnel – is a tactical responsibility. Control is exercised by executives. The word 'execute' means to carry into effect, hence an executive is someone who realises targets set in strategic decisions.

Operational decisions

Operational decisions concern minor administrative matters (e.g. the lengths of production runs, shift rosters, stock levels, etc). Where possible, operational decisions should be taken automatically in accordance with some predetermined decision rule and should not require judgement or discretion (automatically replenishing inventories whenever some minimum predetermined stock level is reached, for instance).

Note that workplace supervisors do not normally make policy decisions. If they do, they are not classified as 'supervisors' but as occupants of higher managerial positions. Supervisors are more concerned with day-to-day decisions regarding such matters as:

- production scheduling and work allocation at the shop floor level
- inspection of employees' work and deciding whether this satisfies minimum quality standards
- training of operatives
- dealing with employee grievances.

Policies

A policy is a set of ground rules and criteria to be applied when taking decisions relating to a particular function or activity. Thus, the existence of a policy establishes boundaries that restrict the scope and nature of decisions concerning a specific issue. Examples of policies are:

- internal promotion
- only recruiting new people who possess certain levels of academic qualification
- advertising in print rather than broadcast media
- requiring at least three quotations for all purchases exceeding a particular value
- not settling suppliers' invoices until the month following delivery.

Advantages to having policies are that problems arising within the area covered by a policy do not have to be analysed each and every time they appear (decisions are simply applied in accordance with company policy); precedents are established; and delegation becomes easier. Managements develop policy guidelines to facilitate the co-ordination of diverse operations and to ensure that all decisions are compatible with the overall aims of the organisation. Coherent policies avoid confusion and lead to consistency of action in the area concerned.

2. Role of the board of directors

In a business, the top level of management is the board of directors. Although the term 'director' is commonly used to describe any top administrator, in Britain it also has a technical meaning in that the directors of a public limited company must be elected by shareholders. Protection of shareholders' interests is therefore the primary duty of a director.

Size of the board

An efficient size for the board of a large company would appear to be somewhere between eight and twelve. If the board were too small each director would carry too heavy a workload, and it would lack the range of skills and experience that a larger board could provide. A board with too many directors would be equally ineffective. Decision making would be slow; there would be too much debate and not enough action; experiences would overlap and efforts would be duplicated.

Part-time and full-time directors

Often, boards contain part-time (non-executive) directors as well as full-time members. The full-time directors will be in charge of specific functions (accounts, marketing, production, etc.) and will work for the firm as executives in addition to taking strategic decisions in board meetings. Daily involvement with the firm's operations and staff gives full-time directors intimate knowledge of the organisation's structure and performance. However, because they depend on the firm for their jobs they might not be truly objective in assessing long-term company prospects. From a shareholders' point of view it might be best to liquidate a company and use the proceeds more profitably elsewhere, but the directors would then lose their full-time jobs, and thus might oppose this course of action. Moreover, a full-time director's regular contacts with staff in his or her own department could lead a full-time director to resist necessary reorganisations likely to create staff redundancies.

Part-time directors may not have the detailed knowledge of the company that full-timers possess, but they may be more impartial and objective when considering the company's affairs. Often, part-timers bring specific skills to the board. Part-timers might, for example, be specialist consultants, tax accountants, or lawyers. Sometimes, firms themselves place representatives on the boards of other companies. It is not unusual to find major suppliers, customers, or creditors occupying seats on the board. Part-time directors have only limited time to devote to the affairs of the companies they assist. Also, a part-timer may lack positive commitment to the organisation.

What boards of directors do

Boards spend much of their time discussing organisational and economic problems rather than technical problems, which are typically dealt with by specialist committees. Examples of matters dealt with by boards of directors are:

- obtaining loans
- choosing capital structures
- discussing proposed large-scale expenditures
- assessing risks of default by major customers (a large bad debt can force a company into liquidation)
- initiating strategic objectives
- defining departmental structures and responsibilities
- selecting senior managers (who are not directors).

Decisions regarding mergers and takeovers are particularly important for the boards of public limited companies. Directors must decide whether to buy other firms, form consortia or merge with competitors. Also, a board may find itself having to recommend acceptance or rejection of an attempted takeover of the firm in question from outside.

3. Problem solving

Often, business decisions can be taken quickly without need for careful thought: the best choice might be obvious, or the consequences of a bad decision might be so trivial that only cursory attention to detail is required. For major decisions, however, managers must think hard about the various courses of action available and their likely results. Information must be gathered and viable options listed. All possible outcomes should be considered and, since management decisions usually involve choices under uncertainty, probabilities of the success of particular actions must be estimated.

Decisions are taken to solve problems. Predetermined problem-solving strategies can be applied in most circumstances. The following approach to problem-solving methodology is based on the work of the mathematician G. Polya:

(a) *Understand the problem.* State what it is that has to be decided. Define the problem as carefully and in as much detail as possible. Ensure that no relevant facts have been left out.

(b) *Consider auxiliary problems.* Perhaps the same problem has already appeared but in a slightly different form. If so, examine the consequences of the previous solution. Even if a specific problem has not been seen before, a related or similar problem might have been solved. Solutions to kindred problems can offer hints on how to tackle the problem in question. Possibly, the problem can be restated to make it resemble one previously encountered.

(c) *Devise a plan for solving the problem.* Dissect the problem into smaller component parts. State any assumptions necessary for a satisfactory outcome. Compare the resources necessary for implementing solutions with those available. Consider *all* feasible options (not just some of them) and choose the most attractive in terms of benefits to the organisation and the probability of success.

(d) *Check the results.* Monitor the effectiveness of the solution selected. Maintain careful records so that the solution to this problem can be used to solve similar problems which may arise in the future.

4. The rational model of decision making

This is a model defining the steps that a rational decision maker *ought* to follow when making rational decisions. It also concerns the barriers that prevent rationality in decision making.

Rational decisions are those which achieve objectives as efficiently as possible in the context of the environment in which the decision is made. The steps involved (which are similar in principle to Polya's problem-solving methodology as described above) are as follows:

- Identify the problem.
- Set objectives.
- Search for alternative solutions.
- List and describe possible alternative courses of action.
- Evaluate the alternatives.

- Select a solution.
- Implement the chosen solution.
- Appraise the effectiveness of the solution.

Difficulties with the model

Several difficulties attach to the rational decision-making model:

(a) The problem to which the model is to be applied must *itself* be well understood and clearly defined. This might not be the case in practice because the decision maker may not know what the problem actually is in the first place.

(b) Much time and effort is needed to research and apply the technique. (Rule-of-thumb approaches might be quicker and cheaper.)

(c) Disagreements may arise regarding which solution is best. Tedious and troublesome interpersonal and interdepartmental negotiations might then be needed to resolve differences.

(d) Solving one problem can create other problems. Often, alternative outcomes are closely intertwined, and many side-effects and implications result from the choice of any one solution.

5. Limiting factors and bounded rationality

A limiting factor is a constraint or barrier that stands in the way of achieving the best solution to a problem. The existence of limiting factors restricts the range of decisions that can be made. Limiting factors must always be taken into account in decision-taking procedures; indeed, management should actively search for them whenever a particular solution is being considered.

Recognition of the importance of limiting factors led to the 'bounded rationality' model, which asserts that sometimes it is more logical to select a convenient and low-risk outcome to a problem than attempt a theoretically superior solution. The justification for this is threefold:

1 The time and other resources needed to discover the optimum solution to a highly complex problem might be so great that the costs involved exceed the benefits derived from the theoretically best outcome.
2 In practice, managers rarely possess all the information necessary to identify all the factors involved in the optimum solution.
3 Even if the theoretically best solution is obvious, the firm might not possess the facilities needed to guarantee its implementation.

6. Satisficing behaviour

In the course of decision making, managers must rationalise, weigh up possibilities and evaluate large amounts of information. But individuals have only limited powers of comprehension; they cannot possibly take into account all conceivable aspects of a complicated business problem or all the data that might be needed to solve it, and there is a substantial element (albeit unconscious) of non-rational, emotional sentiment in many aspects of human behaviour.

According to H.A. Simon, people can only handle a few ideas and a little information at a time. Thus, they seek easy, straightforward solutions to problems rather than attempt to find optimum outcomes that in all circumstances would be best. In Simon's terminology, managerial behaviour is 'satisficing' rather than maximising. Managers use simple rules of thumb that enable them to overcome whatever problem happens to be at hand; they are satisfied with adequate, as opposed to optimum, returns.

7. Brainstorming

This means churning out ideas without considering their feasibility. Every idea on an aspect of the problem mentioned by any participant is listed. However, participants are not allowed to discuss or criticise the contributions of other members, as this might inhibit creative thinking. Participants are encouraged to be as inventive and imaginative as possible, looking at problems from different angles rather than head on. Hopefully, one idea will generate others so that ideas build on themselves.

Proposals resulting from a brainstorming session are considered in a separate meeting at which the costs, benefits and feasibility of each idea are then investigated in detail and the most promising followed up.

Morphological analysis (MA)

This is an extension of brainstorming which seeks to discover fresh ideas by cross-referencing concepts. Consider for example a manufacturing firm that is considering an extension to its range of products. Suppose three new products, A, B and C are technically feasible and that three markets – teenage consumers, the middle aged, and retired people – exist. To conduct a morphological analysis, management lists the products and states how each might be used in each market, thus creating $3 \times 3 = 9$ new ideas for desirable features for the intended new products. Then a third dimension could be added, consisting of (say) three ways of designing the packaging of the products, hence enabling the generation of further ideas (e.g. how best to package product C for the teenage market). This will generate $3 \times 3 \times 3 = 27$ ideas, and so on. Each idea is then critically evaluated, leaving only the best for critical investigation.

Morphological analysis adds form and structure to a brainstorming exercise. As many dimensions may be added as are deemed necessary, with a consequent proliferation of ideas. The problems with MA are that:

(a) Too many ideas might be generated – more than can be properly evaluated in the time available.

(b) Possibly, only one or two options can realistically be implemented so that the remainder of the ideas is superfluous.

8. Synergy

Synergy results from arranging the work of a group in such a way that its *collective* output is greater than the aggregate of members' individual contributions. The idea is neatly summarised by the phrase 'making two plus two equal five'.

Synergy can occur between people, between sections of a firm, or even between separate businesses, for the following reasons.

(a) Group members may spur each other on towards the achievement of a common objective.

(b) Collective effort can stimulate innovation, effort and efficiency and generally bolster group morale.

(c) There is cross-fertilisation of ideas. Individual knowledge, talents and experience are combined.

(d) Management competencies can be carried forward from one group of activities to another.

Examples of synergy occur where:

(a) advertising and public relations undertaken for one product will benefit others

(b) the results of research into one area of operations may be profitably used elsewhere

(c) spare capacity can be reduced by the integration of production processes

(d) the same distribution channel can be used for marketing several products

(e) it is cheaper and more efficient to undertake two activities together rather than one after another

(f) large discounts are available for bulk purchases

(g) brand identities reinforce each other.

Joint activities by two or more businesses might:

(a) develop products and markets more quickly and inexpensively

(b) improve the organisation's overall cash flow position through using money generated in some areas to finance others that are currently short of cash

(c) enhance the collective corporate image of the firms involved.

Consequences of synergy include possibilities for lower selling prices, improved market share, higher returns on research and technical development, increased profitability and a greater return on capital employed.

9. Quality of decisions

Conflicts sometimes occur between the *quality* of a decision, and its *acceptability* to the people who must carry it out. High-quality decisions use objective facts, expert technical knowledge, and possibly a sophisticated decision-making technique (operations research methods, for instance). An acceptable decision is one that satisfies subordinates' needs and generates positive rewards for interested parties. Unfortunately, efficiency and acceptability do not always go hand in hand; a high-quality decision might be unacceptable to those expected to execute the work.

The acceptability of a decision can often be increased through joint decision making and the active participation of subordinates and others with an interest in the outcome. In businesses, joint decision making frequently occurs through committees.

10. Committees

A committee is a group of people to which an issue is referred for consideration, investigation or resolution. Committees may or may not be empowered to implement their decisions, and can be temporary and *ad hoc*, or permanent. The advantages of decision making through committees are as follows:

(a) Increased communications between people and departments leading to easier co-ordination and management control.

(b) Utilisation of the talents and creative abilities of several people. An individual might not recognise some key elements in a problem, or be aware of all potential solutions.

(c) Shared responsibility for decisions. No one person has to bear sole liability for mistakes.

(d) Extensive discussion of issues. Problems can be examined in depth. Opposing views will emerge, the consideration of which should improve the quality of final decisions.

(e) Compromises between conflicting positions will have to be reached. Hence, arbitrary or extreme decisions can be avoided.

(f) Representatives from many interest groups can take part in organisational decision making. In principle, this should encourage acceptance of joint decisions by all who are involved in the decision-making process. Participation should raise enthusiasm for the implementation of decisions.

(g) Avoidance of the concentration of power into small numbers of hands. Individuals are required to justify their intentions before colleagues, who may challenge the views expressed.

11. Disadvantages of decision making through committees

Although widely used, committees are not always the best medium for taking decisions. Problems faced by committees include the following:

(a) *High operating costs.* Typically, committee members are highly paid managers whose time could be profitably spent elsewhere. The wage cost of a committee of, say, ten people meeting for half a day will be very substantial. Decisions taken by individuals require only one person's time.

(b) *Discussion of trivial issues.* Each committee member has a right to express

221

opinions and to cross-examine and challenge the views of other participants. Sometimes members reiterate sentiments that have already been expressed in slightly different forms. Personal conflicts can develop; arguments might be tedious, long-winded and add little to the quality of debate.

(c) *Indecision*. Unanimity of opinion within a committee is rare. Were participants to agree on all issues there would be little need for a committee; decisions reflecting members' views could be taken by a single representative. Committee decisions, therefore, are usually compromises that do not fully satisfy every interested party. The problem is acute in committees which require unanimous agreement for decisions rather than a simple majority vote. Here, minority groups hold great power. They can hold up a committee's work through withholding their consent to particular proposals.

(d) *Abrogation of individual responsibility*. Collective decisions do not require individuals to assume personal responsibility for mistakes. Thus it is hard to identify blameworthy staff. Guilty parties can hide behind ambiguities created by joint decision making; it is difficult to investigate how a bad decision came to be taken within a particular committee.

(e) *Slow decision making*. The larger the committee and the more it discusses issues, the longer it takes to reach decisions. Some important items on meeting agendas might not be dealt with in the time allowed, and so may be held over until the next scheduled meeting. Exceptionally difficult problems are often referred to sub-committees, thus increasing further the delay in reaching final decisions.

(f) *The possibility of groupthink*, i.e. the tendency for like-minded people within a cohesive group to agree on issues without challenging each others' ideas or realising that the consensus which seemingly emerges may not represent the actual views of the group. The problem is commonest in groups with strong, charismatic leaders and when group members devote little mental effort to analysing the situation in hand (Janis 1972).

Progress test 15

1. Explain the difference between strategic decisions and tactical decisions.

2. Describe the steps involved in 'rational' decision making.

3. Define the term 'bounded rationality'.

4. Explain the conflicts that might arise between the quality of a decision and the acceptability of the decision.

5. What is a committee?

6. List the disadvantages of taking decisions through committees.

16

THE MANAGEMENT OF ORGANISATIONS

PLANNING AND OBJECTIVES

1. Introduction

All organisations have to be managed; otherwise they quickly collapse. Although there is a wide range of types and forms of organisation and organisation structure available to those who have to design and run enterprises (*see* Chapters 20 and 21), most organisations need to concern themselves with similar managerial tasks. The management of nearly every organisation must:

- plan
- establish objectives
- control operations
- appraise its employees.

2. Planning

Planning means deciding now what to do in the future given the occurrence of certain predicted or intended events. It requires the analysis of present circumstances, the precise definition of objectives, and the design of strategies and tactics for achieving goals. Planning is troublesome and expensive: troublesome because it requires forecasts of the future, expensive because it absorbs large amounts of time. Nevertheless, planning has a number of advantages:

(a) The organisation will be ready to adapt future activities to meet changing circumstances.

(b) Careful consideration of likely future events may lead to the discovery of new and profitable opportunities. Foreseeable pitfalls might be avoided.

(c) Measures to influence future events can be initiated by the organisation itself.

(d) Decisions concerning future activities can be taken in advance, unhurriedly, using all the data that is available and considering all possible options. This avoids decision making in crisis situations with management unable to study all relevant issues judiciously and at length.

(e) Planning forces the firm to assess critically the feasibility of its objectives. Management is forced to recognise its own strengths and weaknesses.

(f) In preparing a plan, management can co-ordinate and integrate the firm's activities, avoid duplication of effort, and eliminate unnecessary waste.

(g) The planning process requires that people and departments meet, discuss, exchange ideas and co-operate. This encourages initiative and team spirit, and participating staff will be motivated towards achieving the targets set.

3. Approaches to planning

There are three basic approaches to organisational planning:

1 'Top-down' planning, which means that senior management plans and establishes targets for *all* levels of authority within the firm.
2 'Bottom-up' planning, whereby each department prepares an estimate of what it believes it can achieve and submits this to higher management for approval.
3 A method whereby senior management imposes general objectives, but then leaves individual departments to attain them as they think fit.

Specification of objectives

The first stage in the planning process is the specification of 'objectives', i.e. statements of what the organisation wants to do – as opposed to policies, which state how objectives are to be achieved. The more concrete the organisation's objectives, the easier the choice of policies necessary for their attainment. Higher-level targets will be subdivided into specific objectives (preferably expressed in quantitative terms) to be achieved within predetermined periods.

Forecasts

Forecasts might be needed before targets can be set. A forecast is a prediction of future events. This differs from a plan, which is a predetermined response to anticipated future events.

In business, accurate forecasts are notoriously difficult to achieve. Environmental change can occur quickly: production techniques become obsolete, employment and other laws alter, new labour-relations problems emerge. Usually, therefore, the shorter the forecast period, the more accurate its predictions.

Because long-term forecasts are subject to great uncertainty, many firms prepare both short- and long-term forecasts – the former in detail, the latter in outline only. It is not worth spending enormous amounts of money on long-range predictions of highly uncertain events.

4. Principles of planning

Organisations should normally apply the following principles when preparing a plan:

(a) The plan should be as detailed as expenditure constraints allow.

(b) Plans should not extend too far into the future (accurate prediction of the distant future is extremely unlikely).

(c) *All* alternative courses of action available should be considered and not just some of them.

(d) Side effects and implications of the actions envisaged should be examined.

(e) Instructions to individuals and departments must be incorporated into the plan. What is the point of preparing an expensive and detailed plan if no one assumes responsibility for its implementation?

(f) Plans should be concise and easy to understand.

5. Objectives

An objective is something the business needs to achieve in order to fulfil its mission. The clearer the organisation's objectives, the more self-evident is the choice of tactics needed to attain them. The following rules should be observed when setting objectives:

(a) Objectives should be consistent. For example, the maximisation of short-term returns usually implies frequently switching from one market or line of activity to another, and would not be consistent with an objective of attaining long-term security and steady growth.

(b) Objectives should follow a hierarchy, with the most general at the top and the most detailed and specific at the bottom.

(c) Each objective should be accompanied by statements of:

  (*i*) who is responsible for its attainment
  (*ii*) when the objective is to be achieved
  (*iii*) how the objective is to be accomplished, including a specification of the resources necessary and where and how they will be acquired.

(d) All objectives should relate directly and identifiably to the mission of the business.

(e) Criteria for deciding whether an objective has been achieved should be predetermined.

(f) Wherever possible, objectives should be stated in quantitative terms and, where extensive written instructions are required, should be written in simple English.

(g) Objectives should be reasonable: failure to achieve unrealistic objectives can lead to disillusion and a collapse in morale.

Typically, objectives relate to such matters as financial returns, rates of growth, market shares, introduction of new products, efficiency improvements, cost-cutting programmes, removal of competitors, and so on.

225

Setting targets

The term 'management by objectives' (MBO) is used to describe the process whereby organisational objectives are segmented into departmental targets and then into objectives for individual employees. Superiors and subordinates meet and jointly agree subordinates' job specifications and goals, preferably in quantitative terms. Management by objectives supposedly motivates employees through involving them in the determination of objectives, and should help them develop their individual careers. Subordinates who exceed their targets might experience a sense of satisfaction in their achievements, and the causes of success can be isolated, analysed, and applied elsewhere.

6. Advantages of target setting

The advantages of MBO are that:

(a) It forces all employees to think carefully about their roles and objectives, about why tasks are necessary and how best to get things done.

(b) Targets are clarified and mechanisms are created for monitoring performance.

(c) Crucial elements are identified in each job, creating useful information for determining training and recruitment needs.

(d) Subordinates' personal achievements are recognised and rewarded.

(e) Performance is appraised against quantifiable targets, not subjective criteria.

(f) There is forced co-ordination of activities between departments, between junior and senior management, and between short- and long-term goals.

(g) Superiors and subordinates are obliged to communicate. In consequence, superiors can identify which subordinates are ready for promotion and appreciate the help subordinates will need to prepare for this.

7. Disadvantages of MBO

Drawbacks to management by objectives include:

(a) The danger of meaningless attempts to quantify activities that are basically unquantifiable. How, for example, can the objectives of a manager whose role is purely advisory be quantified?

(b) Possible encouragement of myopic emphasis on immediate quantifiable goals to the detriment of nebulous but nonetheless important longer-term objectives.

(c) Difficulties created through subordinates not being given the resources or authority necessary for completion of allotted tasks.

(d) The enormous amount of time consumed by regular consultations between higher and lower executives. A system whereby superiors simply impose targets on subordinates, without consultation, might be more effective. Moreover firms operating in highly uncertain, rapidly changing market environments may need to alter their objectives so frequently that MBO procedures become impractical.

(e) Tendencies of senior managers to pay more attention to subordinates' personal qualities than to their work.

(f) Possible concentration of effort on the achievement of individual rather than organisational goals.

ORGANISATIONAL CONTROLS

8. Control

Control has three aspects: establishing standards and targets; monitoring activities and comparing actual with target performance; and implementing measures to remedy deficiencies. Control links inputs to outputs and provides feedback to those in command. The firm's corporate plan should represent a comprehensive statement of the intended activities and goals of a variety of functions and departments. Thus, mechanisms are needed to ensure that plans are implemented and the work of disparate sections effectively controlled. Further purposes of control are:

- to improve operational efficiency
- to facilitate the management of change
- to develop a common culture within the organisation
- to assist the application of modern management methods such as just-in-time and total quality management.

Control systems are needed for both strategic and operational purposes. Strategic control involves establishing benchmarks for determining whether current strategies should be altered and, if so, how and when. It requires information on key external events and environments, and the data collected has to be far more wide-ranging than that necessary for operational control.

An effective control system will enable the rapid deployment of resources to their most efficient uses; disperse management expertise throughout the organisation; and generate comprehensive information on the activities of subsidiary units. In general, the less expensive the control process the better. Thus, automatic control systems that require minimal human intervention are normally more efficient than systems which require constant supervision. Control systems need to contain three major elements: information input, data evaluation, and feedback to the controlling authority. Rapid feedback is essential, otherwise problems could develop faster than the controller's capacity to correct them. Action should always be taken when targets are not achieved, since there is little point in installing a sophisticated control mechanism only to ignore the deficiencies it reveals.

The first stage in the control process is the careful description of all current activities. Achievements are compared with targets and, if necessary, corrective action is taken or targets are amended to more realistic levels. Problems inevitably occur. Among the more substantial are the possibilities that:

(a) Current activities may not be reported accurately, comprehensively, or in sufficient detail.

(b) Inappropriate criteria might be used when setting performance objectives, resulting in unattainable targets which render the entire system inoperable.

(c) Historical records of relevant activities could be inadequate.

(d) Information retrieval systems may be faulty.

Control systems usually (and perhaps necessarily) involve some degree of bureaucracy, but should not be allowed to inhibit creativity and innovation within the firm. The system should follow from the determination of strategies and plans, and not itself influence how strategies are formulated.

9. Control procedures

Procedures are standard ways of doing things. The main advantages to having standard procedures are that unqualified and/or recently appointed employees can complete tasks without having to set up administrative frameworks or take decisions, and that duplication of effort may be avoided. Further benefits are that:

(a) There is no need for staff to exercise discretion when undertaking tasks.

(b) Written records of standard procedures can be kept in a manual.

(c) There is less scope for arguments between people and departments regarding how work should be completed.

Problems with the application of standard procedures arise when:

(a) they become out of date but are still utilised

(b) personnel apply them without any thought and in inappropriate situations

(c) procedures are regarded as convenient devices for solving problems that in fact require careful analysis and discussion

(d) they become part of a rigid bureaucracy, stifling innovation and creativity.

Procedures should be reviewed periodically in order to assess their value and to determine which should be revised or discarded.

10. Principles of control

The more clearly specified are a company's mission, strategies and policies then the more obvious and consistent will be the plans it produces, and the more self-evident the types of control mechanism it needs to apply. The following general principles should be adopted when devising a control system:

(a) Controls should focus on the key variables that determine the success or failure of the business. Obviously the control of routine duties is important, but the consequences of inadequate control will be nowhere near as catastrophic for the organisation as a whole as neglecting to control success factors that are absolutely critical for the well-being of the firm.

(b) Reports submitted through the system should relate to issues rather than individual performance. Inaccurate information will be submitted if a report might reveal failure to meet standards, with consequent penalties for the person or section concerned.

(c) Early feedback on problems should be generated.

(d) The control system should itself be subject to control. Performance of the system should be regularly monitored, especially in relation to its ability to co-ordinate the work of various sections and departments.

(e) Control information needs to be presented to people in formats that appeal to them and which they fully understand.

(f) The system should be financially cost-effective.

(g) Control mechanisms need to be sufficiently flexible to operate effectively even if corporate plans have to be altered.

The information on which a control system is based needs to be accurate, comprehensive and directly relevant to the firm's activities. It should be as objective as possible, and preferably stated in quantitative terms. Note however that some information necessary for effective control will inevitably be subjective – assessments of staff morale or customer satisfaction for example.

11. Budgeting

This is perhaps the commonest of all control and resource allocation techniques. Budgets compare actual costs and achievements with planned achievements and allocations of financial and other resources. Upper spending limits (or minimum performance standards – sales or production levels, for instance) are specified for each of a number of functions (purchase of supplies, secretarial assistance, office equipment, etc.) over a predetermined period, usually, but not necessarily, of 12 months.

Advantages of budgeting

In preparing budgets, management is forced to think hard about resource requirements and their relationship with corporate objectives. Further benefits are that:

(a) Budgets impose financial discipline on those responsible for their administration.

(b) Spendthrift departments are identified and can be penalised by reductions in further allocations.

229

(c) Cost increases which cause rapid exhaustion of existing budgets can be isolated and their effects on the organisation as a whole assessed.

(d) The meetings, discussions, joint decision making and general co-ordination of activities necessitated by budget planning encourage co-operation and common approaches to organisational problems.

(e) The organisation's strategies are set out in quantitative terms; hence, departments and individuals can be given targets against which their subsequent performances can be compared.

12. Fixed versus flexible budgets

Budgets may be fixed or flexible. Fixed budgets assume constant levels of activity and resource costs. Flexible budgets relate amounts allocated to appropriate performance indices. Production budgets, for example, are frequently determined by the volume of sales achieved – it is assumed that increasing sales will require additional resources to sustain and continue expansion. Another approach to flexible budgeting is the simultaneous specification of not one but several different budgets for the same department or activity. The budget actually applied will depend on the particular circumstances prevailing at the moment of implementation. Here, the firm recognises the impossibility of foreseeing all future circumstances and so makes allowances for several contingencies.

Methods for allocating fixed budgets

Allocations of fixed budgets may relate to operations or to responsibilities. In the former case, expected costs are aggregated to various departmental headings and the totals then allotted to various departmental budgets. If, conversely, budgets are related to responsibilities then: (*i*) individuals specify how much they think they will need in order to attain certain objectives; (*ii*) resources are distributed; and (*iii*) individuals assume personal responsibility for administering the amounts received.

The 'zero-based' approach to budget allocation attempts to solve the problem of managers deliberately overspending in order to increase future allocations. There is no presumption whatsoever that the amount given this budgetary period will be repeated. Indeed, each departmental budget is initially set at zero, assuming thereby that no funds will be made available at all. Hence, heads of department must argue for new allocations at the start of *each* period. Managers are forced to review periodically their plans and working methods and are thus encouraged to identify high-cost activities. The obvious drawback to zero-base budgeting is the amount of time that managers must devote to periodic assessments of costs and functions and spend in repeated presentation of budget proposals.

13. Disadvantages of budgeting

Despite its widespread use, budgetary control has many problems. The major difficulties are listed below:

(a) Cost consciousness, essential for effective budgeting, can be carried too far. It may lead managers into cutting costs by unreasonable amounts. Managers who keep well within their budgets earn the approval of their seniors. Hence, some managers might regard cutting costs as more important than implementation of measures necessary to improve the overall performance of the organisation. Failure to invest will reduce expenditures, but the organisation might suffer in the longer term.

(b) Too much detail in a budget will increase the probability that not all of its constituent parts will be satisfied. The more specific the forecasts embodied in a budget, the higher the likelihood they will be inaccurate. Moreover, the preparation of excessively detailed budgets is time consuming and unjustifiably expensive.

(c) Some budgets are overspent, others underspent. Thus, a mechanism is necessary (referred to as 'virement') for transferring unused balances to areas that require extra funds. So why bother with budgets in the first instance?

(d) Budgets can hide inefficiencies. Once a budget has been set the manager in charge of it may seek to spend the entire amount allotted even though, objectively, not all the funds are needed. Naturally, managers tend to use fully all resources put at their command. In consequence, wasteful expenditure might occur simply to exhaust outstanding balances.

(e) It is difficult to distinguish between a budget that has been exceeded because of genuine additional spending requirements and one exceeded through administrative incompetence. Indeed, managers may deliberately overspend in order to have their allocations increased in the next budgetary period.

(f) Typically, budgets are determined following bids made by heads of departments in meetings of budget committees. Resources are limited, so not all bids can be met. Heads of departments realise this and hence put in exaggerated bids anticipating cuts that will leave the amounts actually allocated to them roughly equal to their requirements. Budgetary control becomes haphazard in these circumstances.

14. Fostering entrepreneurial attitudes

Some organisations will only allocate budgets to individuals, thereafter making recipient managers *personally* responsible for achieving objectives within their budget constraints.

This is done to encourage the entrepreneurial spirit in managerial employees. An entrepreneur is someone who organises, manages, and assumes the risks of a business in the hope of earning profit. Entrepreneurs bring together all the activities of a firm and direct them towards the attainment of a common objective. In the past, entrepreneurship has been associated with the ownership of businesses. Today, however, paid managerial employees frequently undertake entrepreneural tasks, and the concept is now connected as much with efficient co-ordination and the *spirit* of enterprise as with the personal assumption of financial risk.

Indeed, the separation of ownership from control is sometimes inevitable. In a public limited company, for instance, shareholders carry all the company's risks but are rarely involved in management (which is undertaken by a board of salaried directors). Yet the elected directors will themselves be expected by shareholders to be 'entrepreneurial' in approach – to behave 'as if' they owned the business.

Intrapreneurship

The term 'intrapreneurship' is sometimes used to describe the existence of entrepreneurial attitudes within employees of large organisations. One way of encouraging intrapreneurship is for the organisation to create strategic business units (*see* 21:**21**) and then treat these as independent self-financing enterprises (which 'buy in' inputs from other parts of the organisation) for the purposes of budgeting and control.

Examples of intrapreneurial attitudes are the desire to seize opportunities, willingness to acquire resources quickly and at high cost, short-term profit-maximising orientations, and being prepared to put resources at risk. These contrast with bureaucratic perspectives that focus on long-term stability, the need to work within budget constraints, reliance on established personal contacts and communication systems, the establishment of hierarchies, and the development of continuity in resource supply.

15. Performance appraisal

The term 'performance appraisal' (PA) described the process of monitoring employees' achievements and deficiencies in order to build upon their strengths and remedy their weaknesses. Organisations often keep records specifically designed for appraisal purposes; and workers might be interviewed periodically by their departmental heads to review recent events and activities. Knowledge that an appraisal is soon to occur might motivate an employee into increased effort aimed at enhancing the outcome of the appraisal. Moreover, managers' opinions of subordinates' work are formally stated, and subordinates can challenge allegations of inadequate performance.

Other advantages of PA include the following:

(a) It generates useful information about employees and the true nature of their duties. Unknown skills and competences might be uncovered. Data on these can be incorporated into the firm's human resource plan and hence used to assist in avoiding redundancies, in career and management succession planning and in identifying needs for training and staff development.

(b) Manager and subordinate are compelled to meet and discuss common work-related problems. Appraisees become aware of what exactly is expected of them, and of their status in the eyes of higher authority. Through forcing superior and subordinate to investigate problems jointly, PA guarantees the participation of lower-grade employees in matters that affect their working lives. Subordinates might be better motivated in consequence of such involvement.

(c) PA monitors the feasibility of targets set in management by objectives programmes. Subordinates are able to inform higher management of problems encountered while implementing policies.

(d) Known and rational criteria can be instituted to determine pay and promotion decisions.

16. Problems with performance appraisal

There are a number of problems with performance appraisal, including the following:

(a) Dangers of favouritism, bias and stereotyping (*see* 14:6) by managers who conduct appraisals

(b) Possibilities that inconsistent criteria will be applied by different managers when assessing the calibres of subordinates

(c) All the information relevant to a particular case might not be available

(d) Information might not be interpreted objectively

(e) Assessors might seek to rate every subordinate as 'fair' for all performance categories

(f) Assessors might focus on specific cases of outstandingly bad performance while ignoring the employee's average overall ability

(g) Appraisal systems require appraising managers to undertake extra work, which they might be reluctant to accept. Hence the process becomes a ritualistic chore to be completed as quickly as possible in a manner that causes the least comment from those affected by the scheme.

Douglas McGregor noted the great reluctance with which many managers undertake assessment responsibilities, preferring to treat subordinates as professional colleagues rather than as inferiors upon whom they are entitled to pass judgement. Senior managers, McGregor asserted, dislike 'playing God'. Usually they are fully cognisant of their own biases and thus rightly seek to avoid situations where prejudice could arise. Also, subordinates may bitterly resent their personal qualities being commented upon, seeing the appraisal as a patronising exercise designed to humiliate or to punish past inadequacies in their work.

Appraisal requires concentration, diligence and competence in the manager conducting the appraisal. Training in appraisal techniques is required, followed by substantial guided experience in their practical application. McGregor pointed out the facts that: (*i*) few manager receive any instruction in appraisal methods; and (*ii*) even managers who are properly trained might not possess all the information needed to undertake fair appraisals. They may be out of touch with current working practices or unfamiliar with environmental problems affecting subordinates' work.

233

STRATEGIC MANAGEMENT

Business strategy may be defined as the totality of management decisions that determine the purpose and direction of the enterprise and hence its fundamental goals, activities, and the policies it selects in order to attain its objectives. The strategies adopted will determine the internal character of the organisation, how it relates to the outside world, the range of its products, the markets in which it operates, and its intentions for the future. Strategic decisions are the most important that senior management has to take, as they commit extensive resources and have substantial consequences for the life of the organisation. Decisions made at the strategic level set precedents for lower echelons and cascade down to affect functional, divisional and departmental operations.

17. Advantages and problems of formulating strategies

The advantages to having a strategy are as follows:

(a) Strategies provide the business with definite criteria against which to evaluate performance.

(b) The process of formulating a strategy forces the company to analyse its position and hence identify and remedy internal weaknesses.

(c) Reactions to changes in competitors' behaviour may be predetermined.

(d) The company can decide in advance how it will respond to predictable changes in customer tastes and spending patterns.

(e) Co-ordination of divisions, subsidiaries, and other component parts of the organisation is made easier. The existence of a strategy provides a focal point towards which all the firm's energies may be directed.

(f) External threats and opportunities will be identified.

(g) Important decisions are taken only after considering all the facts, not in chaotic short-run crisis situations.

(h) Long-term investments will be properly evaluated.

(i) Speculation about possible future events and circumstances may cause the firm to discover ways of influencing the future for its own benefit.

Problems with strategy formulation include the high risk of inaccuracy of long-term forecasts, possible sudden and unexpected changes in environments (laws or technical regulations for example), and the costs and time involved. In consequence, some businesses do not bother formulating strategies, preferring instead to respond to situations, opportunistically, as they arise.

There are five major steps in creating and implementing a corporate strategy:

(a) Definition of mission and corporate objectives.

(b) Analysis of internal and external situations.

(c) Specification of alternatives.

(d) Evaluation of alternatives and choice of strategy.

(e) Development of plans and policies to meet strategic aims.

18. The questions to ask

In determining their strategies firms often find it useful to ask three fundamental questions:

(a) What business are we in?

(b) What business do we want to be in?

(c) What do we have to do to get where we want to be?

Careful analysis of the answers to these questions can indicate whether the firm should diversify its product range, enter new markets, change its prices, alter existing distribution channels, or make other fundamental changes.

What business are we in?

Is a motor vehicle manufacturer in the engineering business (focusing therefore on the production of engines and car bodies); or is it in the general transport business and thus needs to be interested in *all* forms of transport (air, sea, electrically powered vehicles and so on) regardless of purely technical considerations? Should a stationery firm regard itself as a paper business, or in business communications (including graphic design, photocopying machines, electronic mail equipment, etc.) as a whole?

Failure to define a company's range of interests sufficiently widely makes it vulnerable to predatory competitors and to the adverse effects of technical change, since the obsolescence of a product or process or an alteration in a competitor's prices or product line may create enormous difficulties for the supplying firm.

What business do we want to be in?

Firms need to examine the profitabilities of various markets, market segments and product line. They should ask, 'What *else* can we do to improve our performance?'

What do we have to do to get where we want to be?

This might involve product repositioning, structural reorganisation, new investment, and/or a change in the capital structure of the firm.

19. Missions

A mission statement is a declaration of an organisation's fundamental purpose: why it exists, how it sees itself, what it wishes to do, its beliefs and its long-term aspirations. Thus it is a statement of intent, combined perhaps with an outline of the basic ground rules that management has determined will govern the firm's behaviour. Normally a mission statement will define the company's core business(es) and its strategic aims and objectives – but without going into detail. Accordingly, the statement has a dual purpose: to provide guidance on how the business will operate on a day-to-day basis, and to map out its desired future situation.

The statement needs to be broad in order to accommodate (*i*) necessary changes in strategies resulting from altered circumstances and the emergence of fresh opportunities, and (*ii*) the requirements of interested parties such as shareholders, employees, functional departments, outside regulatory bodies, etc.

The discipline of preparing a mission statement compels management to clarify basic issues affecting the organisation, relate the firm's strengths and weaknesses to its competitive environment, identify external constraints, and develop a central focus for all the company's activities. Advocates of mission statements argue that only through careful analysis of a business's mission may effective strategies be devised: the more concrete the mission statement the more obvious are the strategies needed to satisfy the firm's mission. Also the possession of a mission statement affirms the organisation's long-term commitment to essential values and activities, and generates an aura of confidence and credibility to the outside world. Other advantages to having a mission statement are that it:

(a) encourages top management to adopt a 'strategic vision' derived from a coherent philosophy concerning what the business is about, where it is headed and what it needs to do to get where it wants to be

(b) acts as a 'corporate constitution' against which the firm's behaviour (including acts with ethical and social implications) may be evaluated

(c) presents the firm and its employees with the challenge of attaining the mission, hence facilitating the implementation of change

(d) enables total company resources to be allocated according to the priorities explicit or implicit in the organisation's mission.

Once management has decided what the organisation exists to do it can then devise appropriate strategies and plans and is in a position to detail the corporate skills needed to attain key objectives.

Problems with mission statements

Among the many problems associated with mission statements the following are especially important:

(a) Mission statements can be so vague as to be meaningless. Imprecision invites conflicting interpretations and lack of understanding.

(b) Practical operational benefits resulting from mission statements may be difficult to identify.

(c) Departmental boundaries and interests often inhibit the adoption by all individuals and sections of a uniform view on the firm's basic goals and values.

(d) Staff changes, poor vertical communications within organisations and disinterest among employees frequently result in the majority of a firm's workers not even knowing that the company has a mission statement, let alone its contents.

(e) Companies with well-publicised mission statements sometimes take and implement decisions that are inconsistent with the contents of the statement, and in so doing bring the entire concept into disrepute. Individuals and departments might pursue their own interests independently, losing sight of the need to relate decisions to the organisation's overall mission.

(f) The common pursuit of a clearly defined mission by all employees might inhibit their creativity and responsiveness to changing environments.

(g) Arguably, today's business world is altering so rapidly and extensively that no statement of mission can be relevant for more than a very short period, so why bother drafting a mission statement? In a ferociously competitive situation the need to take decisions at odds with a company's mission might be inevitable. Blind adherence to a pre-existing mission could guarantee failure.

(h) Mission statements need to be followed up by the development of strategies and plans for their implementation. Failure to devise action plans means the effort devoted to formulating the mission will have been wasted, and can lead to cynicism and disillusion.

Too often the language of mission statements comprises hackneyed cliches assembled with little genuine concern for their relevance to the business in question. Indeed, books are available containing sample words and phrases to include in impressive looking statements. These words and phrases appear again and again in the missions of various enterprises. Examples include:

- people are our greatest asset
- dedication to excellence and customer care
- steadfast maintenance of values
- thrust, imagination, innovatory potential, internationalist perspectives, building on progress, creatively harnessing change, respecting the contributions of others, inspirational pursuit of objectives, etc.

These slogans decorate a company's staff handbooks and promotional literature, but make little difference to how the business is actually managed. Note moreover how some of the world's most elaborate mission statements have been published by companies engaged in ethically dubious (even fraudulent) practices.

Progress test 16

1. List the advantages and disadvantages of planning.

2. Explain the difference between planning and forecasting.

3. Define 'bottom-up planning'.

4. Define the term 'management by objectives'.

5. What are the disadvantages of management by objectives?

6. Explain the difference between 'open-loop' and 'closed-loop' control systems.

7. List the main problems associated with budgeting.

8. Define 'intrapreneurship'.

9. What are the disadvantages of performance appraisal?

17

CHANGE IN ORGANISATIONS

THE NATURE OF CHANGE

1. Causes of change

The cultural, political, economic, technical and legal frameworks within which organisations operate are today liable to rapid and far-reaching change. New products are introduced; new materials are discovered; new markets and competitors regularly emerge. There have been technological revolutions in transport and communications, electronics, and the analysis and transmission of information. New economic alliances develop; there has been an explosion in world trade.

Change is inevitable: the problem is how best to harness change and use its consequences for the benefit of the organisation. Some change can be initiated by the organisation itself, otherwise the organisation must learn how to respond and adapt quickly and effectively to the requirements of completely new circumstances.

2. Environmental change

A change in any one of an organisation's environments can create difficulties. Indeed, entire industries have been devastated by external change. Consider, for example, the changeover from conventional typewriting to word-processing. Firms producing ordinary typewriters were – in a limited sense – in the same industry as the manufacturers of WPs (i.e. the creation of letters, memoranda, reports and other 'hard copy' documents) but the skills of their employees and their processes of manufacture had an essentially 'mechanical' orientation. They made and assembled typing keys, carriage returns, roller bars, etc. and were not in a position to transfer these engineering skills to the computer-based technologies that word-processing involves (microelectronics, computer-programming, software design, and so on). Even the materials from which WPs are constructed (circuit boards, microchips, plastic keyboards) are different from those in a typewriter.

Forecasting change

The accurate prediction of future technological (and market) environments is extremely difficult. Not all environmental factors can be investigated (there are simply too many of them) so a handful of seemingly *relevant* external variables must be selected for research. Normally, these variables will concern:

(a) *Marketing* – the activities of competitors, trends in consumer taste and behaviour, changes in the size and structure of the market.

(b) *Legislation* – government attitudes to the industry, impending statutes, licensing arrangements and possibilities of increased state control.

(c) *Technology* – production methods and their efficiency, new inventions, materials, processes and costs.

Planning for change

There are two ways of planning for environmental change. The first is to predict the external changes that might occur and then detail: (*i*) how the organisation would be affected by them; and (*ii*) how the organisation should respond. Alternatively, the planner may begin with a list of the firm's functions, followed by a listing of all the environmental factors that might affect these functions. The latter course is usually the easier of the two since it is concrete, and named individuals can be made responsible for listing relevant factors in each functional department. However, some important variables may be overlooked.

3. Techonological change

New technologies affect materials, processes, work locations and organisational forms. Change might result from new inventions, or from discoveries or increased accessibility of resources not previously available. Technical change is necessary for progress, though its acceptance among those who will be affected by it may be extremely difficult to achieve. Changes might involve modifications to existing products or methods, or the need to replace with new products those items that have been rendered obsolete by the pace of technical development. Increasingly, technical change implies organisational change; and recognition of the inevitability of change should therefore be incorporated into an organisation's long-term corporate strategy.

4. Other sources of environmental change

Other environmental changes that might affect a firm include the following:

(a) *A change in the age structure of the population.* Spending patterns of younger people typically differ from those of the older generation, thereby creating new demands for products.

(b) *Changes in lifestyles.* Basic attitudes towards fundamental aspects of life – diet, family size, style of clothing, form of occupation of dwellings (leasehold or freehold, houses or flats, independent or joint occupation), attitudes towards work and leisure – all alter over time.

(c) *Changes in the labour force.* Developments in the educational system can improve the competence of workers entering the labour market. Note the importance in fast-changing environments of adaptability in skills. Traditional craft-based abilities have been rendered obsolete by new technologies. The skilled worker of today must be able to transfer competence in one area of work to other types of occupation. This fact has fundamental implications for the make-up of training programmes. Note also how general improvements in the educational system lead to increasingly well-qualified junior staff. Better educated workers, moreover, will have new expectations of how they should be treated at work.

IMPLICATIONS FOR MANAGEMENT AND THE ORGANISATION

5. Management of change

There are five steps in the process of implementing change:

1 Precise definition of the operational changes that are needed.
2 Definition of how the new working methods will affect particular people and groups.
3 Identification of attitudes and perspectives currently held by employees and how these support current working practices.
4 Statement of the attitudes and perspectives necessary to enable people to adapt successfully to new environments and working methods.
5 Implementation of measures designed to change existing attitudes.

Four strategic alternatives are available:

1 Altering *technologies* by introducing new equipment, methods, materials and systems. Existing staff may need to be retrained to handle a new technology, or different staff might be required.
2 Altering *structures*. This can involve organisation design; centralisation or decentralisation of functions, respecification of authority and accountability systems, etc.
3 Altering *tasks*, i.e. changing the content of employees' jobs, increasing or decreasing the extent of the division of labour within the organisation, and so on.
4 Altering the *people* who do the work. Here, management focuses on solving the human problems created by change, using some of the techniques discussed below.

6. Techniques for managing change

To the extent that firms themselves initiate change they can control and modify its consequences. Thus, some large businesses make one or more senior managers specifically responsible for the identification of problem areas requiring change, and for its implementation. These individuals monitor external events and assess their implications for existing administrative structures. Further methods for handling change include the following:

(a) Creation by the organisation of a financial reserve specifically intended to protect employees from the adverse consequences of unforeseen change. These funds might be used to retrain employees in new skills, pay the moving expenses of workers who need to be redeployed, and perhaps compensate older employees who prefer to take early retirement rather than retrain in new technology.

(b) Maintenance of existing work groups intact, while changing the content of their duties. Loyalty to a group can be a powerful agent of change.

(c) Preparation of 'skills inventories' of all the attributes, qualifications and experiences possessed by each of the organisation's employees. The information gathered helps management to assess each person's suitability for alternative work and hence to avoid redundancies.

(d) Carefully explaining to workers the causes and potential consequences of likely changes to things that will affect them.

(e) Ensuring (as far as possible) employees' security of tenure and informing workers of the measures that have been implemented to achieve this.

(f) Instructing employees in how to cope with change, emphasising the need for transferable rather than purely job-specific skills. Demonstrations of the interrelations between various types of work should be included in formal training programmes. Also, training courses should encourage workers to adopt working attitudes that are consistent with the realities of a fast-changing world.

(g) Introduction of employee bonus schemes that encourage the speedy implementation of change.

7. Force field analysis

Effective management of change requires an understanding of the dynamics of change and its root causes both within the organisation and in the wider business environment. Hence it is necessary to explore the forces that facilitate or inhibit the implementation of change. This exercise is sometimes referred to as force field analysis, the idea for which was first developed by K. Lewin in 1935. Lewin's model focused on the identification and systematic analysis of those elements within an organisation which seek to promote change ('driving forces') and those which resist new methods ('inhibitors'). Organisational behaviour, Lewin suggested, depends on the relative strengths of driving forces and inhibitors, and the equilibrium that emerges from their opposition. Examples of driving forces are improved inputs and working methods, pressures exerted by senior management, competition between groups, and the introduction of new technology. Inhibitors to change include the existence within an organisation of an inappropriate organisational culture, fear of the unknown, inadequate training of workers, and the narrow-minded pursuit of self-interest by individuals at the expense of attaining organisational goals.

A force field analysis can be illustrated in a diagram that shows the strengths of the enabling and constraining factors as arrows proportional in length to the perceived relative force of each element. Figure 17.1 is an example. Advantages of force field analysis are that:

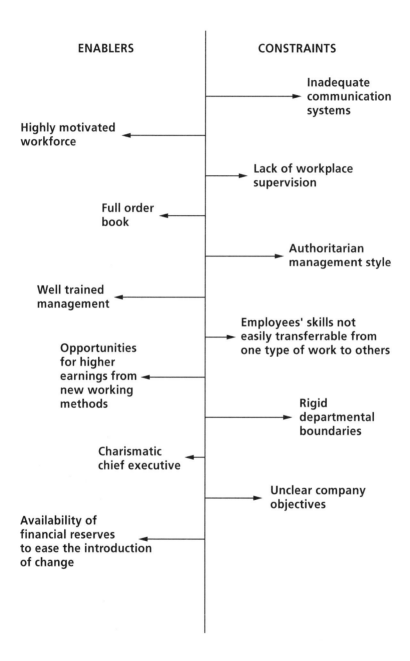

ENABLERS   **CONSTRAINTS**

Inadequate communication systems

Highly motivated workforce

Lack of workplace supervision

Full order book

Authoritarian management style

Well trained management

Employees' skills not easily transferrable from one type of work to others

Opportunities for higher earnings from new working methods

Rigid departmental boundaries

Charismatic chief executive

Unclear company objectives

Availability of financial reserves to ease the introduction of change

Fig. 17.1 Example of a simple force field analysis

- It recognises the dynamic nature of the change process.
- Key factors facilitating or impeding change are (hopefully) highlighted.
- The method is straightforward, understandable, and applicable in very many situations.
- A wide range of people can be consulted in order to identify relevant constraints and enablers.

Problems with the method include the following:

(a) A force field diagram represents a 'snap-shot' of a particular situation at a specific moment in time. By the time decisions are taken on the basis of this snap-shot the entire situation might have changed.

(b) The analysis says nothing about the costs of implementing change or of the techniques necessary.

(c) Attention focuses on enablers and inhibitors and not on whether the intended change is itself worth undertaking, i.e. it is 'process-driven' rather than results-orientated.

(d) Quantification of the values of change factors is crude and subjective.

(e) Sometimes a factor can be interpreted either as an enabler or as a constraint. Also factors might inter-relate and affect each other.

(f) The lists of possible enablers and inhibitors are so extensive that important variables might be missed.

Force field analysis might be effected via special brainstorming sessions or as part of a firm's overall strategy formulation and corporate planning processes.

8. Resistance to change

Employees (including managers) resist change for many reasons, including the following:

- feelings of insecurity generated by an intended change
- disruption of existing relations and patterns of behaviour
- threats to individual status and financial reward
- the influence of group norms and values that oppose change
- doubts regarding the technical feasibility of proposed changes
- the threat of having to retrain and acquire new skills in order to cope with altered working methods
- feeling of personal inadequacy *vis-à-vis* new technologies, e.g. fear of not being able to understand a recently installed computer system
- resentment over not having been consulted about a change
- the realisation that skills and experience acquired at great effort over many years are no longer of value to the organisation.

9. Management systems and resistance to change

R.M. Kanter completed a celebrated study of 115 examples of successful innovation occurring within American companies, concluding that certain management attitudes and practices invariably inhibited the introduction of change. Examples of these attitudes and practices were:

(a) suspicion of new ideas or of suggestions emanating from the base of the organisation

(b) management through committees

(c) allowing one department to criticise and interfere with another's proposals

(d) assuming that high-ranking employees know more about the organisation than low-ranking employees

(e) assigning unpleasant tasks (dismissal of employees for example) to subordinates

(f) not involving subordinates in decisions to restructure the organisation

(g) exercising tight supervision and control

(h) perceiving subordinates' problems as indications of their failure, and treating a subordinate's discussion of a problem as an admission of his or her incompetence

(i) telling subordinates that they are not indispensable

(j) regularly criticising subordinates but only rarely praising them.

10. Overcoming resistance to change

Kurt Lewin suggested three steps for overcoming resistance to change:

1 *Unfreezing* – getting rid of existing practices and ideas that stand in the way of change.
2 *Changing* – teaching employees to think and perform differently.
3 *Refreezing* – establishing new norms and standard practices.

There are a number of alternative ways in which the programme might be implemented. Kotter and Schlesinger outline four possible approaches:

1 *Education and communication.* This approach aims to make employees fully aware of all aspects of the situation and to convince them that change is necessary.
2 *Participation and involvement.* Hopefully, participation by employees in deciding exactly how to implement change will stimulate their commitment to new methods.
3 *Negotiation and agreement.* This is appropriate where several distinct interest groups may be discerned, some of which may be adversely affected by intended changes.

4 *Manipulation.* Here, management carefully selects the information about a proposed change that is to be given to workers in order to present the change in the most favourable manner. There is a danger, however, that employees may recognise management's manipulation of data and bitterly resent the fact that they are being manipulated.

Role of planning

Forward planning is essential for the effective management of change. The advantages of planning include the following:

(a) The organisation will be ready to adapt future activities to meet changing circumstances.

(b) Careful consideration of likely future events might lead to the discovery of new and profitable opportunities. Foreseeable pitfalls might be avoided.

(c) Measures to influence future events can be initiated by the organisation itself.

(d) Decisions concerning future activities can be taken in advance, unhurriedly, using all the data available and considering all available options. This avoids decision making in crisis situations with management unable to study all relevant issues judiciously and at length.

(e) Planning forces the organisation to assess critically the feasibility of its objectives. Management is forced to recognise its own strengths and weaknesses.

(f) In preparing a plan, management can co-ordinate and integrate the firm's activities, avoid duplication of effort, and eliminate unnecessary waste.

(g) The planning process requires that people and departments meet, discuss, exchange ideas and co-operate. This encourages initiative and team spirit, and participating staff will be motivated towards achieving the targets set.

11. Human resource planning

This involves the comparison of an organisation's existing labour resources with forecast labour demand and hence the scheduling of activities for acquiring, training, redeploying and possibly discarding labour. It seeks to ensure that an adequate supply of labour is available precisely when required. Specific human resource planning duties include:

(a) estimation of labour turnover for each grade of employee and the examination of the effects of high or low turnover rates on the organisation's performance

(b) analysis of the consequences of changes in working practices and hours

(c) predicting future labour shortages

(d) devising schemes for handling the human problems arising from labour deficits or surpluses

(e) introduction of early retirement and other natural wastage procedures

(f) analysis of the skills, educational backgrounds, experience, capacities and potential of employees.

12. Chaos

Arguably, disorder and confusion are endemic to business situations, so that management theory and practice should focus on the best means for responding to uncertainty and change. Scientists have been interested in the theory of chaos for generations, seeking to understand the effects on macro-systems of micro events (e.g. a butterfly flapping its wings in northern Siberia can generate a chain of events leading to a hurricane in the USA). The number of possible combinations of micro events and potential outcomes was so immense that new thinking on the nature of 'prediction' and 'uncertainty' was required, taking into account the fundamental instability of nature. These ideas have begun to influence management theory as the pace of organisational and environmental change has accelerated to unprecedented levels.

The 'chaos approach' challenges the conventional scientific emphasis on seeking to discover relationships between cause and effect, since the conventional approach assumes regular mechanistic 'laws of the universe'. Rather it is necessary to recognise that every event affects every other event in some way or other, so that there are no clear and direct chains of causality: the consequence of a change in one variable causes something else, which affects other things which themselves have implications for numerous further variables, including that which altered in the first instance. Thus, nature is a continuous feedback system with inputs and outputs mutually interacting. 'Laws of nature' exist, but are far too complex to be explained in terms of straightforward cause-and-effect relationships. Consider for example the determination of the shape of a snow-flake as it drifts towards the ground. The surrounding air quality, temperature and other environmental conditions affect the snowflake, which itself is simultaneously influencing the environment (by lowering its temperature, changing the humidity, etc.), which affects the form of the snowflake, and so on.

A state of equilibrium (balance) in a business situation can be upset by seemingly trivial events (staff transfers, personal disagreements, changes in procedures, etc.) that have knock-on effects which interact and multiply in an extremely complicated manner. Chaos theory has been offered as an explanation for unexpected turmoils on stock exchanges and foreign exchange markets, the instability of world oil and other commodity prices, and the sudden collapse of organisational structures. The chaos approach has many implications for management, including the following:

(a) Managements cannot control long-term future activities because future environments are totally unpredictable (in consequence of the complexity of cause/effect linkages).

(b) Stable environments can suddenly explode into unstable environments for no seemingly apparent reason, and vice-versa. Hence it is necessary to recognise that 'anything can happen' and plan accordingly.

(c) Organisations can appear to be stable and then suddenly become highly unstable.

(d) Unstable organisations need not be unsuccessful.

(e) Dynamic forces are constantly pulling a business in different directions. Examples of such forces are market conditions, regulatory frameworks, decentralisation of decision making, and human desires for excitement or for a quiet life. An organisation that moves towards stability is likely to ossify and lose its innovative edge. Equally, however, movements towards extreme instability can lead the organisation to collapse.

(f) Firms must be flexible and responsive to environmental change. They need to have effective information-gathering systems and to focus on short-term rather than long-term activities.

(g) Long-term planning is basically useless, as it is not possible to predict future environments.

(h) Mission statements should be regularly updated.

(i) Statistical forecasts will typically be wrong. Simulation and scenario building is preferable as a means for taking decisions.

To cope with chaotic situations firms need to be able to learn from past and current activities, systematically review the lessons learned from recent experience, and hence develop rapid and flexible responses to fast-changing environments.

Progress test 17

1. On which variables should an organisation focus when investigating the possibility of environmental change?

2. There are two ways of planning for change; what are they?

3. How might technological change affect an organisation?

4. List the major causes of environmental change.

5. What strategic alternatives are available for the management of change?

6. Why do employees sometimes resist change?

7. Lewin suggested three steps for overcoming resistance to change. What were they?

8. Describe the role of forward planning in the management of change.

9. Define the term 'human resource planning'.

18

INFLUENCE OF INFORMATION TECHNOLOGY

1. Information technology in business

Information technology (IT) is the acquisition, processing, storage and dissemination of information using computers. IT has revolutionised office work, and is about to revolutionise telecommunications (i.e. the transmission of information via radio waves or electric cables). Information technology, moreover, lies at the heart of computerised manufacturing systems using robotics, and of modern management information systems.

Determination of an IT strategy is one of the most important of all senior management functions, due to the ever-increasing complexity of modern business and the enormous efficiency improvements that the effective utilisation of IT can create. Further stimuli to the development of an IT strategy might include:

(a) rival firms gaining competitive advantage

(b) information overload within the organisation

(c) environmental turbulence accompanied by an increased need to gather and analyze information from external sources

(d) organisational restructuring and/or being taken over by another firm

(e) ferocious competition in markets both at home and abroad.

Products have to be supplied quickly, economically and at a high level of quality; and only by using modern technologies can most companies keep up with rival firms. Judicious use of IT can lead to a first-rate administrative system, effective decision making, efficient use of resources, and high productivity levels within the firm. IT helps businesses cope with complexity, uncertainty, and the explosion in the volume of information (internal and external) that has become available to companies in recent decades. As organisations become more sophisticated, so too must the techniques and procedures of organisational control – techniques that in today's world are invariably based on IT.

Information technology can be an important source of competitive advantage through:

(a) linking the firm to its customers and suppliers

(b) improving operational efficiency

(c) helping management devise and implement high calibre strategies

(d) creating a fresh entry barrier for firms outside the industry

(e) making it difficult for business customers to switch to alternative suppliers that have incompatible IT systems

(f) facilitating business re-engineering

(g) improving quality management. Note how modern TQM systems rely heavily on computerised production and IT

(h) enabling the firm to respond quickly to environmental change

(i) facilitating the monitoring of key performance indicators

(j) enabling the firm to service niche markets via product differentiation and flexible manufacturing

(k) monitoring suppliers and reducing procurement costs

(l) integrating marketing with production

(m) improving management control.

Rapid conveyance of control information facilitates fast and effective decision taking. The quality of decisions should improve because computerised systems enable operations research models and solution techniques to be applied, and advanced methods of planning and co-ordination to be implemented. Decisions are taken on the basis of more comprehensive information and the likely consequences of a wide range of alternative courses of action can be explored.

2. IT and human resources management

Those who operate IT-driven administrative and production systems typically require a higher level of education and training than the traditional manufacturing worker. At the same time, however, the need for conventional craft skills has diminished. Labour flexibility within a computerised working situation requires *technologies* rather than crafts people. In particular, the range and quality of the information potentially available to everyone in the organisation is greatly increased. Hence, traditional dividing lines between occupational categories break down and the demarcation of jobs can become irrelevant: vertically as well as horizontally. Other important possible consequences of computerisation with implications for human resources management include the following:

(a) Deskilling of tasks in certain parts of the enterprise while new types of skill are required elsewhere, leading perhaps to resentments and conflicts between various categories of worker.

(b) Total integration of all phases of production, office administration and internal communications, causing more frequent and perhaps closer interactions among employees in different sections of the firm and between various levels in the managerial hierarchy.

The competencies needed to succeed within a computerised work environment are general in nature and not necessarily related to particular occupations. Hence there is much scope for job rotation, undermining thereby employees' specific control over what were previously highly specialised jobs that could not easily be given to other categories of worker.

IT staff (and computer literate employees generally) frequently occupy key positions in organisations whereby they can cause great disruption through taking industrial action. This could induce management to treat computing personnel more favourably than other categories, and to try and arrange the division and pattern of work so as to ensure that not too much disruptive potential lies in a few pairs of hands.

To the extent that computer staff are treated differently to other types of worker, a number of sources of conflict may arise, as follows:

(a) Sometimes, computer literate staff with specialist qualifications have the same status, earn similar salaries, and occupy the same grades as line managers who – although they contribute a great deal to the organisation's work – are not as well certificated academically and have not had to spend several years studying for professional examinations. Accordingly, those who operate the computerised system might treat with disdain the work of line managers and resent the fact that computing staff and line managers are graded and paid equally. Conversely, line managers may begrudge the computer worker's self-assumed intellectual status.

(b) Those who manage the computerised system might expect to be able to exercise discretion and judgement in the course of their work, but at the same time must comply with the bureaucratic rules and demands of the wider organisation. They are subject to the authority of senior administrators, yet usually are not fully involved in the formulation of the administrative processes that determine the rules.

(c) Other categories of employee (including line managers) might form a coalition against computing staff whose level of education and social status they resent and whom they do not feel should be taking significant decisions on behalf of the company.

3. End-user computing

End-user computing means the imaginative manipulation of computer packages and systems by employees who have no special qualifications or expertise in computing or IT, so that non-specialist package users have maximum discretion in determining the outputs of the system. The implications of end-user computing for business organisation and for human resources management include the following:

(a) There is a levelling out of the performances of the firm's best and worst employees, since the computer will do a lot of the employee's basic work. This makes it difficult to appraise workers' performances accurately and to determine a fair system for rewarding employees.

(b) Opportunities are created for greatly increased productivity among white-collar workers, who will be able to choose how they complete IT-related tasks. This should make their jobs more interesting.

(c) Staff require a flexible approach to their work, must undertake tasks relating to a wider variety of business functions, and need to be able to assess the reliability of outputs from systems that contain information on topics with which they are not familiar.

(d) Workers' capacities to choose *how* they complete IT-related tasks should motivate them and provide numerous possibilities for acquiring experience of higher-level work.

(e) There is less need for middle managers.

(f) Employees have open access to a wide range of the firm's databases. Note how this can create data security problems and possibilities for the deliberate disruption of systems.

(g) Decision making is much faster.

(h) Employees are presented with:

- new alternatives regarding how work can be completed
- more interesting tasks, challenges and responsibilities
- a wider range of duties to be completed
- the need to take an increased number of decisions
- fresh possibilities for restructuring the working day.

Introduction of end-user computing is often accompanied by the 'downsizing' of systems, i.e. the increased use of small but powerful personal computing systems and applications, made possible by the enormous expansion in the capacity of the typical PC that has occurred in recent years. Downsizing implies greater systems flexibility, decentralisation of costs, and improved responsiveness to local needs. On the other hand it can involve a substantial capital outlay, weaken central control, and impose additional workloads on staff in user departments.

Strategic issues related to end-user computing are as follows:

(a) Definition of the role of end-user computing in attaining corporate objectives.

(b) The extent of central management control over end-user computing activities.

(c) Who is to select hardware and software (i.e. the degree of user involvement in the process).

(d) How the system is to be developed, how quickly and by whom (users or specialist IT staff).

Advantages and problems of end-user computing

Advantages of end-user computing are:

(a) Individuals are able to develop their IT skills.

(b) Each section of the firm can use IT at a level of sophistication appropriate for its particular requirements.

(c) The approach encourages creativity and innovation among employees.

Problems with end-user computing include duplication of activities, higher costs, the possible emergence of inconsistencies in working methods, and perhaps a general lowering of the quality of the firm's overall IT activities. Users might not define problems in an appropriate manner, with consequent waste of computing time and resources. Training needs are extensive (and costly) and money has to be spent on technical support (either from a centralised unit or from outside consultants). Note moreover that some individuals might be extremely reluctant to become involved in the system, creating extra work for other people. Further difficulties are that:

(a) End users might not be competent to select the decision support tools that are objectively the best to apply in complex circumstances.

(b) Users might concentrate on short-term issues at the expense of long-term systems development.

(c) Bad IT working practices may be passed on from department to department.

4. Implications for organisational structure

Often the introduction of a new IT system necessitates the rearrangement of the departmental structure of the firm. Computerisation tends to encourage centralisation of administrative procedures. Data is summarised and distributed automatically, circulating around a central control unit which can receive and monitor management information continuously. Requirements for local data interpretation and decision taking might diminish. Less delegation from senior to junior managers is likely in a computerised system because higher management obtains better, faster and more comprehensive information. Consequently senior managers exercise much tighter personal control. Indeed the great bulk of senior managerial work in some industries can, in principle, be conducted from a computer terminal.

The basic issue here is whether to concentrate IT resources into one or more centralised units, or to disperse IT expertise throughout the firm. Some firms have 'information centres' to support sectional IT activities (especially end-user computing). Each centre gives specialist advice to a number of departments, has access to sophisticated software, and may undertake more difficult computing tasks. The problem is that the centres could lack detailed knowledge of sectional IT requirements and become 'marginalised' within the organisation. Other alternatives are the creation of a single centralised department to oversee all IT activities, or widespread dispersion of responsibility for IT throughout the firm.

253

Centralisation

Advantages to the creation of a centralised department include:

(a) rapid responses to systems failures

(b) cost savings made possible through the avoidance of duplicated activities

(c) better security

(d) clear responsibility for IT activities

(e) tight control over the system

(f) accumulation of technical expertise within the central unit, together with the application of sophisticated support facilities and software

(g) the ability to recruit highly qualified IT staff, whose talents can be fully utilised in a centralised IT department (a career ladder will exist within the unit)

(h) improved prospects of IT procedures

(i) the fact that staff can be quickly redeployed within the department.

However, centralisation can lead to a splitting off of IT development from the rest of the organisation, and costs may run out of control as IT specialists pursue their particular interests. 'Chinese walls' might be erected between IT and other functions, with IT not being regarded as an integral part of the management structure of the firm. Further problems with centralisation are:

(a) Inflexible attitudes and administrative bureaucracy may emerge.

(b) The centralised unit might lose touch with the goals of major IT user departments.

(c) Long delays may occur before user departments experiencing difficulties can be serviced.

(d) It can be difficult to allocate the costs of the centralised unit to user departments. Should these costs be regarded as a general overhead to be spread across the entire firm (thus penalising sections that do not use the unit's services), or should IT-intensive departments pay more than the rest?

(e) If the central unit fails, the company's entire IT system will collapse.

Decentralisation

Factors encouraging dispersion of responsibility for IT (via the creation of Information Centres for example – see above) include:

(a) massive increases in the power of desktop computers

(b) the development of high-quality end-user computing software

(c) growing computer literacy among middle managers

(d) the large variations in the IT needs of certain departments.

Dispersion results in IT specialists being closer to end-users and (hopefully) more in tune with their everyday needs. Users are involved with devising and operating the system and should in consequence be better motivated towards making it succeed. Further advantages are that:

(a) Systems that emerge should be immediately relevant to the business's operational requirements (rather than being selected for their purely technical excellence).

(b) Systems are more likely to be flexible and responsive to changing circumstances.

(c) Computer awareness is encouraged throughout the organisation.

(d) End-user computing is facilitated.

(e) Creativity is stimulated.

(f) Information is processed close to where it is to be used.

(g) Decentralised units can tailor their activities to the specific requirements of particular functions and/or departments.

(h) IT costs are directly related to user sections.

(i) IT is more closely integrated into the organisation system of the enterprise.

Problems with dispersion include communication difficulties, computer illiteracy among certain types of staff, and duplication of effort. Costs may be higher and (importantly) not as visible as when the IT function is concentrated into a single unit. Other difficulties are that:

(a) Working methods in various units may become incompatible and lead to poor co-ordination.

(b) Dispersed facilities might not be able to cope with complex and technically sophisticated IT problems.

(c) The role and status of IT specialists might be unclear.

(d) Arguments between dispersed IT staff and functional line managers might develop.

5. Re-engineering

This means the radical redesign of business processes, normally via the use of the latest information technology, in order to enhance their performance. Conventional approaches to efficiency improvement sometimes fail because they focus on automating and speeding up existing systems and processes, merely perpetuating old ways of performing operations rather than addressing fundamental deficiencies and replacing out-of-date systems as a whole. Often, moreover, firms seeking efficiency gains do little more than tinker with the prevailing organisation structure in the naive belief that this alone will lead to the desired result. Problems with simple organisation restructuring are:

(a) The revised structure is likely to become out-of-date very soon after it is implemented.

(b) Frequent alterations in company structure destabilises the organisation and demoralises workers.

(c) Existing employees are likely to be thrust into new and unfamiliar roles for which they lack experience and/or training.

(d) Significant time periods are needed for people to adjust to each restructuring.

Re-engineering, conversely, involves challenging underlying assumptions and changing the basic rules and philosophies concerning the ways a business is managed. Examples of re-engineering include:

- abolition of job descriptions and departmental boundaries
- widespread use of empowerment (see 21:14)
- integration of a large number of operations
- finding new ways of achieving specific outcomes
- creating organisation structures based on desired results rather than on the functional duties needed to attain them, e.g. by having one person overseeing several types of task and assuming full responsibility for reaching a specific objective
- involving users of the outputs to processes in the design and execution of those processes. For example, departments that work on raw materials could be made partially responsible for selecting and controlling suppliers of the raw materials.
- centralisation of control procedures using computers
- having decisions taken on the spot, where work is performed. Note how this implies the removal of some layers in the management hierarchy and hence a 'flattening' of the organisation.

Progress test 18

1. Define information technology.

2. Assess the implications of end-user computing for business management.

3. What is meant by the term 're-engineering'?

19

WORK STUDY AND THE BEHAVIOURAL EFFECTS OF OPERATING SYSTEMS

1. Definition of work study

Work study consists of method study, which is about how work is performed; and work measurement, which concerns the assessment of times taken in completing tasks. Its objectives are the reduction of operating costs (especially labour costs) and the improvement of management control.

Method study

Method study seeks to simplify work, eliminate unnecessary tasks, and avoid duplication of effort. The basic principles of method study follow conventional precepts of the division of labour, and problems experienced by method study practitioners typically involve those human problems that specialisation and the division of labour necessarily entail. Current working practices are investigated analytically in attempts to discover new, more efficient ways of achieving targets. Examples of applications may be found in materials-handling procedures, operation of machinery, factory layout, and the design and utilisation of equipment.

Work measurement

Work measurement, on the other hand, is the systematic and detailed study of operations and movements in work situations. Workers may be timed using stop-watches, or they might be photographed or filmed while performing their work. The aim is to establish how long jobs should take in normal circumstances. These standard times then become yardsticks against which actual performance can be assessed. Another task of work measurement is the evaluation of how much time workers need for rest and relaxation between activities.

2. Contingency and relaxation allowances

Once the elements that make up a job have been defined and their completion times estimated, the work study officer will add a contingency allowance to cover unanticipated delays, and a relaxation allowance for recovery from fatigue.

The size of an appropriate relaxation allowance will depend on the nature of the work. Clerical work, for example, normally attracts an allowance of 15 per cent, whereas labouring usually gets 20 per cent. Factors determining specific allowances are:

- amount of muscular effort involved
- age and physical conditions of workers
- environmental conditions (heat, noise, etc.)
- degrees of stress and mental fatigue associated with the job
- the length of the job cycle (short-cycle work is monotonous and deserving of extra allowance).

Contingency and relaxation allowances are often subject to negotiation between management and trade unions and, of course, disputes over what items should be included frequently occur. Common disputes involve:

(a) whether an allowance should be a single overall figure for all similar jobs and departments, or whether allowances should vary to take account of differing environmental circumstances

(b) whether female workers should receive higher allowances than males or *vice versa*

(c) how often machinery is expected to break down

(d) the frequency of anticipated interruptions in supplies of raw materials.

Once settled, contingency and relaxation allowances are added to basic time to obtain the final standard time for the job.

3. Tiredness and fatigue

Tiredness causes accidents and reduces output. Often, physical tiredness is caused by unbalanced movements. Simultaneous, symmetrical use of both hands produces more work in the longer term than using just one hand at a time. Also, regular repetition of movements develops great speed. The establishment of rhythm means that operatives do not have to think too much about what they are doing. This elimination of hesitation accelerates the movement cycle and reduces fatigue. Note, however, that inefficient movements can themselves become bad habits which, subsequently, are hard to break.

In general, smooth, continuous movements are preferable to jumpy, uneven ones. Smooth movements require less muscular tension and are less tiring.

Fatigue is a more general concept. It means the lack of energy required to complete work satisfactorily. Fatigue can be caused by:

- high levels of noise
- poor lighting
- extreme temperatures or humidity
- badly designed equipment
- over exertion.

All these factors need to be considered when designing working environments. The obvious remedy for over-exertion is to allow the employee to rest. Research suggests that, in general, rest pauses should be short and frequent rather than long and irregular. Workers should rest *before* they begin to feel tired, since once a person has become extremely tired it is difficult for him or her to return to the previous level of output, even after a relatively long interruption.

The functions of rest are to dissipate fatigue, that is to allow the mind to refocus, and the body to recover physiologically from a long period of effort.

4. Noise

The effects of excessive noise levels include fatigue, interference with interpersonal communications, possible long-term deafness, and emotional stress. Also, accident rates tend to be higher in extremely noisy environments.

Deafness may occur gradually and so slowly that the worker is not aware that his or her hearing is being impaired. Noise, moreover, may cause aggression among employees, especially if their concentration is frequently and irregularly disturbed by loud noise.

5. Psychological aspects of work study

An individual's reactions to a work study exercise will depend substantially on his or her attitudes towards the acceptance of change (*see* Chapter 17). If outcomes from a work study project are to be accepted by employees they need to exhibit the following characteristics:

(a) The distribution of work and responsibility emerging from an exercise should be perceived as fair and evenly balanced.

(b) A worker should feel that management and fellow employees regard the worker's job as valuable to the organisation.

(c) Incentive schemes resulting from work study need to demonstrate a clear relationship between effort and reward.

(d) Employees should be aware of expected standards of performance.

(e) Workers need to feel useful as people and not merely appendages to systems and / or machines.

Unless work study is applied sensitively it will encounter resistance at all levels within the organisation, especially from trade unions. Accordingly, most work study practitioners seek to involve union representatives at the outset of an investigation. Consultations with unions typically focus on:

(a) how the study will affect union members

(b) provisions for helping employees who might be adversely affected by the scheme

(c) procedures for resolving disputes and queries arising from the investigation.

Effects on managers

Senior managers may themselves be upset by the activities of work study officers. A manager might believe that his or her authority is being undermined, or that future prospects are threatened.

Often, work study specialists are external consultants specially contracted for the exercise. The outsiders might temporarily 'take over' a manager's department, possibly leaving the manager feeling helpless, hostile and opposed to anything the consultant might do. Close involvement of managers in work study projects, plus (wherever possible) guarantees of continuing job security, can help overcome these difficulties.

6. Ergonomics

Ergonomics concerns the relationships of people with their working environments and how the latter can be adapted to meet human capabilities and needs. Practical applications include factory layout, lighting, heating and ventilation, acoustics, design of instruments and controls, and the design of office furniture. A major function is the study of factors that cause fatigue at work and hence the creation of working conditions conducive to prolonged, energetic activity.

The aim of ergonomics is the improvement of human comfort at work in order to increase efficiency (less fatigue, higher quality output of work, etc.). It is a multidisciplinary subject that draws on the academic disciplines of psychology, physiology, biology, engineering, anthropology and the natural sciences – as well as the practical skills of equipment design and construction.

7. Shift work

A number of problems arise from the practice of two- or three-shift working, including:

(a) disruption of biological rhythms (adrenalin secretions, sleep/waking patterns, body temperature, etc.)

(b) reductions in the quantity and quality of sleep, accompanied by constant tiredness

(c) digestion problems and possible loss of appetite

(d) disruptions to family life, anxieties about child care, social isolation and worsening social relationships.

Shift workers, on average, have severe accidents more frequently than others, and the quality of their output is often lower. There are perhaps two explanations for this. First, there is less continuity of supervision on shift work systems. A manager who supervises each of, say, three shifts for a few weeks or months at a time will regularly have a completely new set of subordinates under his or her command. The manager establishes satisfactory relations with one group and then moves on to another.

Night-shift supervision is especially onerous because no administrative support is available. (Personnel staff, wages clerks, specialist engineers, etc. are at home in bed.) Problems that arise must either be referred to appropriate day-shift managers or decisions must be taken unilaterally without discussing them with colleagues.

Second, shift workers are often unable to relax properly, causing fatigue, inattentiveness and accidents. Several weeks are needed to adapt fully to a new time system, but then days off and weekends – when the worker reverts to a normal lifestyle – disrupt the newly established pattern.

8. Visual display units

Perhaps the most problematic new working 'hazard' (if it is in fact a danger) is the effect on workers of protracted exposure to computer visual display units (VDUs). Critics allege that VDU users (especially those who operate word-processors) suffer eye strain, headaches, muscular dysfunctions, and absorb excessive amounts of radiation over long periods of use. It may be that the heat and static electricity generated by VDUs engender lethargy and general feelings of ill health among long-term users and this might cause persistent tiredness. Pregnant women and foetuses, it is alleged, are especially vulnerable. Staring into a VDU hour after hour can make workers clumsy, drowsy, and unable to think clearly or concentrate for long periods.

9. Behaviour implications of payment and incentive systems

A remuneration policy has two objectives: (*i*) to attract and retain high-calibre workers, and (*ii*) to provide incentives for increased effort. In most western countries, remuneration schemes have tended to move away from direct incentive systems towards other methods which recognise that workers are motivated by factors other than monetary reward. Desires for security, stability of earnings and job satisfaction are also important.

Nevertheless, many contemporary systems contain incentive elements which over time have tended to become increasingly complex. Protracted negotiations between employers and unions have led to complicated structures, and since relatively few incentive systems have been successful, numerous amendments to original formulae have been introduced. It is difficult to state categorically the factors that determine a good wages system. Generally, however, it should:

(a) be mutually acceptable to management and workers

(b) be clear, understandable and simple to operate. Workers should always be able to check their own wages.

(c) relate wages to the quantity and quality of work done

(d) offer a guaranteed minimum below which income cannot fall

(e) not confront the worker with unattainable objectives needed to achieve a reasonable wage

(f) be cheap to operate and not absorb excessive amounts of clerical time

(g) not present the firm with unexpectedly high wage bills

(h) enable beginners and the less competent to earn reasonable amounts

(i) not result in too many overlapping grades and differentials.

10. Time rate systems

In a time rate system workers are paid a predetermined wage per period (hour, day, week or month) regardless of how much they produce. Originally, time rates were applied where output quality was more important than quantity produced. Today they are also used in mass production situations: it seems that the security and status they offer can act as significant motivators to effort and efficiency. Time rates are particularly suitable where excessive working speed could produce accidents, injury or risks to health.

Successful application of time rates requires uninterrupted work flows, and implicit agreement by employees to work reasonably hard. A possible disadvantage of time rates is that lack of incentive might tempt workers to work slowly, thus necessitating close and detailed supervision. Also, idle workers receive the same pay as others, leading to resentment among hard-working employees.

Incentives are possible through awarding high time rates to highly efficient workers, or paying extra bonuses on top of basic wages. Overtime working, however, should not be encouraged in time rate systems as overtime availability might lead to workers going slow during normal working hours.

11. Piece rates

Employees on piece work are paid according to how much they produce regardless of how long is spent completing jobs. Piece work systems seek to stimulate effort and efficiency through providing incentives. Harder work creates higher wages.

Operatives are unlikely to require extensive supervision, are free to determine their own earnings, and are encouraged to initiate improvements to work techniques. However, output quality could diminish and accidents may result from employees attempting to work too quickly.

Since wage payments are determined by workers themselves, the firm will experience an uneven distribution of wage costs through an accounting year, depending on how much work employees decide to do at various times.

Critics of piece work argue that it does not actually lead to higher output, since social and organisational factors ultimately determine how much is produced. Moreover, complicated piece rate systems are expensive to administer and cause arguments between management and employees.

Measured day work

Measured day work is an alternative to straight piece work. It is a fixed hourly rate system – based on work study – where expected standards of performance are determined by work measurement techniques. The employee is paid a time wage, but management establishes and enforces certain minimum production standards. Instead of paying so much per item, management insists that so many items be produced per hour and then pays a predetermined wage for the day's work. Employees are not expected to exceed target output, nor should they produce less.

12. Bonus systems

Bonus schemes are relevant only to situations where work is measurable and the pace of work is subject to the employee's control. Workers should understand how a scheme that affects them operates, and should not experience interruptions to their work.

There is a major difference between bonus schemes based on valuation of output, and those based on valuation of the effort which goes into the production of the output. Effort-based systems fix standard times for waiting periods, clearing up, machine setting and related duties. These periods (computed from average values previously experienced) are paid at a standard predetermined rate without any bonuses because waiting time involves no effort on the worker's part. Output-related schemes, however, pay bonuses on the number of units produced ignoring waiting time.

Group bonuses are sometimes offered to groups of workers to encourage team spirit and lessen the need for supervision. The group bonus is distributed among members either equally or in proportion to individual contributions to total group work completed (measured, perhaps, by individual basic pay). Indirect workers and service staff whose efforts cannot be objectively measured may be included in the scheme. There are two major problems: inefficient workers can reduce the bonus payable to the entire group, and there is less individual incentive for highly productive workers.

Progress test 19

1. Define the term 'work measurement'.

2. What are the adverse effects on workers of excessive levels of noise?

3. What is a 'relaxation allowance'? What is the standard relaxation allowance for a clerical worker?

4. Explain the difference between tiredness and fatigue.

5. Define the term 'ergonomics'.

6. Describe the main problems attached to three-shift working.

7. What health hazards have been alleged to be associated with visual display units?

8. What are the advantages of piece rate payment systems?

9. Explain the differences between effort-based and output-based bonus systems.

Part Four

THE DESIGN OF ORGANISATIONS

20
NATURE OF ORGANISATIONS

1. What is an organisation?

Organisations have social and technical aspects. As social entities, organisations are affected by social and psychological forces; while in their technical aspect they are necessarily influenced by technological and environmental change. Most organisations exhibit the following characteristics:

(a) They are social units deliberately created to achieve certain objectives. Were this not the case they would consist of nothing more than *ad hoc* collections of random and unconnected interpersonal contacts and not be 'organisations' as such.

(b) The division of labour is applied to a greater or lesser degree.

(c) Certain individuals exert power and/or authority over others.

(d) There is some force (management, for example) which guides the organisation towards the attainment of its goals.

THE ORGANISATION AS A SYSTEM

2. Systems view of organisations

Systems theory is discussed in Chapter 3. Organisations can be viewed as conglomerations of interrelating sub-systems. An organisation receives *inputs* of information, materials, human and other resources from the external environment, and transforms these into *outputs* of services and/or goods, which are then returned to the outside world. *Technology* determines the character of the inputs used and outputs created and the techniques by which inputs are transformed into outputs. Social factors affect *how* technology is applied. Accordingly, the major sub-systems of a typical organisation are as follows:

(a) *A technical sub-system* (*see* **7** below), which covers the methods for selecting particular techniques and the knowledge necessary for their implementation.

(b) *An information subsystem* (*see* **4** below) concerned with collecting and analysing information, with internal and external communication (*see* Chapter 14) and with decision making (*see* Chapter 15).

(c) *A managerial sub-system* (*see* **5** below) that sets objectives for the organisation, designs its structure, and relates the organisation's activities to the outside world.

(d) *A psycho-social sub-system* (*see* **3** below) comprising individuals and groups and their modes of interaction. This will be affected by individual perceptions (*see* 4:**14**), group dynamics (*see* 12:**6–7**) and roles (*see* Chapter 9).

Management must co-ordinate and integrate these sub-systems into a unified whole. Classical approaches to management (*see* Chapter 2) concentrated on the technical and managerial sub-systems and sought to develop general principles of management that could be universally applied, regardless of specific circumstances. Conversely, the human relations school (*see* 3:**1**) emphasised the psycho-social sub-system at the expense of all other considerations. Systems theory (and the contingency approach it implied – *see* 3:**27**) sought to consider all the sub-systems jointly and to analyse their interactions.

3. The psycho-social sub-system

All organisations need to be managed, otherwise they quickly collapse. Accordingly, organisation structures must be established and patterns of communication, authority and responsibility set down. The essential characteristics of the social aspect of organisations are as follows:

(a) Human relationships within an organisation develop, people interact and this causes change. *Functional* changes improve the efficiency of the system; *dysfunctional* changes do the reverse. Eventually a *social equilibrium* emerges among the organisation's component parts. This means that people work together reasonably harmoniously and that minor disturbances to existing relationships are resolved quickly and amicably.

(b) Individuals make unwritten *psychological* contracts with the organisation, i.e. they establish their own opinions about how much work they should do and how they expect to be treated by the organisation. A person might not be conscious that he or she is going through this process, but will experience alienation (*see* 7:**2**) and job dissatisfaction if the contract is not 'honoured' by the other side.

(c) Power centres emerge, which may or may not relate to the organisation's formal authority system.

(d) People work together according to rules and predetermined relationships.

4. The information sub-system

To the extent that organisations are open systems (*see* 3:**24**) they are susceptible to rapid and unpredictable environmental change. Hence, every organisation requires an efficient system for gathering and interpreting the information needed to cope with uncertain environments. This has implications for organisation design (*see* Chapter 21) and for the development of internal communication systems. Thus, it might be necessary to alter the configuration of the organisation's work units (departments, sections, divisions, etc.) in order to improve the collection, processing and distribution of information.

Organisations face differing degrees of environmental uncertainty and possess varying capacities to process information. Management's task, therefore, is to match the organisation's structure to its information processing needs.

5. The managerial sub-system

Management is a process that seeks to help the organisation fulfil its objectives in the most efficient ways possible. Accordingly, management concerns:

- allocating resources
- controlling activities and employees
- decision making
- setting targets
- co-ordination
- planning and issuing instructions to ensure that plans are carried out.

The managerial sub-system embraces many aspects of the total organisation, as without management the organisation's entire superstructure would collapse. Its purpose is to relate the organisation to its wider environments through:

- devising and implementing policies
- directing human and other resources towards their most profitable uses
- generally utilising available technologies to the best effect.

Although the basic administrative processes (planning, co-ordinating, etc.) are common to all organisations regardless of their size or how they are owned, certain aspects of management are more important in some organisations than in others. Accordingly, it is conventional to break down the managerial sub-system into further sub-systems, as follows:

(a) *The operational sub-system.* This concerns technical matters and day-to-day decision making and control. It seeks to achieve immediate short-term objectives as quickly and efficiently as possible. Usually, the operational sub-system is self-contained and has inputs and outputs mainly determined by the wider organisation. Thus, its boundaries are clearly defined and it (normally) need not interact with more general surrounding environments.

(b) *The strategy determination sub-system.* Procedures for determining the organisation's strategies necessarily involve relationships with social, legal and other environments that are beyond the organisation's direct control. Hence, strategy determination is undertaken through an *open* sub-system with loosely defined boundaries and numerous interactions with the outside world.

(c) *The co-ordination sub-system.* In order to relate strategies to operations and to adapt the other sub-systems to environmental needs, the organisation might require a separate sub-system to mediate between policy making and day-to-day control. Manifestations of this sub-system include meetings and committees, 'staff' management systems (*see* 21:5), and middle management as a whole.

Note that: (*i*) the same individuals could be involved with all three sub-systems; and (*ii*) the larger and more complex the organisation, the more distinct and separate the sub-systems are likely to be. The management of organisations is further considered in Chapter 16.

TECHNOLOGY AND ITS IMPACT

6. Definition of technology

Technology means the utilisation of the materials and processes necessary to transform inputs into outputs. Understanding technology requires knowledge; operating a technology requires skills (*see* 6:**12**). Technology is created by people and it affects people; especially through the goods it produces and the working conditions (extent of division of labour, employee involvement in operational decision making, use of discretion at work, etc.) it creates.

Typically, new technologies benefit some people through giving them jobs, higher incomes and/or a wider variety of goods, and harm others by creating technological redundancy or making worse the boredom and alienation (*see* 7:**2**) they experience at work.

7. The technical sub-system

Technology determines the physical and economic resources that an organisation has at its disposal. Technology and people interrelate. This relationship is known as the *socio-technical system* of the organisation (*see* **11** below), or as the *technical-human interface*. The characteristics of the technical aspects of organisations are as follows:

(a) As the technology used within an organisation increases, so too will the demand for specialisation of functions in order to cope with the growing complexity of the problems it faces. This creates the need for better co-ordination in order to *integrate* activities and unify effort towards the attainment of the organisation's goals.

(b) New technologies require new work patterns, incentive systems, occupational mobility and fresh attitudes towards the acceptance of change.

(c) Advanced technologies need more professionally-qualified and well-educated employees and fewer manual workers.

(d) Different technologies might demand differing forms of group leadership (*see* Chapter 13) and management style.

The human–machine interface

A human being is a biological system; a machine is a mechanical and/or electronic system. Some additional system, referred to as the human-machine interface, is needed to bring together and regulate relations between the other two. The precise nature of the interface will depend on such factors as:

(a) how much work the machine is expected to do relative to its user (e.g. the extent of the programming needed to operate certain computer packages)

(b) the extent of the user's control over the machine(s)

(c) whether the machine is 'intelligent' in the sense that it can act on feedback information without further human intervention

(d) how easily the user can interact directly with the processes controlled by the machine, e.g. through issuing instructions that evoke an immediate response on an assembly line.

8. Effects of technology

Changes in technology affect: (*i*) physical devices (such as machines, tools, instruments and equipment); and (*ii*) techniques and working methods (procedures, routines, application of specific skills, etc.). Accordingly, technology usually affects:

- the extent of the division of labour
- employee training needs
- the nature of employees' tasks
- organisation structures
- employee job satisfaction and attitudes towards work.

Management has to choose which particular devices and techniques are best for improving efficiency and for achieving organisational goals.

9. Social aspects of mass production

The human relations school's demand for job extension (*see* 8:26) resulted from unfavourable employee reactions to the extensive division of labour embodied in early forms of mass production. Complaints about mass production included the following:

- boredom created by repetitive work
- lack of opportunity to practise occupational skills
- inability to exercise discretion over working methods
- feelings in workers of low occupational status and lack of personal esteem
- resentments against close and detailed supervision
- lack of opportunity for promotion
- feelings of anxiety (*see* 10:8) and isolation.

10. Classification of technology

Charles Perrow classified technical systems into two categories. The first category involved technologies within which: (*i*) problems are familiar; (*ii*) tasks may be performed in routine ways; and (*iii*) work is predictable.

In the other category: (*i*) problems are exceptional and will not have been experienced before; (*ii*) work is unpredictable; and (*iii*) there are few precedents for how to analyse difficulties. According to Perrow, the distinction is crucially important for organisations because it determines:

(a) management methods and leadership style (*see* Chapter 13)

(b) the degree of centralisation (*see* 21:**17**)

(c) the techniques of co-ordination applied (committees, etc.)

(d) the extent of the division of labour within the organisation

(e) the level of motivation of employees (*see* Chapter 8).

11. Empirical studies on work and technology

A number of empirical studies have greatly influenced current thinking about the relationships between work, technology, and the structure of an organisation. One of the first and most important of these was by E.L. Trist and K.W. Bamforth who in the 1940s studied the effects on working groups in the British coal mining industry of the introduction of new mechanised methods.

The new methods disturbed traditional working relationships and practices, and caused social frictions that reduced productivity. Existing small work groups were broken up, with depressing social and psychological consequences. Workers reacted to the new technology in negative and hostile ways, particularly through high rates of absenteeism.

According to the authors, social and technological factors interrelate to influence task performance. Working groups are, therefore, self-contained 'socio-technical' systems in which neither the social nor the technical aspect predominates. Hence, within a given socio-technical system various working methods can be imposed with differing social and psychological consequences. In other words, organisations and jobs within them can be *designed* to suit particular circumstances (*see* Chapter 21).

12. The work of P.R. Lawrence and J.W. Lorsch

Lawrence and Lorsch suggested an 'environmental' approach to work, technology and the theory of organisation. According to the authors, organisations are created to solve 'environmental problems'. Thus, organisations develop separate units (departments, divisions, functions, or whatever) for dealing with various aspects of the outside world.

Lawrence and Lorsch studied ten American firms drawn from three very different industries: plastics, wood, and containers; concluding that the more departments and functions created, and the more precisely defined the duties and responsibilities of each sub-unit, the greater the degree of change and uncertainty in a firm's environment. This process of 'differentiation', as the authors put it, resulted in the various sub-units having different attitudes, patterns of interpersonal communication, formal hierarchies, and time horizons – some units reacted more to short-term problems than to long-run opportunities.

Of the three industries, plastics was found to be the most diverse and unstable and therefore the plastics firms had greater differentiation within their organisation structures. The existence of differentiation created the need for 'integration' of an organisation into a unified whole capable of achieving its objectives. Thus, firms in the plastics industry had many more 'integrative devices' (rules, codes of conduct, standard procedures, appointed co-ordinators, etc.) than others.

Lawrence and Lorsch rejected 'universalistic' prescriptions for organisational problems. Neither the classical nor human behaviour approaches could offer organisational structures that were always suitable in all circumstances.

13. Burns and Stalker

T. Burns and G.M. Stalker investigated the attempts made by a number of Scottish firms to introduce electronics work into their existing manufacturing systems during the late 1950s. As with Lawrence and Lorsch, the authors found that the rate of change of outside environments affected organisational effectiveness.

In stable environments, structured 'mechanistic' organisational forms emerged. Here, individual tasks were clearly defined, there was specialisation and the division of managerial labour, formal hierarchies, and rigid administrative routines. The emphasis was on vertical communication, with only the very senior management having overall knowledge of how the organisation operated. Conversely, firms within volatile environments found that new and unfamiliar problems that did not fit conveniently into existing structures constantly arose. These firms needed to respond quickly to external change and firms with bureaucratic organisations could not accommodate the demands of new technology. Working methods frequently altered, individual roles needed continual redefinition. Looser, horizontal communications systems were appropriate for these circumstances, which demanded *organistic* rather than mechanistic organisational forms.

Organistic structures are flexible, relatively informal, have overlapping individual responsibilities and hence a great capacity to cope with change. Organisations, the authors claimed, possess (at least) three social systems:

1 *A formal authority system* that derives from the organisation's objectives, resources and current technology.
2 *A co-operative system* involving interpersonal relationships, competition for career advancement among employees, and relations between higher and lower authority levels.
3 *A political system* (*see* 14:**11**) relating to departmental and personal attempts to gain internal power.

Each of these systems is affected by the particular organisational form adopted, and they all influence the organisation's ability to accommodate change.

Many of the firms studied failed to introduce electronics work to their production systems successfully. The authors explained this in terms of these firms not being able to alter existing mechanistic structures into organistic forms, so that internal social systems were incapable of coping with the changes necessary for the firms to survive.

273

14. Joan Woodward

Studies conducted by the industrial psychologist Joan Woodward concluded that the *type of technology* used in production was a major factor in determining the suitability of an organisation structure for a manufacturing firm. She claimed that classical systems were best for assembly-line mass production whereas participative organisations were appropriate for small batch production or continuous-process technologies.

Woodward defined continuous-process production as being 'most technologically complex' and small-batch production as least technologically complex. Mass production was between the two. She found that, on the whole, the more technologically complex the organisation: (*i*) the longer the chain of command (*see* 21:**3**); (*ii*) the wider the spans of control (*see* 21:**10**) of senior managers; (*iii*) the higher the proportion of managerial and technically qualified staff relative to manual labour.

Woodward's work has been criticised for the following reasons:

(a) Environmental factors (e.g. the nature of competition, socio-economic trends, legal frameworks, etc.) might be more important than technology in determining organisational structure.

(b) The technology an organisation uses may itself be the *consequence* of organisational structure and not its cause.

15. Implications of the pioneering empirical studies

These studies uncovered the enormous importance of interrelations between organisations and their environments in determining organisational behaviour. Prior to these studies, management theorists had tended to regard organisations as 'closed' systems, whose actions were explained more by internal attitudes, rules and regulations than by outside influences and connections. The new 'open systems' approach to organisations suggested by these (and other) studies, however, emphasises the fact that organisations are very much affected by, and themselves influence, the wider environments in which they exist. An organisation's ability to survive and prosper depends considerably on its ability to adapt to changes in the outside world. The systems approach to organisation and the 'contingency' theories that emerged from it are examined in Chapter 3.

16. Formal and informal organisation

In large organisations, informal or 'shadow' organisational structures sometimes grow up alongside the official system. Formal organisation is that established by management and embodied in organisation charts (*see* 21:**9**), official hierarchies, company rule books, operating manuals, etc. Formal organisation is intended to be permanent, to contribute directly to the attainment of organisational goals, and to facilitate the smooth flow of work.

Informal organisation, conversely, arises naturally and spontaneously as individuals begin to interact. Thus, informal groups emerge to represent people with common interests, each group possessing its own norms, perceptions and internal communications. Informal organisation is important because the informal structures that emerge may develop goals and work routines that run contrary to the interests of the formal system. Often informal structures result from poor management/worker communication within the firm, for example:

- staff not knowing the organisation's true objectives
- absence of procedures for interdepartmental consultation and/or joint departmental decision taking
- a single favoured department dominating others, even to the extent that other departments feel they need its permission to undertake certain actions
- conflicts between individual and organisational objectives, including the pursuit of personal rather than company goals
- higher levels of management casually overruling decisions of subordinates. If senior managers do not back their juniors then the latter will conceal some of their activities and a hidden authority system may arise.

17. Advantages and disadvantages of informal organisation

The disadvantages of informal structures are that they:

(a) establish standards and objectives beyond management control

(b) encourage conformity and lack of initiative

(c) can be highly resistant to change

(d) may generate grapevines (*see* 14:**4**)

(e) create conflicts of loyalty between a person's role in the formal system and his or her role in the informal organisation.

Nevertheless, informal organisation offers a number of benefits:

(a) It can supplement and improve the operation of the formal system.

(b) Informal groups can help individuals relate to their colleagues more easily and thus might assist people in fulfilling personal ambitions and needs.

(c) Communications within the organisation may be greatly improved through the existence of an informal system.

(d) The workloads of formal leaders might be lightened, since some important managerial responsibilities (co-ordination of work, for example) may be undertaken by the informal organisation.

CULTURE AND CHANGE

18. Nature of culture

An organisation's 'culture' (sometimes referred to as its 'organisational climate') comprises its members' shared perceptions of issues, customary ways of doing things, modes of behaviour and attitudes towards work and the nature of the enterprise.

Culture is easier to recognise than to define, involving as it does a complex set of interrelating beliefs, perspectives, motivations, norms and values. It has three primary characteristics: it is *shared* by a group; it is something that people *learn*; and it depends on *environmental* circumstances.

Influence of culture

Positive aspects of organisational culture are that it furnishes employees with a sense of corporate identity, helps generate commitment to the attainment of organisational goals, provides employees with a frame of reference through which to evaluate issues and, by influencing individual perspectives and perceptions, stabilises interpersonal relationships within the firm. Equally, however, a culture might be highly resistant to change, encourage bureaucracy and inflexibility, and lead to short-sighted thinking within the firm.

Culture and strategy

Culture influences senior managers' perceptions of strategic issues and priorities, how they interpret information, their ethical standards, and how power is used to determine the strategic direction of the firm. Culture also impinges upon the implementation of strategy through helping individuals define their particular roles within the firm, and by providing benchmarks for attitudes, motivation and loyalty. Strategies that contradict the prevailing culture may be less likely to succeed than those in consonance with existing cultural norms.

Culture affects business strategy formulation and planning mechanisms in a number of important respects, including:

(a) how well the company's goals are understood and supported by employees

(b) decision making processes (participative, autocratic, etc.) and the management style applied within the enterprise

(c) whether individuals can be relied upon to be self-motivated and to implement strategic plans and decisions

(d) attitudes towards risk

(e) how senior management perceives the very character of the organisation: as a market leader or follower, as traditional and conservative, innovative and trend setting, etc.

(f) organisational drive, vigour and vitality.

Development of culture

The culture of an organisation evolves gradually, and employees may not even be aware that it exists. Organisational culture is important, however, because it helps define how workers feel about their jobs. In particular it affects:

- leadership styles applied within the organisation (*see* 13:**3**)
- individual perceptions of colleagues and situations

- assumptions about how work should be performed
- attitudes towards what is and what is not correct.

Further consequences of organisational culture might (to some extent) include:

- communication patterns, especially in relation to vertical communications (e.g. whether these are restricted to the formal line system – *see* 21:**5**), and whether subordinates can openly criticise their superiors
- approaches to remuneration management (time-based versus performance-related pay structures for instance)
- the degree of formality of company rules, regulations and procedures
- how closely employees identity with the firm
- extent of decentralisation.

A culture will have risen within a particular environmental context and be related to specific organisational needs. Factors contributing to the formation of a culture include the following:

(a) Management's stated objectives and core values. Employees who wish to progress within the organisation will tend to adopt these values in order to win the approval of their superiors.

(b) Induction systems and organisational socialisation techniques (e.g. selection methods and methods for training employees).

(c) Procedures for bonding the worker to the firm. These include the provision of status symbols and fringe benefits, superannuation schemes, company housing loans, possibly the wearing of company uniform, and so on.

Advantages derived from a firm having a strong and distinct organisational culture include:

- the provision of a focal point for employee identification with the enterprise
- agreement within the organisation of the basic goals that need to be pursued
- unification of effort among employees
- potentially higher levels of staff motivation
- easy implementation of agreed norms of behaviour.

Further benefits are that:

- There is a uniform interpretation of what constitutes correct and incorrect behaviour.
- Unanimity of purpose creates social cohesion within the firm and loyalty to the organisation. Hence staff turnover should fall.
- Employee and corporate behaviour will be predictable and consistent over time.
- There is less need for written rules and procedures.
- The organisation's unique character is clearly defined, thus contributing to the projection of a distinct corporate image.
- Internal social systems are stable.

- Employees are presented with clear information about how things should be done.

The problem with organisational culture is that whereas an organisation's needs and activities will regularly change, its underlying culture might remain constant. The continuing existence of out-of-date attitudes and perspectives among employees following changes in organisational structure and working methods is known as 'cultural lag'.

To alter an existing culture the following measures may be required:

(a) injection of new staff into the organisation

(b) introduction of incentive schemes to encourage the acceptance of new approaches and working methods

(c) emphatic managerial endorsement of new ideas, plus an increase in the flow of information between management and workers

(d) deliberate promotion of individuals who possess flexible and appropriate cultural attitudes.

Change agents (*see* 21:**25**) and organisational development (*see* 21:**23**) may be required in order to alter an inappropriate organisational culture. The work of a change agent in this respect is called a 'cultural intervention'.

Cultural fit

Arguably a successful enterprise needs to be able to adapt its organisational culture at will in order to fit its present environment. Within such a culture employees will communicate closely, be prepared to take risks, trust each other and work together as a team, and have high positive regard for themselves, colleagues and the company (Brown 1995). According to D. Denison (1990), flexibility in an organisation's culture:

- enables the firm to respond quickly to changing environments
- facilitates internal organisational design (departmentation, divisionalisation and so on)
- encourages the modification of employee behaviour in an appropriate manner as circumstances change.

Criticisms of this proposition (that an easily adopted organisational culture improves business performance) are that:

- Management can lose control over employees' actions (especially where risk taking is involved).
- The organisation might lack an overall sense of direction.
- Interpersonal relations may become unstable.
- A culture that is extremely hostile towards the firm's management could arise.

Although it is clearly important for management to understand and, if possible, determine the culture that exists within an organisation, a preoccupation with cultural matters can itself create difficulties. Employees may feel they are being manipulated, and hence react in a negative manner. Also the process of culture change is never-ending, so that enormous amounts of time and resources may be devoted to relatively minor cultural problems and issues.

19. Cultural norms

Certain group norms (*see* 12:**3**) will be regarded by organisation members as applicable in all circumstances at all times. Such norms (or values) are referred to as 'cultural absolutes'. A 'cultural imperative' is something that an individual must do in order to fit in with group norms and a firm's organisational culture. This contrasts with a 'cultural exclusive', i.e. something that must *not* be done for the maintenance of cultural harmony, and a 'cultural adiaphora', which is an act without cultural implications.

Cultural norms are *learned* by new entrants to a group. The process whereby an individual acquires cultural norms via learning (*see* Chapter 6) is known as *enculturation*.

Differing cultural norms among organisations can lead to acclimatisation difficulties (known as 'culture shock') for managers moving between firms with disparate organisational climates. Examples are transfers from large to small companies, from centralised to decentralised administrative structures, or from a firm with an authoritarian management style to a firm in which participative management is common.

Culture space (C-space)

This is a term coined by Max Boisot to describe the cultural implications of the knowledge and information existing within an organisation and how such knowledge and information is used. Boisot distinguishes between personal knowledge, organisational knowledge (e.g. patents and other intellectual property), public knowledge such as that found in textbooks and official reports, and 'common sense'. Organisations, he suggests, are typically based on just one of these types of knowledge. In consequence, particular patterns of interpersonal relationships arise.

20. Types of organisational culture

Charles Handy distinguished four types of culture: power; role; task; and person. One of these might dominate the entire organisation, or different cultures may exist in various parts of the firm. The *power culture* stems from a single central source, as in a small business that has begun to expand. Here, there are few rules and procedures and few committees. All important decisions are taken by a handful of people and precedents are followed. A *role culture*, in contrast, is highly bureaucratic. It operates through formal roles and procedures and there are clearly defined rules for settling disputes. Organisations dominated by a role culture offer security and predictability, but since they are rigidly structured, cannot adapt quickly to accommodate change (as can a power culture organisation).

The *task culture* is job- or project-oriented and manifest in matrix organisation structures (*see* 22:**2**). There is no single dominant leader; all group members

279

concentrate on completing the collective task. A task culture will encourage flexibility in approach and is ideal for an environment of change. Job satisfaction is high and there is much group cohesion. A *person culture* might arise in an organisation which exists only to serve the people within it. Examples are partnerships, consultancy firms, and professional organisations.

According to Handy, none of these cultures is better than the others. A culture arises, he argues, from historical circumstances, the existing environment, technology and the human needs of people within the organisation.

21. Social values

A social value is a moral principle or standard against which the desirability of certain modes of behaviour may be assessed. Values help determine what an individual considers important, personal priorities, and how he or she assesses other people's worth. Examples of how values can influence perspectives include the situations where (*i*) 'masculine' values within an organisation inhibit the promotion of gender equal opportunities, (*ii*) 'individualistic' values encourage non-conformism and the pursuit of self-interest, or (*iii*) collectivist values affect industrial relations, the degree of employee participation in management decisions, etc. Other core values might concern the work ethic, honesty, social responsibility, choice of career, and so on.

Values change over time; some may disappear entirely as environmental circumstances alter. Also, values may vary across industries and from state to state (Japanese and British values, for instance, differ significantly).

NATIONAL CULTURE

22. Importance of national culture

A nation's culture is easier to recognise than to define. We speak readily of 'Japanese culture', 'British culture', and so on; yet it is extremely difficult to specify precisely what is meant by these terms. National culture involves a complex set of interrelating beliefs and ways of living, and it is almost impossible to acquire a complete knowledge and understanding of another country's culture without residing there for several years. However, national culture is important because it represents a collective frame of reference (*see* 10:**16**) through which a wide range of issues and events are perceived, including:

(a) how symbols, sounds and pictures are interpreted by individuals (this has many implications for advertising and marketing)

(b) socialisation and friendship patterns

(c) social institutions and legal frameworks

(d) aesthetics and language.

Additionally, national culture affects personal attitudes towards such matters as:

- the accumulation of wealth and material possessions
- the upbringing and education of children
- sexuality
- morality
- social class (*see* 7:**10**)
- the role of women in society
- respect for authority
- how the underprivileged should be treated
- religion, politics and many other socio-economic issues (though note how religion can itself influence national culture).

Managers need to know about cultural differences among nations in order to be able:

- to communicate effectively with customers, suppliers, business associates and partners in other countries, and with foreign employees (Subhash and Tucker 1995)
- to conduct negotiations and understand the nuances of the bargaining postures of the other parties to a negotiation
- to predict trends in social behaviour likely to affect the firm's foreign operations
- to understand ethical standards and concepts of social responsibility in various countries (Ferraro 1990)
- to predict how cultural differences will affect consumer reactions to advertisements and other promotional forms.

23. Effects of national culture on business

National culture helps determine consumer behaviour, consumption patterns, family size and structure, and decision making within families. Cultural influences are evident, moreover, in certain aspects of a country's demographic makeup (kinship patterns, social mobility and social stratification, for example) and in the authority and occupational status systems that emerge from the management styles of firms.

Community attitudes towards entrepreneurship are affected by national culture. Such attitudes have implications for new business startups, the introduction of new technologies, acceptance of risk, and government policies for business development (including taxes and laws on competition).

A country's culture is especially significant for the advertising and marketing of goods, influencing topics such as:

(a) How customers perceive the characteristics of products

(b) The degrees of quality, elegance, urbanity, etc. expected in goods

(c) The style of advertising adopted in different countries. British advertising, for example, makes extensive use of humour whereas German advertising tends to stick to the facts. Even the postures depicted in advertisements (standing, sitting, lying down, etc.) can have meanings determined by cultural considerations, and might be interpreted differently (e.g. as friendly, antagonistic or superior) in different states.

24. Culture and language

The world has about 3000 distinct languages and around 10,000 dialects. A number of countries have more than one language. Canada for example recognises English and French; Belgium has Flemish in the north, French in the south, and German in the south east. India has 15 main languages and around 800 dialects; around 200 dialects were spoken in the former USSR. Some ex-colonies of Western nations have an 'official' language used for public administration, government communications and the administration of justice, and which is taught in schools alongside the local language or dialect. Typically the official language is English or French (according to the former occupying power) and is used to maintain the unity of the country in the face of numerous regional languages, dialects and (often) ethnic groups. An interesting development has been the adoption of English as the official 'corporate language' of a number of multinational firms that are not based in English-speaking nations (Philips in the Netherlands for instance). Hence intra-firm communications between branches, subsidiaries, etc., in various parts of the world are conducted in English, with company executives being expected to be able to communicate in English as a matter of course.

Non-linguistic influences

The meaning of body language also differs from nation to nation. For example, disagreement is indicated by shaking the head from side to side in some countries (the UK for example), or by nodding the head or perhaps by waving a hand in front of the face in certain parts of the world. Showing the soles of the feet to another person (as when putting feet on a desk or placing a foot on the knee) is considered a grave insult in some regions. Further examples of culturally sensitive body language are joining together the thumb and index finger, the 'thumbs up' sign, folding the arms, and sitting cross-legged (as is the case in some Middle Eastern countries). An important cultural difference affecting the conduct of international business relates to the ways in which individuals express (or conceal) their disagreement with other people's statements. Openness and plain speaking is the norm in Western Europe and North America, but not in the Far East – where it may be considered extremely impolite to disagree with a stranger. Many misunderstandings arise from this situation, with Westerners believing that they have successfully negotiated a deal whereas in fact the other side has no intention of confirming the bargain.

Culture affects how people think, quite independently of what they do or the words they utter. Examples are whether people approach issues analytically rather than intuitively, and whether individuals inwardly feel they should be organised and methodical, rather than 'taking life as it comes'. Attitudes towards space and time also differ between nations. Turning up late for an appointment is regarded as a great insult in some countries, as normal in others, or as acceptable only for high ranking social groups. Multinational firms operating in some parts of the world experience great difficulty in getting locally recruited workers to attend work punctually and for pre-set periods. Similarly, different cultures have different norms regarding the physical distance that one person should stand away from another in various circumstances. Physical nearness to other people is regarded as correct in some cultures but rude (representing a violation of 'personal space') in others. Handholding and other forms of physical contact have different meanings in disparate societies.

25. Analysis of national cultures

In 1945 G. P. Murdock published a highly influential study of what he referred to as 'cultural universals', i.e. aspects of culture supposedly found in all societies. To the extent that cultural universals exist, societies can be regarded as essentially the same and cultural differences between them relatively unimportant. Examples of cultural universals are interest in sport, bodily adornment, courtship, household hygiene, sexual taboos, gift giving, status differentiation, etc. Subsequent approaches to the analysis of culture and the consequences of cultural analysis have focused on lifestyle and, in particular, the taxonomy of cultures into 'high context' or 'low context' categories. The former relates to that which is internalised and/or embedded within the person and not expressed in an explicit manner (Hofstede 1980). Individuals who share the same high-context culture do not feel any need to explain their thoughts or behaviour to each other. Hence high-context culture relies heavily on non-verbal communication. Japan is frequently cited as an example of a country with a high-context culture. Communication within a high-context culture is fast and efficient, but can break down in relation to outsiders who may not be able to comprehend what the high-context group believes or is talking about. Behaviour within a high-context culture is stable and predictable. A problem is that the nature of a particular high-context culture might be misunderstood by outsiders in consequence of the latter's stereotyping of the former's members. In a low-context culture, conversely, communications need to be explicit: words, signs, symbols, rituals, etc. are used to rationalise, communicate and explain cultural norms and social activities. Low-context cultures emphasise individualism rather than collectivism. Communications are clear and precise, and it is necessary to argue and persuade when presenting propositions. Members' values, attitudes, perceptions and patterns of behaviour are diverse and liable to change quickly. It is sometimes suggested that the USA is a good example of a low-context culture.

These issues are important for international businesses, which need to understand the nuances of specific foreign culturally high-context or low context groups in order to design marketing campaigns and promotional messages that will appeal to them.

Norms and values

A major part of cultural analysis is the identification and characterisation of group norms within various societies. Group norms are shared perceptions of how things should be done or common attitudes feelings or beliefs. As norms emerge, individuals begin behaving according to how they feel other group members expect them to behave. Entrants to an existing society will feel isolated and insecure and hence will actively seek out established norms that will act as a guide to how that person ought to behave. Norms, therefore, facilitate the integration of an individual into a social group, and thus will be eagerly accepted by new members.

Social values are moral principles or standards against which the desirability of certain modes of behaviour may be assessed. Values help determine what an individual considers important, personal priorities, and how he or she assesses other people's worth. Values change over time; some may disappear entirely as environmental circumstances alter. Also, values may vary across industries and from state to state. Nevertheless social values contribute greatly to 'national temperament', a concept easier to recognise than to define, encompassing as it does such matters as tolerance of opposing viewpoints, display of emotion, self-discipline, degree of formality of relationships, etc. National values affect the acceptability of specific messages and symbols, and make important contributions to national culture. For example, 'masculine' values help determine the influence of advertisements that contain assertive messages, that emphasise toughness and vigour, and appeal to the competitive instinct.

'Individualistic' values within consumers imply a preference for advertisements with non-conformist, egocentric themes that focus on the pursuit of self-interest, self-control, etc. Other core values might relate to honesty, social responsibility, ambition and so on. The aim is to discover the existence of similar values within groups of consumers in different countries and hence present a common value-specific theme when promoting a product in disparate states.

26. Self-referencing

A managers awareness of national differences should not be clouded by stereotyping (*see* 4:**14**). Self-stereotyping can also be important, and create problems. Thus for example managers from countries generally regarded as superefficient may regard *themselves* as superefficient, regardless of whether this is actually the case. Equally serious is the problem of cultural 'self referencing', i.e. the (unconscious) preassumption by an individual that the culture of his or her own country is the appropriate one against which other cultures should be assessed. Rather it is necessary to look at problems and issues from *foreign* as well as home country norms and perspectives and identify clearly the difference between the two. Local nationals should be consulted, as they will be sensitive to local cultural influences and will understand the 'inner logic' of the local way of life. *Ethnocentrism* can cost an international business dear. Ethnocentrism is the tendency to regard one's own nation, group or culture as superior and to compare the standards of other nations, groups or cultures against this belief. It can lead to fundamental misunderstandings of foreign consumer attitudes and business practices, to inefficiency, and bad relations with host country governments. Ethnocentrism contrasts with polycentrism, which regards other nations, groups and cultures as different but of equal value, and with *geocentrism* that sees some but not all nations, groups and cultures as being of equal status. (The term geocentric is also used by some writers to describe the management approach adopted by companies which co-ordinate all their activities on the global scale, planning and resourcing without regard for national considerations.) A possible disadvantage with polycentrism is that it can cause a firm (inappropriately) to avoid transferring excellent home country practices intact to other nations. Also, delegation of duties to local subsidiaries may be excessive, leading to problems of control and co-ordination.

To overcome potential biases when evaluation foreign cultures, the following procedure might be adopted:

(a) Define the issue or problem to be studied in terms of the cultural norms, traits and perspectives of the home country.

(b) Repeat this exercise, without applying value judgements, using the cultural norms, traits and perspectives of residents of the foreign country.

(c) Compare the results of (a) and (b) and identify cultural differences that emerge from the analysis.

(d) Consider how these cultural differences might influence the interpretation of the original issue or problem.

(e) Redefine the issue or problem having removed cultural bias.

Progress test 20

1. What are the major characteristics of an organisation? List the main sub-systems of an organisation.

2. Define the term 'psycho-social sub-system'.

3. Define 'technology'. In what sense might an organisation be regarded as a technical system?

4. Explain the social implications of mass production.

5. Why did C. Perrow believe in the importance of classifying technology into two distinct categories?

6. What were the major conclusions of the empirical studies conducted by Joan Woodward?

7. Define the term 'informal organisation'.

8. List the main variables affected by organisational culture.

21
THE DESIGN OF ORGANISATIONS

APPROACHES TO DESIGN AND CONTROL

1. Introduction

Modern management theories (*see* **4** below and Chapter 3) strongly suggest that there is no unique organisational structure that is always applicable to every situation. Rather, choices are necessary and organisations need to be *designed* to suit the requirements of specific sets of circumstances. In particular, management must resolve the following issues:

(a) the extent to which individual employees should specialise and how precisely the division of labour should be applied

(b) whether and to what extent employees' responsibilities should overlap

(c) the spans of control (*see* **10** below) of various managers

(d) how individual and departmental activities are to be co-ordinated and controlled

(e) whether to organise the firm around products, functions or people.

Four major factors affect these choices:

1 *How much information flows through the firm.* If information flows smoothly through the business and if interpersonal and interdepartmental relations are good, a relatively complicated organisation structure may be appropriate.
2 *Employees' attitudes, morale, abilities and educational attainments.* Organisations which use highly qualified staff for specialist tasks may need to adjust their organisation structures to meet the emotional requirements of this type of worker.
3 *The firm's goals.* A change in objectives might create the need for a new organisation structure. Consider, for example, a business which operates in a fast-moving, technically sophisticated industry and finds that a competitor introduces a new product which renders all existing models obsolete. The firm must react instantly by altering its own product line. This can involve complete reorganisation of methods of production, marketing and administration. A flexible structure that can be quickly altered is most appropriate in this case.

4 *The nature of the external environment.* Examples of variables affecting wider commercial environments are the laws and/or customs of society, market structures, the degree of market uncertainty, local business practices, perhaps even the local political system.

2. Organisation theory

To organise work is to break it down into units for allocation to people and departments. The system for distributing tasks constitutes the 'organisational structure' of the enterprise. This structure defines the framework within which activities occur. *Organisation theory* is the study of organisational structures, of how organisations function, the performance of organisations and how groups and individuals within them behave.

Organisations are composed of people. Control of an organisation, therefore, necessarily involves the regulation of human activity and the arrangement of people into hierarchies and working groups. Patterns of authority, responsibility and accountability must be fashioned and employees made aware of their duties. Individuals need to know the extent of their personal authority and whom they should obey.

3. The classical approach to organisation theory

This cannot be attributed to any one person; rather it is a conglomeration of the ideas of many people developed over several decades. The fundamental proposition is that people should be selected and trained to fit into the organisation – the organisation itself need not be structured to suit the human needs of particular members of staff. Rigid organisational patterns are specified and individuals are allocated to various positions according to their perceived suitability for those particular jobs. The principal tenets of the classical theory are outlined below.

Specialisation and the division of labour

Resolution of a job into simple, routine operations usually increases the speed and precision of the work. Less skill is needed for easy and repetitive tasks, so fewer highly qualified employees are required.

The concept of the division of labour can be applied to managerial work. Advocates of the classical approach would recommend that managers be responsible for a single function and not assume overall control of a wide range of activities. Hence, specialised skills are developed and individual performance improves.

In the managerial context, division of labour creates the need for a pyramid structure of authority and control. At the apex of the pyramid is the managing director (or equivalent chief executive), then come senior executives, line and staff managers, supervisors and, finally, operatives. Higher managers must co-ordinate the efforts of subordinates. The lower the manager's position in the hierarchy, the more specialised the duties performed.

Unbroken chain of command

There should be a clear line of authority running from the top of the managerial pyramid to its base. A break in the chain of command means that instructions issued by senior managers will not be implemented: chaos and disruption might then ensue.

Unity of command

A subordinate should be directly responsible to one superior only. Instructions to the subordinate should not be issued from different sources, otherwise orders received could conflict and the subordinate would have to choose which to obey.

Application of this principle is difficult in practice because of the strong influences sometimes exerted by informal authority systems. A person might in theory be responsible to a single superior, but in reality may behave according to standards determined by someone else.

The classical theory recommends narrow spans of control (*see* **10** below). It assumes that only small numbers of immediate subordinates can effectively be managed by one superior.

Management by exception

F.W. Taylor (*see* Chapter 2) recommended that subordinates should submit to their superiors only brief, condensed reports on normal operations but extensive analyses of deviations from past average performance or targets set by higher management. Routine matters should be dealt with at low levels, leaving senior managers free to devote their time to unusual problems and major policy issues.

Delegation

The assignment of duties to subordinates, accompanied by the devolution of authority necessary to implement decisions, is essential for the efficient administration of large organisations because top management does not have the time or specialist knowledge to take all important decisions. Care is necessary in the choice of duties for delegation, and higher management must ensure that subordinates selected to receive delegated work are competent to complete it successfully. Recipients of delegated authority must be given all necessary resources and information. Systematic delegation is crucial for management development programmes. Work of increasing difficulty can be delegated thus gradually improving a subordinate's capacity to act independently.

4. Reactions to the classical approach

All organisation theorists have asked the same questions – how best to structure and administer working groups – but their answers have differed according to the schools of thought to which they belonged. The basic disagreement concerns the extent to which universal prescriptions – the idea that there is always one best way of organising a business (or other administrative unit) regardless of circumstances – may reasonably be applied.

The human relations approach

According to the human relations school (*see* Chapter 3) organisations should be designed to accommodate the social and human needs of the people who work within them. They should encourage personal initiative and release creative potential. Rigid organisation forms are said to inhibit the innate enthusiasm of junior managerial staff, hence reducing efficiency. Advocates of this theory recommend participative management. Targets jointly determined by subordinate and superior will be more readily accepted than those arbitrarily imposed.

Contingency theories

The contingency school (*see* 3:**27**) insists that the general application of any of the previously discussed principles will, in practice, be doomed to failure. Instead, organisations should be individually structured to meet the requirements of specific circumstances. The contingency approach is therefore the antithesis of the classical proposition that authority and responsibility systems should be constant and predetermined. Rather, management should examine the influence of a number of key variables and then select an organisational structure that provides the 'best fit' to the needs of the situation. The variables to be examined include:

- technology
- environments
- nature of employees' work duties
- the firm's labour and product markets.

5. Line and staff organisation

Line managers are directly responsible for achieving the organisation's objectives, and exert direct authority over their subordinates. Line authority flows through the chain of command, from the apex of the organisation to its base. Often, the chain of command is illustrated by means of an 'organisation chart' (*see* **9** below).

Typical line management positions are: managing director, production director, general manager, works manager, sales manager, first line supervisor. Each position in the line system identifies points of contact between manager and subordinates, showing the authority of its occupant and to whom that person is responsible. Vertical communications proceed only through the line system; if a manager cannot handle a problem it is referred upwards to superiors. Equally, work may only be delegated to the subordinates of a specific position.

Staff managers

Staff managers advise line managers but do not possess authority to implement important decisions. Line executives might ask staff managers for advice, but are not obliged to accept their recommendations. Examples of managers likely to occupy staff rather than line positions are lawyers, researchers, industrial relations specialists, or technical experts.

Often, staff and line organisations are mixed. Such a combination is called a 'functional' organisation. It means that staff managers are empowered to implement their own decisions within carefully specified areas of activity. A personnel officer, for example, might be authorised to choose media to carry job advertisements, but not to select candidates for particular posts. Another example would be a training officer who is empowered to insist that members of other departments attend certain training courses, even if the line managers in charge of the individuals concerned are not keen on the idea.

Hence, 'functional authority' in this context means a specialist staff manager's right to control the activities of other departments within the limits of the function. Line managers are *obliged* to accept the staff manager's advice in certain prespecified matters relating to the relevant function.

6. Personal staff

Note the distinction between a 'staff manager' and a manager's 'personal staff'. The former is a position in the managerial hierarchy (e.g. company lawyer or training officer), whereas the latter consist of helpers who assist a manager (line or staff) to fulfil his or her duties. Personal staff are adjuncts to the line or staff manager concerned, who is solely responsible for his or her activities regardless of the inputs of personal staff. Examples of personal staff are personal assistants, secretaries, research assistants, etc., who provide services to one person, section or department rather than to the organisation as a whole.

7. Advantages and disadvantages of various systems

In practice it is frequently difficult to distinguish between line and staff organisation and to define who exactly is a line executive as opposed to a staff manager! However, advantages and disadvantages apply to each system. The *advantages* of line organisation are that:

- There is an unambiguous chain of command.
- Each person's area of responsibility is clearly defined.
- Everyone knows to whom they are accountable.
- It is coherent and easy to understand.
- It embodies a logical division of labour.
- Decision taking can be fast and effective (orders have to be obeyed immediately).

Disadvantages of line systems include the following:

- Staff advisers are relegated to subsidiary roles which, as highly qualified specialists, they may resent having to occupy.
- Line systems rely heavily on a small number of key personnel whose resignation or illness may cause great disruption.
- Power is concentrated into the hands of a few line managers who might not be sufficiently mature, experienced or competent to exercise it responsibly or effectively.
- Line managers might be overworked, have to take too many decisions, and thus be subject to excessive amounts of stress.

For staff organisation the *advantages* are that:

- Line managers do not become immersed in detailed analysis of what to them are secondary issues.
- Staff specialists are left free to develop their personal expertise.
- Executive decisions are taken by people who have been trained and are sufficiently experienced to take them.

Staff organisation *disadvantages* are as follows:

- Possible confusion over who is responsible for what and who has authority over whom.
- Line managers might rely too heavily on staff specialists' advice.
- Line managers may receive so much advice from staff specialists that vital points are missed.
- Experts are not able directly to implement their expert recommendations.

'Functional' organisation has the following *advantages:*

- It lifts the burden of routine decision making from line executives.
- Expert decisions can be implemented immediately.
- Fewer line managers are required.

The *disadvantages* of a 'functional' organisation are that:

- Organisational structures become extremely complex.
- Much co-ordination of activities is required.
- Duplication of effort may occur.

8. Conflicts between line and staff managers

Conflicts between line managers and staff managers may result from the following factors:

(a) Line managers' jealousy of staff specialists' superior knowledge and qualifications.

(b) Staff managers giving their advice in unintelligible technical jargon.

(c) Line managers not implementing staff managers' recommendations.

(d) Differences in the backgrounds and lifestyles of line and staff managers (the latter might be younger and more outward looking than line managers).

(e) Resistance to change by line executives.

(f) Staff managers' possible lack of concern for wider organisational objectives beyond the confines of their particular specialisations.

(g) Employees perhaps taking more notice of staff managers' recommendations than line managers' directives.

(h) Staff managers giving advice that is theoretically sound, but impractical.

9. Organisation charts

Authority and accountability systems are often described in 'organisation charts'. An organisation chart is a diagram showing the locations of individuals, jobs or departments within the hierarchy of an organisation. Figure 21.1 is an example of a (simplified) organisation chart for a large company. Figure 21.2 is a hypothetical organisation chart for a production department in a manufacturing firm.

The purpose of an organisation chart is to resolve ambiguities about who does what. Associated with each position in the diagram will be a job specification stating precisely the duties and responsibilities of the post. Horizontal as well as vertical linkages can be included to highlight areas of mutual concern and joint responsibility, though the resulting diagram might be complicated and difficult to understand. A major benefit of preparing an organisation chart is that it forces management to concentrate hard on questions of accountability within the firm. Also, new employees – who will be given a copy of the organisation chart on appointment – will be in no doubt about their roles and responsibilities. There are, however, some problems:

(a) A chart will show desired organisation structure at a specific moment in time. Yet business environments change continuously. New and different organisational forms might become appropriate as circumstances alter. Charts can rapidly become out of date, and the efforts involved in their preparation will then have been wasted.

(b) Formal rather than informal relationships are illustrated. In reality, however, actual behaviour is frequently influenced by informal communications. Indeed, informal channels can be faster and more efficient than the official system. Rigid adherence to bureaucratic formal procedures can inhibit initiative and effective decision taking.

(c) Even on a formal level, relationships may, in practice, be more complex than can be portrayed on diagrams. Some responsibilities can be allotted to any one of several different departments. If work is distributed haphazardly there is little point in preparing an organisation chart in the first instance.

10. Spans of control

The number of immediate subordinates controlled by a manager is known as the manager's span of control. A wide span involves many subordinates (say 15 to 20) all of whom report directly to one superior. Whether a span is too wide or too narrow depends on individual circumstances, though in practice the general rule that no manager should control more than six subordinates is commonly applied.

Complex relationships result from wide spans of control because of competing demands made on the superior's limited time by immediate subordinates of equal rank. Also, subordinates themselves have others under them. Consequently, wide spans of control will cause senior managers to accumulate large numbers of indirect subordinates.

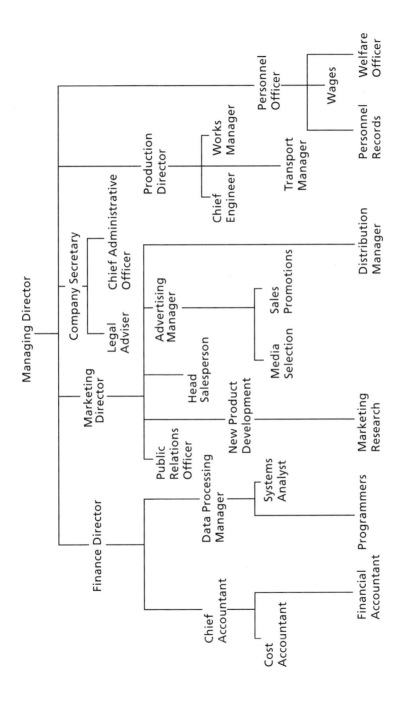

Fig. 21.1 Large company organisation chart

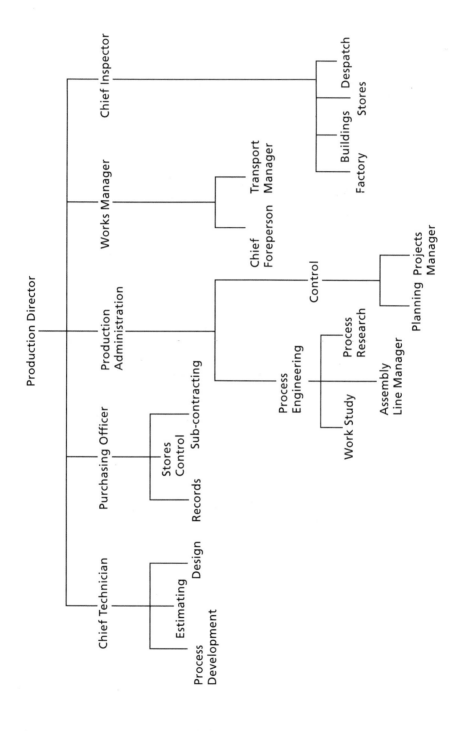

Fig. 21.2 Production department organisation chart

The optimum span

The size of an optimum span of control will depend on such factors as the following:

(a) *The complexity of the work to be done.* If the issues confronting higher management are technical and complicated there will be advantages to their having relatively few subordinates. Then, senior executives will have time to assess properly the suggestions of subordinates and not be overburdened with minor problems arising from lower levels.

(b) *Organisational diversity and the efficiency of internal communications.* Wide geographical distance between departments makes wide spans of control physically difficult to administer. Were face-to-face contacts between manager and subordinates impossible, communications would rely on telephone calls, letters, memoranda, and similar indirect methods. Interruptions in information flows and other communication breakdowns cause loss of effective control.

(c) *The quality of the individual manager.* Some people are better able to handle large numbers of subordinates than others. A manager's abilities depend on training and experience as well as personal characteristics. The degree of authority given the manager is another important consideration in assessing his or her optimum span of control.

(d) *The calibre of subordinates.* Well-trained, enthusiastic and competent subordinates need less control and supervision than others. In these circumstances, a wide span of control can reasonably be applied.

Delayering

This is a technique of downsizing and efficiency improvement that consciously seeks to increase senior managers' spans of control. It has been applied most commonly in tall managerial hierarchies containing several levels of middle management, each individual executive controlling the work of just a few immediate subordinates. A major justification for delayering an administrative system is the advent of computer-assisted management which sometimes enables managers simultaneously to oversee the work of up to 30–35 subordinates. This saves money and speeds up the flow of communications within the firm. Conditions for successful delayering are as follows:

(a) It needs to be completed as part of an overall strategy for restructuring an organisation; not as a panic measure during a financial crisis.

(b) Paperwork and administrative bureaucracy must be reduced and simplified so as to enable the remaining executives to perform effectively.

(c) The company's most talented people should not be delayered just because they happen to occupy a certain position in the management hierarchy.

(d) Delayering should be done in a single 'big bang'; otherwise uncertainties concerning the possibility of further delayering exercises can greatly demotivate the surviving workforce.

11. Tall versus flat structures

Narrow spans of control create numerous levels of authority within the organisation and therefore long chains of command. The advantages of a 'tall' organisation with many levels between top and bottom are as follows:

(a) Managers may devote their full attention to the demands of their subordinates.

(b) It recognises that an individual's capacity to supervise others is limited and that it is better to deal with a small number of subordinates properly than to have contact with many subordinates but only in casual ways.

(c) There is less need to co-ordinate the activities of subordinates than in a flat structure.

(d) Duplication of effort among subordinates is unlikely.

(e) Communications are facilitated.

(f) Employees are presented with a career ladder and thus can expect regular promotion through the system.

(g) It facilitates specialisation of functions and the creation of logically determined work units.

'Flat' organisations have the following advantages:

(a) Managers are forced to delegate work; hence, subordinates acquire experience of higher-level duties.

(b) Morale may improve on account of the majority of employees being on the same level.

(c) Low supervision costs.

(d) Subordinates are given more discretion over how they achieve their objectives.

(e) Few personal assistants (*see* **6** above) and staff advisers (*see* **5** above) are necessary because there are fewer levels.

(f) Managers and subordinates meet directly without having to communicate through intermediaries. Thus, information will not be lost or misinterpreted as it passes up and down the organisation.

(g) Managers remain in touch with activities at the base of the organisation.

12. Linking-pin organisation

This is a form of organisation recommended by the psychologist R. Likert. Each manager is required to be a 'linking-pin' between three distinct groups:

(a) the manager's peer group of other managers at the same level of authority

(b) the manager's superiors one step up in the organisational hierarchy

(c) the manager's subordinates.

Hence the manager needs to have direct communications in three directions – upwards, downwards and horizontally – e.g. by serving on various committees at each of the three levels. The advantages claimed for this approach are that through creating overlaps between each manager's area of responsibility it:

(a) integrates the activities of all levels within the organisation

(b) enhances communications between levels

(c) encourages employee participation in decision making at higher levels

(d) motivates the individual manager.

13. The inverted management pyramid

This is an approach to organisation and management that seeks to turn upside down the traditional organisational pyramid that has a chief executive at the apex of the system, with senior executives underneath, middle managers below the senior management team, and so on. Critics of these orthodox hierarchies allege that customers are implicitly placed at the very bottom of the structure – beneath the lowest level of employees. Yet without customers there can be no business in the first place! Thus customers should be at the very top of the system, not at its base. Moreover, through inverting the conventional pyramid, front-line (customer contact) staff are recognised as occupying a crucially important role. Middle management supports front-line employees in the performance of their duties; senior management facilitates middle ranking executives while, at the bottom of the system, the chief executive supports the senior management team and, indirectly, everyone else within the organisation. Problems with the implementation of the concept are that:

- It is likely to be opposed by middle managers who fear losing their power and influence.
- Existing interpersonal relationships and understandings are disrupted.
- The absence of a conspicuous figurehead may cause the organisation to lack strategic vision.
- It is unclear as to who is to issue directives.

Opponents of the idea of the inverted management pyramid claim that conventional hierarchies offer an efficient device for devolving authority and accountability within organisations, and that customers should not figure in an organisation chart (of whatever variety) in the first place. Rather the *raison-d'etre* of the pyramid is itself to serve customer requirements.

14. Empowerment

An employee's feeling of being in control and of significantly contributing to an organisation's development can be greatly enhanced by 'empowering' that person to complete tasks and attain targets independently, without constantly having to refer back to management for permission to take certain actions. The employee is trusted to take sensible decisions. Hence, for example, salespeople might be empowered to offer special discounts to prospective customers, production operatives can be empowered to decide the speed of an assembly line, and work teams may be empowered to determine the extent and intensity of the use of robots within a section of a firm. The aim is to enable employees who actually have to deal with problems to implement solutions quickly and without recourse to supervisors and/or higher levels of management. This is increasingly necessary as large and bureaucratic organisations delayer management hierarchies in the search for administrative efficiency and lower costs. Removal of one or more entire layers of the management pyramid is a fast and sometimes highly effective means for streamlining management communication and control.

Empowerment differs from 'delegation' in that whereas the latter is the devolution of duties from boss to subordinate (albeit with the authority to implement decisions), empowerment is a general approach to operational management, requiring not just the passing down of power and responsibility through a hierarchy but also that the individual workers actively contribute to improving the performance of tasks. Benefits to empowerment include:

- the encouragement of individual creativity and initiative, commitment to the enterprise and team spirit
- decision taking at the most suitable levels
- facilitation of performance management
- faster and more flexible responses to customer requirements
- higher levels of self-confidence and motivation among employees
- better relations between management and front-line (customer contact) employees
- a 'meeting of minds' *vis-à-vis* customers and the firm's staff regarding what constitutes product quality (Schneider *et al* 1980)
- receipt of valuable ideas for new products from front-line employees
- provision of an early warning system regarding customer dissatisfaction
- immediate correction of mistakes.

Problems with empowerment are that greater care has to be exercised when hiring employees, who then need more training than in conventional circumstances. Staff might take bad decisions, and customers may be treated differently leading to resentments among those not receiving favours. The entire organisation might need to be redesigned in order to make empowerment operationally effective.

Bowen and Lawler (1992) suggest that four conditions need to apply in order for empowerment to succeed, namely that employees receive:

- information concerning the organisation's performance
- power to make decisions that genuinely influence the direction and performance of the organisation
- knowledge enabling them to understand and contribute to organisational performance
- rewards that are based on the organisation's performance.

STRUCTURAL OPTIONS

15. Creation of departments

A 'department' is a set of activities under a manager's jurisdiction. Division of the firm's work into units creates the need for departments, which can be defined in terms of: function performed; a product; market; or person.

Functional departments

These are established to deal with particular varieties of work. Examples are production, accounts, advertising, transport and administrative departments. Major functional departments contain sections. Thus an advertising department can be subdivided into sections for media selection, sales promotions, package design and other promotional activities.

Definitions of the responsibilities of functional departments follow logically and naturally from the work of the organisation. Normally divisions will parallel occupational distinctions so that, for instance, everyone concerned with selling will be in the marketing department; everyone involved in manufacture will be in production, and so on.

Although it is easy to understand, functional departmentation may encourage narrow and introspective attitudes. Departments with wider responsibilities could provide staff with challenging environments that stimulate effort and initiative.

Product departmentation

This means creating departments each of which deals with a single product or service. Staff within the department control all activities associated with the good, including the purchase of raw materials, administration, processing, and the sale and distribution of the final output.

Senior departmental managers acquire a wider range of general managerial skills than they would in functional departments and they accumulate expert knowledge of the problems involved in the design and manufacture of their own product.

Such specialised experience might be essential for efficient administration in firms producing technically complicated goods. A further advantage of product departmentation is that it makes co-ordination between relevant management functions and stages of production easier to achieve.

Market departmentation

This can occur by geographical region or customer type. Regional sales departments are an example. Local factors can then figure in decision making, and it might be cheaper to locate offices near to customers. Otherwise the departmentation could relate to customer size (e.g. having special facilities for large buyers), or to retail or wholesale distribution channels, export or home markets, etc. Problems of co-ordination might ensue, and control could be difficult.

In small family businesses it is common for departments to develop around *specific people*. As new functional needs arise they are allocated according to the interests of the family members so that, eventually, each department controls a variety of unrelated tasks. A partner in a small firm might be interested in finance and advertising. Thus, all things concerned with these functions will be dealt with in that partner's own department.

16. Autonomous work groups

The principles of job design (*see* 8:**26**) can be applied to the tasks performed by working groups. Accordingly, *autonomous work groups* may be created in such a way that:

(a) Each group has a complete and self-contained task to perform.

(b) Groups are given the authority needed to implement their own decisions.

(c) Group members themselves choose the methods whereby work is completed and then monitor and appraise their own performances.

(d) Each group member is trained to the level where he or she can undertake most or preferably all the jobs performed within the group, so that frequent job rotation is possible.

The technique was pioneered at the Volvo truck assembly unit in Sweden. There, each team:

- selected its own leader
- allocated work among team members
- set its own pace of work
- established its own targets (subject to constraints imposed by higher management)
- assumed full responsibility for quality control.

Volvo reported the following results:

- Productivity increased
- Management/employee communications were enhanced
- Quality improved
- Labour turnover reduced dramatically.

However, the benefits of specialisation were lost and labour cost per unit of output remained (by international standards) substantial. Autonomous work groups are more appropriate for organisations which operate participative management styles (*see* 3:**9**) and have decentralised organisation structures (*see* **18** below). Also the work completed by each team needs to consist of self-contained units rather than a flow production process in which it is impossible to establish where one set of tasks finishes and another begins.

17. Centralisation

In a centralised organisation, all major decisions are taken by a central administrative body which issues binding directives to lower levels of authority. Subordinates are bound by fixed rules and procedures, and exercise little discretion in the course of their work. Note, however, that as organisations grow, it becomes physically impossible for top management to take *all* decisions, so that some decentralisation – by delegation of decision-making responsibilities to subordinates – becomes inevitable. Nevertheless, some organisations prefer to centralise decision taking as tightly as possible, for the following reasons:

(a) All employees are subject to direct and immediate control.

(b) Departments and sections can be provided with detailed operating instructions.

(c) There is no question of decentralised units competing with each other to undertake similar tasks.

(d) Employees' performances can be rapidly appraised.

(e) There is unified decision making as the activities of all sections can be related to the objectives of the organisation as a whole.

(f) Correct working methods can be imposed on all units within the organisation.

(g) The efforts of diverse units can be synchronised.

(h) Administration is simplified.

(i) New strategies can be implemented quickly.

The *disadvantages* of centralisation include the following:

(a) Local expertise is not fully utilised.

(b) The organisation becomes less flexible and possibly more bureaucratic (*see* 2:**9**) and incapable of accommodating change.

(c) Centralised managers will receive so much information that important points might be misinterpreted or overlooked.

(d) Subordinates might deliberately disobey the detailed instructions they receive, preferring to operate through unofficial and informal decentralised organisation systems.

18. Decentralisation

There is perhaps a natural tendency for large organisations to decentralise, since this allows 'local' control over operations, thus enabling the central authority to concentrate on long-term strategic plans. Decentralisation may occur through the creation of subsidiary companies, through increasing the decision-making authority of individual managers, or through the divisionalisation of a firm. Factors encouraging decentralisation include the following:

(a) *Rapid growth of the organisation.* The larger the organisation, the harder it becomes for top management to take all important decisions.

(b) *Variability in the external environment,* hence creating a need for rapid response to external change.

(c) *The need to allocate separate budgets* to functions, sections and departments.

The *advantages* of decentralisation include the following:

(a) Senior executives can devote their time to strategic planning while leaving operational matters to expert local managers. Those at the top can take an overall bird's-eye view of the situation. The word 'local' in this context need not refer to geographical location. Rather it means nearness to operations and to the units where the decisions taken have to be applied.

(b) Local initiative is encouraged.

(c) The organisation becomes responsive to local conditions.

(d) There is less red tape and hence faster decision taking.

(e) Local circumstances are taken into account when policies are determined.

(f) Managerial jobs in decentralised units become more interesting so that the organisation can attract better-quality managerial staff.

(g) Decentralised managers acquire the experience needed for more senior positions.

19. Divisionalisation

This is a popular form of decentralisation. It avoids the cost and inconvenience of setting up subsidiary companies, and divisional managers can be made subject to close central control.

Divisions may be established for different products, for geographical markets, customer type (retail or wholesale, for example), organisational function (purchasing, finance, etc.) or method of production. Heads of division are given targets, but are left to achieve them in their own ways. Organisation within a division may itself be centralised or decentralised.

There is a difference between divisionalisation and decentralisation in that the latter simply means passing authority to others – perhaps to the bottom levels of a conventional line and staff system – whereas the former is the consequence of growth and diversification, and involves the creation of new and quasi-autonomous organisational units.

The advantages of divisionalisation, apart from the general benefits of decentralisation already mentioned, relate to:

(a) Its value as a training medium for the development of divisional managers for top level posts in the parent organisation.

(b) The relative ease with which divisional activities can be integrated at higher levels of control.

(c) The motivation afforded to local managers who are encouraged to use individual initiative when dealing with local problems. Note, however, that total decentralisation of an organisation by divisionalisation is impossible, since any decision arising at the divisional level that has policy implications for the organisation as a whole must be endorsed by central control.

Appraising divisions

An important task when creating divisions is to ensure that their performances can be easily measured and appraised, as sometimes one or more divisions subsidise others without anyone being aware of the fact. Problems attached to devising an appraisal scheme for divisions include:

(a) deciding whether each division is to be regarded as a cost centre in its own right ('buying in' materials and services from other divisions)

(b) choice of criteria for measuring profitability (absolute money values, rates of return on capital employed, etc.)

(c) assessing the effects of company policies on the profits made by a particular division (e.g. the effects of artificially-low input prices from other divisions)

(d) overhead allocations *vis-à-vis* shared common services (administrative premises, for instance) and relating these to estimates for divisional rates of return on capital employed

(e) deciding whether divisions should manage their own idle cash balances or turn them over to a central treasury for investment outside the division (externally or elsewhere in the company).

20. Disadvantages of divisionalisation

These include the following:

(a) Senior managers may lack the training and expertise necessary to co-ordinate decentralised units effectively.

(b) Divisions might not be large enough to justify each one providing a full range of their own internal services, and thus may not be cost-effective.

(c) Divisions might fight each other for control over resources and to undertake certain functions.

(d) Bad external publicity attracted by one division will rub off on the rest.

(e) Activities might be duplicated.

(f) Potential economies of scale (e.g. cost savings through the integration of processes, discounts for bulk purchasing of supplies, etc.) could be lost.

(g) The benefits of specialisation of functions become difficult to obtain. Each division might have its own accountant, administrative staff, etc. rather than these people being centralised into single units serving the entire organisation.

21. Strategic business units (SBUs)

These are groupings of a business's activities which are then treated as self-contained entities for the purposes of strategic planning and control. An SBU could be a division of a company, a department, a collection of departments, a subsidiary, or a function undertaken within the firm (e.g. all the firm's marketing activities might be regarded as an independent SBU). Often, SBUs cut across existing divisional, functional and departmental boundaries. Having defined SBUs, management then gives each unit a budget and the authority to administer its own resources.

The idea was invented by the US General Electric Company which, dissatisfied with its existing divisional structure, rearranged all the enterprise's activities into SBUs, some of which bore little relation to traditional departments, divisions or profit centres. Thus, for example, a number of food preparation appliances previously manufactured and sold through several independent divisions were merged into a single 'housewares' SBU.

Similarly, a firm might produce television sets in one division, radios in the next, and car stereo systems in another. Yet for strategy and planning purposes all three activities could be conveniently lumped together into a self-contained administrative unit. To make sense, an SBU should:

(a) comprise compatible elements each possessing a direct and identifiable link with the unit as a whole

(b) be easy to appraise (which requires that its performance can be compared with something similar within or outside the organisation)

(c) contribute significantly towards the attainment of the organisation's goals.

SBUs are most appropriate for highly diversified businesses the activities of which can be grouped under distinct headings.

Advantages to the creation and use of SBUs are:

(a) They reduce the total number of administrative units that senior management has to monitor and control.

(b) Use of SBUs enables management to operate two levels of strategy: overall corporate decisions that affect the nature and direction of the enterprise; and unit level strategies relevant to specific operating environments. This facilitates the linking up of strategy development with strategy implementation.

(c) Important decisions can be taken in discrete business units.

(d) SBU organisation provides a planning framework that cuts across organisational boundaries.

(e) Units are encouraged to behave entrepreneurally.

(f) Decision making can be related to specific consumer groups and resource categories.

The main problems with SBUs are how to co-ordinate many disparate activities simultaneously and how to assess the financial and other contributions of various activities to a particular unit. SBUs are not suitable for vertically integrated companies supplying a limited range of products.

OTHER CONSIDERATIONS

22. Organisational size and employee performance

The size of an organisation exerts several influences on the relevance of a particular organisational structure and on the attitudes and behaviour of its employees. Specifically, large organisations:

- have more extensive and complex communication systems
- contain a wider variety of interest groups
- require more co-ordination
- project relatively authoritarian images to their employees
- are perceived to offer greater opportunity for employee development and promotion
- have access to many specialist support services
- possess a large number of levels of management
- require much delegation of authority
- have many departments
- tend to be more bureaucratic than smaller organisations.

23. Structure and technology

The technology an organisation uses affects its structure and operations in the following ways:

(a) An organisation that operates in a high-technology environment must (normally) be involved in research and development.

(b) High-tech firms need to employ large numbers of technically qualified staff.

(c) Substantial amounts of training are necessary in high-tech organisations.

(d) Technology affects the nature and extent of the division of labour within the organisation and hence employee job satisfaction and morale.

(e) Complex technology may require narrow spans of control.

(f) A high-tech organisation will usually require a sophisticated management information system.

24. Structure and markets

The markets in which a firm operates can influence its structure. A number of market characteristics might affect organisation structure, including the following:

(a) *Number of customers and their location.* This will help determine whether the firm is organised by product or by market.

(b) *Extent of competition.* Fiercely competitive environments require organisational structures that can be quickly and easily modified (in order to introduce new products and/or change distribution systems).

(c) *The degree of market segmentation.* Market segmentation means splitting up a total market into sub-units (e.g. for teenage consumers, middle-aged men, consumers with different income levels, lifestyles, etc.) and then modifying product characteristics and promotional methods to fit in with the needs of each market segment. This affects the size of production runs and the number and structure of departments within the firm.

25. Organisation development and the role of the change agent

The term 'organisational development' (OD) is sometimes used to describe the process whereby management periodically and systematically audits the adequacy of its existing organisation structure for meeting current operational requirements. OD examines the effectiveness of internal communications, employees' awareness of company goals and procedures, the efficiency of decision taking, and the organisation's ability to respond to change.

Individuals responsible for implementing OD exercises are often referred to as 'change agents'. A change agent could be a member of the existing management, or an outside consultant hired specifically for the task. He or she might suggest:

- training and management development for employees
- creation of new departments and/or working groups
- restructuring departmental or individual responsibilities
- rearranging communication patterns.

It is important that senior management be quite clear about its expectations of an OD exercise, and be willing to finance and implement its recommendations. There is little point in commissioning an OD survey if its findings are largely ignored!

26. In-house change agents

Current employees are familiar with the existing organisation structure and (importantly) know exactly where to look for information. Internal staff are fully accountable for their actions; indeed, their future careers might depend on the success of OD assignments. They are, moreover, constantly and immediately available and subject to senior management's direct control. On the other hand, in-house staff:

(a) are not exposed to penetrating expert criticism from independent outsiders

(b) usually have limited experience of other industries and organisations

(c) may lack insight and creativity

(d) might not possess the management skills necessary to complete the work satisfactorily.

27. Role of the external consultant

Frequently, external rather than in-house change agents are better equipped to deal with organisational problems. Outsiders will take a more objective view of the organisation's activities and structural requirements, and will bring to the firm their experience of OD exercises implemented elsewhere. Outside consultants have no vested interests in the welfare of particular departments and are not involved in internal departmental politics. External advice is especially valuable when unusual organisational difficulties are experienced for the first time and an outside expert can explain their causes, consequences, and how they have been overcome in other organisations. The consultant might conduct research, test employee attitudes and opinions, suggest solutions to particular problems, discover new methods for organising work, and may be involved in the mundane implementation of his or her recommendations.

Further *advantages* of using an outsider include:

(a) They need not be afraid to ask embarrassing questions of anyone in the organisation, including top management.

(b) Few overhead costs are incurred.

(c) Expert consultants have up-to-the-minute knowledge of specialist techniques.

(d) The need to earn a profit will motivate a consultancy firm to provide an excellent service.

(e) An external consultant will have a wide range of contacts with other experts in the field.

(f) Internal staff will benefit simply by observing how an expert consultant tackles the job. This can be extremely useful for training and developing managerial employees.

In effect, using a consultant enables the organisation to benefit from other organisations' mistakes, since work undertaken for other clients will have enabled the consultant to acquire wide-ranging experience and skills.

The *disadvantages* of using external consultants include the following:

(a) If the consultant's work is unsatisfactory the effects of his or her bad recommendations might not be felt for several months, by which time the consultant will have disappeared.

(b) Outsiders' long-term careers will not suffer if a particular organisation development project fails, so that consultants might not possess the same level of motivation as in-house staff.

(c) A consultant will not possess detailed knowledge of the day-to-day operations of the firm.

(d) An outsider's actual competence and qualifications might not be as good as he or she initially claimed.

(e) Use of a consultant will probably be more expensive than using an existing member of staff.

Progress test 21

1. List the essential components of the classical approach to organisation theory.

2. What is a 'staff' manager?

3. Explain the difference between a staff manager and a manager's personal staff.

4. List the advantages of line organisation.

5. What are the major possible causes of conflict between line managers and staff managers?

6. What is the main purpose of an organisation chart?

7. Define the term 'span of control'.

8. List the advantages of a 'tall' organisation structure.

9. Define the term 'linking-pin' organisation.

10. What is an 'autonomous work group'?

11. What are the commonest criteria used for creating departments?

12. List the advantages of decentralised organisation.

13. Explain the difference between decentralisation and divisionalisation.

14. Define the term 'strategic business unit'.

15. Explain the significance of organisation size for organisation structure.

16. Define the term 'organisation development'.

17. How might the technology an organisation uses affect its structure?

18. What is a 'change agent'?

22

RECENT DEVELOPMENTS IN THE PRACTICE OF ORGANISATIONAL DESIGN

1. Introduction

An organisation is put together from constituent elements. What these elements are and how they are united depend on the history of the enterprise, current technologies, working practices, and external legal and other environments.

This chapter briefly examines some contemporary influences on organisational design. The topics discussed are as follows:

- organisation structures suitable for part-time, casual and other 'flexible' workers
- networking
- honeycomb systems
- project teams
- organising for the efficient management of professionally qualified staff
- autonomous work groups (cells)
- Japanese approaches to organisation and management.

The virtual organisation

The term 'virtual organisation' is sometimes used to describe an organisation that exhibits the following characteristics:

- a small highly centralised core
- subcontracting to outside firms of the maximum number of business functions
- few (if any) departments
- no manufacturing plant (all manufacturing is contracted to outside firms)
- wide spans of control (*see* 21:**10**)
- extensive use of the latest information technology.

Advantages to virtual organisations are their flexibility and ability to undertake extensive operations from a small capital base. A virtual organisation might comprise a partnership among individuals or a joint venture among firms, with membership of the venture or partnership regularly changing. Hence the boundaries of the organisation and the scope of its activities might be subject to constant alteration.

MATRIX STRUCTURES

2. Project teams and matrix organisation

Matrix organisation is a means for creating project teams that cut across departmental boundaries. Individuals are seconded from their 'home' departments onto various project committees and thus have a number of bosses – their head of department and the team leaders of the groups to which they are temporarily attached. The idea is illustrated in Figure 22.1.

Manager A (a management services officer, for instance) has to be involved in, say, projects 1 and 4. Manager B is necessarily connected with projects 1 and 2, and so on. Instead of relating to projects (e.g. introducing a new product, acquiring new premises), the columns of the matrix could denote functions – such as credit control, cost reduction, or industrial relations – whereas the rows might describe sections within an organisation, e.g. sales, production control, or purchasing.

In either situation, reading down the columns shows who needs to become involved in the groups that are to oversee each project or function, while reading across the rows indicates the contributions of each person or section to the overall organisation. Committees may now be assembled to supervise the administration of each project or function.

Of course, a real matrix would be far more extensive and detailed than the above. It would name individual people within departments and identify their areas of activity. Sub-matrices can be drafted for departments and sections.

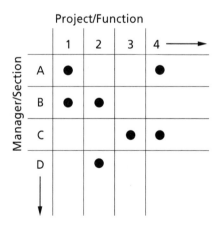

Fig. 22.1 Matrix organisation

Teams are multidisciplinary, cutting across traditional occupational divisions, departments and distinctions between line and staff. Matrix structure, moreover, creates numerous opportunities for employee participation in decision taking and the rapid development of general managerial skills. The system is extremely flexible (teams can be set up and disbanded at will). Matrix structures are especially useful for: (*i*) managing complex projects where immediate access to several highly specialised professional skills is required; and (*ii*) managing strategic business units (*see* 21:**21**). Often, SBUs do not correspond to existing divisions or departments so that it becomes necessary to establish a team representing each aspect of the work of the unit to oversee the unit's activities.

3. Advantages of matrix structures

Matrix organisation offers a practical and coherent device for analysing the makeup of an enterprise. Personal and departmental contributions to the organisation are systematically classified and crucial activities that absorb large amounts of effort and resources are highlighted. The method is commonly used where several departments performing related duties are grouped together into divisions. In this way, interdepartmental communications are enhanced and duplication of effort can be avoided. Further advantages are that:

(a) There is much face-to-face communication between managers with interests in the same projects.

(b) Project teams can be immediately disbanded following a project's completion.

(c) Departmental boundaries do not interfere with the completion of projects.

(d) Team leaders become focal points for all matters pertaining to particular projects or functions.

(e) It encourages flexible attitudes.

(f) Specialised professional knowledge relevant to a project or function is instantly available.

(g) Interdisciplinary co-operation is encouraged.

(h) Junior managers develop broad perspectives on problems and issues.

(i) Top management is left free to concentrate on strategic planning.

4. Disadvantages of matrix structures

Matrix organisation deliberately violates the principle of unity of command (*see* 21:**3**). Team leaders are responsible for projects, though heads of department retain executive authority over their staff. In consequence, team members might receive conflicting instructions from heads of department on the one hand and project team leaders on the other! It is important to establish at the outset: (*i*) who, ultimately, each individual should obey; and (*ii*) whether subordinates are to regard themselves first and foremost as members of a department or as members of a particular project team. Usually, departments take precedence, as projects last only for limited periods, and individuals will normally be assigned to a number of projects at the same time. Other problems are that:

(a) Matrix systems are more complicated and costly to administer than other forms of organisation.

(b) They might offer fewer discrete promotion opportunities than hierarchical systems.

(c) Teams rather than individuals are appraised (unsatisfactory employees may thus be difficult to identify).

(d) Unoffical links between members of various project teams may emerge, which subvert teams' abilities to achieve their objectives.

(e) Staff need to be trained in the methods of matrix management and the cost of such training could be substantial.

(f) There could be much duplication of effort within the organisation.

(g) Managers need to spend much time in committees (*see* 15:8).

(h) Disputes may arise regarding who should do what and who is in charge of whom.

(i) Conflicts may occur between the decisions of individual line managers and the collective decisions of project teams (which normally are given their own budgets and authority to implement decisions).

(j) Matrix structures might encourage managers to develop their political and negotiating skills at the expense of their managerial abilities.

(k) The system may severely overwork certain key managers.

(l) Team members may be unclear about the precise nature of their roles in the team and in the organisation.

5. Operative cell structure

This is a Japanese idea applicable to manufacturing businesses. In Britain it is usually associated with just-in-time stock control (JIT) (i.e. scheduling work-flows so precisely that only minimal stocks of work-in-progress need be held; work from each previous stage in the production process arrives 'just-in-time'). Workers in each cell are responsible for quality and production control, and are put in charge of the repair and maintenance of equipment and the timing of movements of work from one cell to the next.

Operatives' jobs thus become more interesting. Workers function as a team and hence are expected to cover for each other's absences, latecoming, etc. Responsibility for errors is shared by the entire group. Errors might lead to lost bonuses for everyone involved.

The success of this type of organisation depends critically on cell members' ability to work as a team, i.e. to co-operate and *voluntarily* co-ordinate their activities in order to achieve group objectives. There is need for: (*i*) participants to develop a common bond; (*ii*) extensive interaction between group members; (*iii*) participants to offer mutual support and share common perceptions of events; and (*iv*) a fair distribution of work and responsibility within the group, especially for unpleasant or exceptionally demanding duties.

Sound supervisory training for those in charge of such systems is essential.

FLEXIBLE WORKFORCES

6. Managing a flexible workforce

Organisations increasingly employ labour on a part-time, casual, *ad hoc* and/or sub-contract basis. Three major factors explain the trend towards 'flexible' work in the United Kingdom:

1 Organisations often find that their permanent full-time employees are not fully utilised throughout the year (sometimes not even through an entire working week) so that contract labour hired for short periods and/or to undertake specific assignments is much cheaper than employing permanent staff.
2 The size of the labour force can be varied at will.
3 Widespread redundancies and unprecedented high unemployment in the 1980s and early 90s has released a large supply of workers willing – through choice or economic necessity – to work casually.

Core and peripheral workers

Clearly, new work patterns demand fresh approaches to labour management and the design of organisations. The common approach is to distinguish between 'core' and 'peripheral' workers. Core workers comprise full-time permanent employees who have security of tenure, receive training and enjoy numerous fringe benefits. In return, however, their contracts of employment demand total job flexibility: they must stand ready to do whatever work is available, irrespective of occupational divisions, at any time. Core workers have no job description other than to complete any tasks that need doing.

Peripheral workers, conversely, are hired on short term and/or part-time contracts, whenever extra labour is required. They exercise little discretion over how they perform their work and (generally) do not have 'careers'. Peripheral staff might include job sharers, agency employees, self-employed consultants and sub-contract labour as well as casuals and part-timers; indeed, anyone who can be hired and fired quickly and easily as market conditions change might be categorised as a peripheral worker.

7. Advantages and disadvantages of flexible workforces

The *advantages* to the organisation of operating a flexible labour system are that:

(a) It need not be concerned about superannuation, promotion, annual pay rises or sick pay (other than the statutory minimum) for flexible workers.

(b) Unions are often uninterested in having part-time or casual employees as members (regarding casuals as a threat to full-time jobs).

(c) Unsatisfactory non-permanent workers may be easily discarded (few of them are covered by existing employment protection legislation).

The *disadvantages* are that casually-employed staff often lack commitment to their work, have (usually) received less training than full-time colleagues, and frequently resent being employed part-time and/or on short-term contracts. Also, numerous frictions can arise from the employment of casual workers alongside permanent employees. Casual staff resent having to do the same work as full-time colleagues for lower pay and without equivalent conditions of service. Permanent workers, on the other hand, may regard casual employees as inferior and a danger to their security of employment, particularly where the overwhelming majority of casual workers are women and/or belong to an ethnic minority.

There are few opportunities for job enrichment in such circumstances; morale is usually low and rates of absenteeism and staff turnover are high. Even though casual workers are not normally unionised, industrial disputes still occur and because they are not resolved through agreed management/union procedures they are likely to be highly disruptive in the longer term. Grievances persist indefinitely in casual labour systems, transmitted from one generation of casual workers to the next without any possibility of resolution.

8. Difficulties attached to managing a flexible workforce

In order to manage a flexible workforce effectively the organisation needs separate policies in each of the following areas:

(a) appraising the calibres of peripheral workers (especially those who work off the premises)

(b) achieving the wholehearted participation of peripherals in the meetings, committees, etc. necessary for effective decision taking within the organisation

(c) preventing permanent employees resenting 'special' treatment afforded to flexible staff (e.g. if common grading and promotion systems apply to both core and peripheral workers)

(d) controlling the quality of recruitment of peripherals

(e) securing loyalty among flexible workers

(f) arranging for the supervision of peripheral employees and deciding whether this should be done by other peripherals in a higher grade or by core employees. Note that flexible workers are not usually capable of handling crises or the sudden influx of extra work since they lack the resources, information, experience and authority necessary for this – leading perhaps to overwork among core staff.

9. Improving the performances of flexible workers

Profit sharing, holiday and sick pay, and paid time off for the training of flexible workers are among the many strategies that might be employed to overcome some of these difficulties. Further devices include:

(a) paying peripheral workers to attend general discussions about the firm's objectives

(b) making peripherals responsible for the quality of their outputs

(c) offering fringe benefits (superannuation, for example) to peripherals

(d) providing contractually-binding guarantees of re-entry to jobs after a break in continuity of service

(e) devising grievance and appeals procedures, consultation systems, etc. suitable for casually-employed staff.

Networking (*see* **10** below), job sharing and formal career break systems can be used to improve the motivation of flexible employees (though note the problem of the 'two Monday mornings' syndrome frequently attached to job sharing arrangements). Such schemes:

(a) enhance the morale of flexible workers, who are made to feel wanted and of real value to the organisation

(b) enable individuals to choose how and when they do their work

(c) help employers of flexible labour to retain their best peripheral workers

(d) help overcome problems of low commitment, poor communication and shoddy work among casually-employed staff.

Induction of flexible workers into existing work groups is especially important, as it is essential that peripherals feel part of the team and are introduced to the wider aspects of the organisation.

OTHER FLEXIBLE STRUCTURES

10. Networking

With networking, employees and/or sub-contractors work from home, communicating with head office through a home-based computer, telephone calls, and through face-to-face meetings at prearranged times. Networking is increasingly popular among professional workers who possess a specific technical competence, the exercise of which does not require their physical presence in any particular place. Examples are design, computer programming, technical writing, and similar skills. Indeed anything that can be undertaken from a self-contained home office is amenable to networking. The advantages include:

(a) the time saved in not having to commute to work (in London this can amount to three or four hours per day)

(b) a more relaxed working environment leading to greater creativity, more output, and a higher level of enthusiasm for work

(c) freedom from arbitrary routines, flexible starting and finishing times, absence of set meal breaks, etc. (work may be completed when the individual most feels like it)

(d) not having to endure the numerous unwanted interruptions inevitably attached to working in the head office of a large organisation

(e) being able to fit work between transporting children to and from school

(f) saving on premises costs for the employing organisation.

A network can be based on one of two employment models. The options are:

(a) To bind the networker to a single firm through paying that person a regular wage, deducting PAYE and Class 1 National Insurance, providing superannuation, and perhaps also a company car and other fringe benefits.

(b) Treating networkers as self-employed sub-contract labour entirely responsible for their own tax and National Insurance, and paying them an *ad hoc* lump sum for each assignment.

In the former case the employer needs systems for: (*i*) periodically appraising networkers' performances; (*ii*) finding new ways of improving efficiency; and (*iii*) generally controlling networkers' efforts. Here, individuals are treated as if they were full-time and permanent employees who, circumstantially, do not work at head office. Under option **(a)**, control is exercised by the setting of targets, work inspections, visits to the person's home by senior managers, etc.

In the latter (self-employed) situation the firm risks losing the individual to other employers (a networker engaged in this manner has no legal commitment to any particular organisation other than to complete the assignment in hand) and it cannot directly control working methods (if it did, the Inland Revenue would not allow the networker to have self-employed status). Assignments are *ad hoc* and the networker has no security of tenure. Particular difficulties arise here if the firm has invested large sums in the networker's training, or if valuable company equipment is used in the networker's home office, or if highly confidential information is involved.

In general, the problems of networking include the following:

(a) Ambiguity of status *vis-à-vis* the employing firm. Networkers are typically employees on long-term and continuing (albeit *ad hoc*) assignments. Yet their work rarely carries the prestige normally attached to a permanent head-office post.

(b) Inability to rise through the ranks of the organisation to a senior line management position. Networkers are specialists and, because of their isolation on the outer fringes of the firm, cannot acquire the general management experience needed for a top job.

(c) Lack of direct control over networkers. How can head office know the extent of the work actually required to complete a particular job or whether certain work might be deskilled and done elsewhere at lower cost?

(d) Co-ordination difficulties, especially where projects critically depend on each of several isolated networkers meeting tight deadlines.

(e) Feelings of insularity; loneliness; and the inability to communicate as frequently as the job requires. Networkers who are constantly on the phone and/or travelling to see colleagues might just as well work at head office.

(f) The need to employ head-office managers specifically to liaise with networkers, to supply their input requirements, deal with their problems, arrange their meetings, etc.

(g) Ambiguities regarding the ownership of copyright of ideas, designs, programmes, etc. created by networkers at home; especially if the worker is self-employed.

11. Honeycomb and motherhood structures

A *honeycomb* structure comprises a conglomeration of 'cells' each corresponding to a particular functional area. The organisation recruits employees who are already trained and competent in relevant specialisations, adding or deleting cells as circumstances change. If, for example, a company acquires its own fleet of vehicles it might add a transport management cell to its organisation structure, hiring an experienced and qualified transport manager and associated staff from outside the firm.

The advantage of a honeycomb system is the speed and convenience with which a business can expand or contract its operations (through creating or disbanding cells). Disadvantages are that staff engaged in such a manner will feel little commitment to the enterprise (qualified specialists can easily move to other firms) and labour turnover may be high.

Motherhood systems, conversely, are structured around generalist managers; recruited young and without experience but then trained and developed within the company. Staff become committed to the business, undertake a wide range of duties, experience several types of work and become steeped in the organisation's culture and working practices. There is a coherent management succession scheme and guaranteed continuity of operations within the firm, but employees may lack the detailed knowledge of specialised functions possessed by outside experts. Also, because of the long periods necessary to train new entrants, motherhood firms cannot expand or contract their field of activities as readily as honeycomb companies.

12. The work of Charles Handy (b.1932)

According to Charles Handy, changes in economic conditions, working practices and social attitudes have led to fundamental alterations in organisational
culture and hence in approaches to organisational design; especially considering
the need of so many companies to introduce flexible work patterns and to
downsize the extents of their operations. Another important factor contributing
to new perspectives on organisational structuring is the widespread decline of
labour-intensive processes and their replacement by 'knowledge-based' production methods. Modern organisations, Handy suggests, increasingly evolve from
the 'shamrock' form, through the 'federal' structure and eventually into the
'triple I' system (Handy 1989).

The shamrock organisation

This is analogous to the shamrock plant (which has three interlocking leaves) in
that it comprises three distinct groups of employee, each with its own unique
set of terms and conditions of employment. The first 'leaf' is a small number of
core workers (*see* **6**) on permanent contracts and who run the system. They are
loyal to the firm, progressive and flexible in outlook, and are handsomely
rewarded for their contributions. The core is well-trained, competent and highly
effective. Alongside the core is the second group in the system: the 'contractual
fringe', comprising contract workers remunerated on a payments by results
basis. The third leaf consists of casually employed part-time employees hired
and fired according to the state of market demand for the firm's output. Individuals take this sort of work either because they cannot obtain full time jobs or
through preference for part-time employment. In some shamrock organisations
there is a fourth leaf: the customer. Here the purchaser of the firm's goods or
services undertakes certain tasks formerly carried out by employees, e.g. self-as-
sembly furniture, self-service in supermarkets and in restaurants, and so on. The
customer assumes the role of *de facto* subcontractor.

Advantages to the shamrock form of organisation include a high level of
output from a limited number of workers, absence of red tape and bureaucracy
and the ability to respond quickly to alterations in market conditions. Problems
are the absence of feelings of loyalty towards the enterprise among many
employees (whose jobs are liable to end at any time), and the organisation's
heavy reliance on a handful of core workers.

The federal organisation

Small firms with 'lean' organisations might enter into close collaborative arrangements in order to acquire the resources and scope for action of large
companies. Members share a common business identity, while retaining independent managements and business systems. Thus there is innovation and
creativity within each shamrock organisation, while the federation as a whole
develops a 'critical mass' capable of competing effectively in turbulent markets.

The triple I organisation

Eventually the organisation might progress to become a 'triple I' enterprise based on 'ideas, information and intelligence'. The triple I firm is a 'learning organisation' (*see* 6:**14**) with core workers possessing a wide range of conceptual, analytical, informational and general business skills. Managers of such firms need to be facilitators, advisors and coaches as well as decision makers *per se*.

STRUCTURES FOR PROFESSIONAL STAFF

13. Organisation structures for professionally qualified staff

The nature of professional bodies is described in 11:**9–10**. Special problems attach to the management of professionally qualified employees. The following difficulties are particularly worthy of mention:

(a) Assessing the performance, calibre and professional competence of certain categories of professionally qualified staff (lawyers or research scientists, for instance). The typical line manager does not possess enough knowledge of the professionally qualified subordinate's field to be able to make rational judgments about his or her ability.

(b) Enabling professionals to utilise their professional skills to the full. Professionally qualified employees often complain that their talents are not fully utilised by employing companies; that they are asked to undertake mundane duties for which professional qualifications are not really required, and that the extent to which they are expected to exercise 'professional' judgment is not clearly defined. Thus, for instance, a qualified accountant might be asked simply to 'do the books' and not be involved in the (many) broader management functions for which he or she has been trained; or a solicitor may be expected to handle routine legal paperwork that could easily be dealt with by a solicitor's clerk.

(c) Deciding how much independent discretion a professionally qualified employee should be allowed, and to what extent he or she requires special facilities.

(d) Integrating the professional into the existing organisation structure. Note how the co-ordination of a large organisation's activities normally involves the establishment of hierarchies, with upper ranks controlling and superintending the work of subordinates.

Professional work, however, might not be conveniently managed in this way – particularly where professional discretion and creativity are required. The professional carries ultimate responsibility for his or her professional decisions. Thus, for example, a lawyer must *personally* decide whether a civil action against a debtor is likely to succeed, or an accountant must personally decide whether a company's books are accurate and lawfully presented.

Relations with line management

Conventional line and staff systems might not be suitable when large numbers of professionals are employed because:

(a) Line managers may become overwhelmed with requests for decisions on professional matters which they do not really understand.

(b) Overworked line managers might ignore important advice offered by professionals.

(c) Professionals may find they are increasingly involved in the mundane administration needed to implement professional decisions.

(d) Many issues cannot be unambiguously assigned to 'administrative' or 'professional' categories, since they require research and administrative action as well as professional discretion; thus they can be regarded as *either* professional or administrative matters.

14. Fitting the professional to the organisation

Either the professionally qualified employee must adapt his or her perspectives and working methods to fit in with the bureaucracy of the organisation, or the organisation itself must change its ways. The former option is more common, for whereas the professional contributes a particular function which *partially* satisfies the organisation's needs, the line management system is necessary for *all* the organisation's work. Thus, most firms will choose to subordinate their professional staff to the requirements of the existing system.

Alternatively, an organisation that is dominated by professionals (a research centre, for instance) might adopt a 'federal' organisation structure in which individuals enjoy great personal autonomy in how they undertake their work, but have separate administrations to perform routine management tasks. In effect, two distinct organisations operate simultaneously and side by side.

Professional support services

Large organisations (government departments or multinational corporations, for example) sometimes establish self-governing subsidiary bodies that concentrate entirely on the provision of a particular professional service. (The economic advisory unit of the civil service or the legal departments of the commercial banks are cases in point.) Within these subsidiary 'professional organisations' the conventional administrator/professional relationship – with the professional being a subordinate adviser to the line management system – is reversed. Professionals hold executive authority and take decisions while administrators give advice. The role of the administrator here is to offer advice about the organisational, financial and other implications of intended professional decisions, though professionals and *not* administrators take the final decisions. Administrators concentrate on achieving efficiency and economy, and on tactical rather than strategic planning. Usually, the administrator of a professional unit will not reach the top of that particular organisation.

15. Conflicts between professionals and line managers

Unfortunately, the separation of the professional from the normal line of command can undermine the authority of the central administration. Note particularly how professional immunity from the ordinary rules of superior/subordinate relationships will be closely observed by non-professional staff, who may question why they too should not be allowed to innovate, take important decisions, and not fear adverse criticism from higher authority about the decisions they take.

A number of specific sources of conflict between professional and line management employees may be discerned, including the following:

(a) Often, professionally qualified staff have the same status, earn similar salaries, and occupy the same grades as line managers who – although they contribute a great deal to the organisation's work (much more perhaps than their professional colleagues) – are not as well certificated academically and have not had to spend several years studying for professional examinations. Accordingly, those who perform professional jobs might treat with disdain the work of line managers and resent the fact that professional and line managers are graded and paid equally.

(b) Line managers may begrudge the professional workers' self-assumed intellectual status, and not be prepared to concede that professional duties sometimes require special support services and working arrangements.

(c) Professionals expect to be able to exercise discretion and expert judgment in the course of their work, but at the same time must comply with the bureaucratic rules and demands of the wider organisation. They are subject to the authority of senior administrators, yet usually are not fully involved in the formulation of the administrative processes that determine the rules. The values of the professional worker – autonomy, commitment to certain professional ideals, ethical standards, diffusion of knowledge within the profession, etc. – might directly contradict the requirements of a company in which the primary need is to get work done quickly, cheaply and as efficiently as possible.

(d) As professions have developed, so too have the ancillary services needed to support them. Thus, a company lawyer may need a trained and specialist legal secretary, access to expensive legal texts, a legal database, a qualified legal executive (solicitor's clerk), and so on. Support staff are directly responsible to the professional manager concerned, and not to the wider administrative system. An (expensive) organisation within an organisation is created, absorbing resources that line managers may prefer to see used elsewhere.

JAPANESE MANAGEMENT

16. Japanese management

The enormous success of Japanese companies in world markets has caused intense interest among western management theorists in the Japanese approach to organisation and management.

In fact, many aspects of Japanese management were imported into Japan from the USA, although they were severely modified to fit into the Japanese way of life and cultural traditions.

Origins of the Japanese approach

Today, Japanese companies have an impressive record for good industrial relations. But this has not always been the case: during the late 1940s and early 1950s Japanese industry experienced many protracted and damaging nation-wide industrial disputes. Japanese firms, moreover, had a bad reputation for producing poor-quality output.

Many factors contributed to these difficulties: disruptions caused by the war, large-scale shifts of population between regions and from agriculture to industry, chronic shortages of skills and material resources, etc.

Meanwhile, the American occupation of the Japanese mainland had caused a thorough overhaul of Japanese social, economic and industrial organisations, and had encouraged Japanese firms to look to the USA for practical guidance on business organisation and management. Accordingly, the (then) latest American methods – work study, scientific quality control, corporate strategy, techniques for employee appraisal and management by objectives, and so on – were transported to Japan.

Importantly, however, these techniques were altered to suit Japanese conditions and the perspectives of Japanese workers. The system retained its great respect for status and authority, but became intensely competitive and egalitarian in many ways, especially in business management. Meritocratic recruitment, careful organisation, and great concern for staff training and development started to be implemented in large Japanese enterprises.

What emerged was a distinct (and highly successful) industrial philosophy based on customer care, new product development, careful targeting of international markets, and great concern for the reliability of products.

17. Characteristics of Japanese management

W. Ouchi, a westerner who studied Japanese management closely, summarised the Japanese approach as comprising three strategies and six associated techniques. The strategies are as follows:

1 Commitment to life-long employment.
2 Projection of the philosophy and objectives of the organisation to the individual worker; making workers feel they belong in a clearly defined corporate entity.
3 Careful selection of new entrants and intensive socialisation of recruits into the existing value system.

The strategies are implemented through six techniques:

1 Seniority-based promotion systems. Recruits expect to spend their entire careers with a single firm. They acquire experience of various aspects of the business through job rotation and steady (but slow) progression through the management hierarchy. Since there is but limited opportunity for promotion,

most transfers are lateral. This develops generalist rather than specialist management skills, and well-rounded management personalities.

2 Continuous training and appraisal which, combined with guaranteed job security, enable managers to construct long-term career plans. Managers thus experience less stress than their western counterparts.

3 Group-centred activities. Tasks are assigned to groups rather than individuals.

4 Open communication both within work groups and between management and labour. Managers and workers dress alike and eat in the same works canteen.

5 Worker participation in decision making, based on consultation with all who will be affected by a proposed change.

6 A production-centred approach with, nonetheless, great concern for the welfare of the employee. There is no great social divide between management and workers.

In Japan, payments systems are seniority-based. The longer an employee has been with the firm, the more he or she is paid. Another important feature of the Japanese corporation is that it will have just one trade union representing all its employees. Unions are company-based rather than covering entire industries or professions.

18. Benefits of the Japanese approach

The following advantages have been claimed for the Japanese system:

(a) Because Japanese managers experience many internal transfers within their employing company during their careers, they obtain a wide-ranging appreciation of all aspects of the company's operations.

(b) Single status for all employees can significantly improve loyalty to the organisation, morale, and team spirit.

(c) Employees invest so much of their life energy in a single employing organisation that they become totally committed to its long-term survival. There is much training, job rotation, employee participation in operational decision making, and hence an improvement in the general quality of operations at the grass roots level.

(d) The need to protect employees' jobs regardless of economic circumstances forces management to adopt a long-term view of the organisation's strategies; in particular to seek a constantly expanding market share in preference to immediate short-term profits thus creating the ability to provide long-run security of employment. This drive for market share arguably leads to:

(*i*) rapid and frequent adaptation of existing products rather than new product innovation in order to avoid high-risk activities that threaten jobs
(*ii*) aggressive marketing, low-price policies, numerous dealer incentives and high expenditures on advertising.

(e) Emphasis on group work rather than individual discretion encourages harmony within the workforce, consensus between management and labour, and a high degree of employee co-operation.

19. Critical comments regarding Japanese management

A number of critical comments can be directed against Japanese approaches to organisation and management, including:

(a) There is much discrimination against women in Japanese industry (employers often require female employees to resign on marriage).

(b) Although most large Japanese companies publicly espouse life-long employment, in fact only one quarter of Japanese workers are employed under a contract that actually guarantees life-long employment; and there is compulsory retirement (normally) at age 55 for employees with such contracts.

(c) The emphasis on conformity and obedience to authority might itself eventually become a barrier to the introduction of new methods and the acceptance of change.

(d) While the rewards to those who survive the severe initial screening process for entry to management in large and well-established Japanese companies are extremely high, income is unevenly divided and only a minority of people actually benefit. There are still very many Japanese employees who by western standards are not particularly affluent.

(e) The new generation of younger Japanese managers may resent restrictions on the speed at which they can progress through an organisation and thus might themselves eventually become the agents of change who will disrupt the system.

20. Problems in transferring Japanese methods to Britain

Several attempts have been made to transfer the Japanese approach to Britain, with mixed results. The major barriers to successful transfer appear to have been as follows:

(a) Few UK workers are culturally attuned to the idea that they should be personally responsible for the quality of their output (as is standard practice in Japan). Rigorous inspection by independent quality-control personnel has always been the norm in this country.

(b) Often, Japanese approaches are only partially applied. For example, management may expect enthusiastic employee participation in, say, a quality-improvement programme while totally rejecting the idea that workers should participate in any other aspect of the firm's operations.

(c) Single status is rare in British industry. Management is predominantly hierarchical, with numerous status symbols attached to each level.

(d) British companies do not offer life-long employment regardless of the state of trade. Indeed, the incidence of part-time, temporary and casual employment (*see* **6** above) has increased enormously in Britain over the last quarter century.

(e) UK workers are typically recruited to undertake specific jobs, and are not expected to remain with a company doing several different jobs over their entire careers.

Progress test 22

1. Define 'matrix organisation'. What are the disadvantages of matrix organisation?

2. What are the factors that explain current trends towards temporary and part-time employment?

3. Explain the difference between core and peripheral workers.

4. List the major difficulties attached to managing a flexible workforce.

5. Define 'networking'.

6. Explain the difference between honeycomb and motherhood organisation structures.

7. List the main problems associated with devising an organisation structure suitable for managing professionally-qualified staff.

8. Describe the key elements of the Japanese approach to management.

APPENDIX 1

References and Bibliography

Adair, J. (1983), *Effective Leadership*, Gower, Aldershot.

Alderfer, C.P (1972), *Existence, Relatedness and Growth: Human Needs in Organisational Settings*, The Free Press, New York.

Allport, F.H. (1924), *Social Psychology*, Houghton Mifflin, Boston.

Ansoff, H.I. (1990), *Implanting Strategic Management*, Prentice-Hall.

Argyris, C. (1957), *Personality and Organisation*, Harper and Row.

Argyris, C. and Schon, D. (1978), *Organisational Learning: A Theory of Action Perspective*, Addison-Wesley.

Barnard, C. (1938), *Functions of the Executive*, Harvard University Press.

Beer, M. Spector, B.A., Lawrence, P.R. and Walton, R.E. (1985), *Human Resource Management*, The Free Press.

Belbin, R.M. (1981), *Management Teams: Why they Succeed or Fail*, Butterworth-Heinemann.

Berne, E. (1964), *Games People Play*, Penguin.

Blake, R.R. and Mouton, J.S. (1964), *The Managerial Grid*, Gulf Publishing.

Bowen, D.E. and Lawler, E.E. (1992), 'The empowerment of service workers: what, how and when', *Sloan Management Review*, Spring 1992, 31–39.

Brown, A. (1995), *Organisational Culture*, Pitman.

Burns, T. and Stalker, G.M. (1961), *The Management of Innovation*, Tavistock Publications.

Clark, N. (1994), *Team Building: A Practical Guide for Trainers*, McGraw-Hill.

Denison, D. (1990), *Corporate Culture and Organisational Effectiveness*, Wiley.

Deutsch, M. (1969), 'Social science, IQ and race differences revisited', *Harvard Education Review*, 39, 1–35.

Drory, A. and Romm, T. (1990), 'The definition of organisational politics: a review', *Human Relations*, Nov. 1990, 1133–54.

Drucker, P.F. (1954), *The Practice of Management*, Harper and Row.

Drucker, P.F. (1989), *Managing for Results*, Heinemann.

Drucker, P.F. (1987), *The Effective Executive*, Harper and Row, New York.

Eagly, A.H. and Johnson, B.T. (1990), 'Gender and leadership style: a meta-analysis', *Psychological Bulletin*, September 1990, 233–256.

Eagly, A.H. and Karau, S.J. (1991), 'Gender and the emergence of leaders: a meta-analysis', *Journal of Personality and Social Psychology*, May 1991, 685–710.

Farrell, D. and Petersen, J.C. (1988), 'Patterns of political behaviour in organisations', *Organisation Studies*, 9 (2), 406–407.

Fayol, H. (1916), *General and Industrial Management*, English translation Pitman 1949.

Fielder, F.E. (1967), *A Theory of Leadership Effectiveness*, McGraw-Hill, New York.

Follett, M.P. (1942), *Dynamic Administration: Collected Papers of Mary Parker Follett*, Harper.

Fox, A. (1966), 'Industrial Sociology and Industrial Relations', *Royal Commission on Trade Unions and Employers' Associations Research Paper No. 3*, HMSO.

French, J.R.P., and Raven, B.H. (1959), 'The bases of social power', in D. Cartwright (Ed.), *Studies in Social Power*, University of Michigan Press.

Furnham, A. (1990), *Personality at Work: the Role of Individual Differences*, Routledge, Chapman and Hall.

Gier, R.N. (1979), *Understanding Scientific Reasoning*, Holt, Rinehart and Winston.

Gilbreth, F.B. and Gilbreth, L. (1914), *The Psychology of Management*, Sturgis and Walton.

Gilbreth, F.B. and Gilbreth, L. (1916), *Fatigue Study*, Sturgis and Walton.

Glaser, B.G. and Strauss, A.L. (1967), *The Discovery of Grounded Theory: Strategies for Qualitative Research*, Chicago, Aldine.

Grant, J. (1988), 'Women as managers: What they can offer to organisations', *Organisational Dynamics*, Winter 1988, 56–63.

Guest, D. (1987), 'Human resource management and industrial relations', *Journal of Management Studies*, 24 (5), 503–21.

Hall, D.T., *Careers in Management*, Goodyear, Calif., 1976.

Hammer, M. and Champy, J. (1993), *Re-engineering the Corporation: A Manifesto for Business Revolution*, Nicholas Brealey.

Hamner, W.C. (1974), 'Reinforcement theory and contingency management in organisational settings', in Tosi, H.I. and Hammer, W.C. (Eds.), *Organisational Behaviour and Management: A Contingency Approach*, Chicago, St Clair Press.

Handy, C. (1976), *Understanding Organisations*, Penguin, 1976.

Handy, C. (1989), *The Age of Unreason*, Pan.

Hersey, P. and Blanchard, K.H. (1989), *The Management of Organisational Behaviour*, 3rd edn., Prentice Hall.

Herzberg, F. (1966), *Work and the Nature of Man*, New York, World Publishing Co.

Hull, C.L. (1943), *Principles of Behaviour*, New York, Appleton Century Croft.

Hunt, J. (1969), 'Has compensatory education failed?' *Harvard Educational Review*, Series 2, 130–152.

IRRR (Industrial Relations Review and Report) (1994), 'Team building and development', *Employee Development Bulletin*, 55, July 1994, 2–11.

Janis, I.L. (1972), *Victims of Groupthink*, Houghton Mifflin.

Jensen, A.R. (1969), 'How much can we boost IQ and scholastic achievement?', *Harvard Educational Review*, 31, 1–23.

Kanter, R.M. (1983), *The Change Masters*, Simon and Schuster.

Katz, R.L. (1974), 'Skills of an effective administrator', *Harvard Business Review*, Sept/Oct. 1974, 90–101.

Ker, S. and Jermier, J.M. (1978), 'Substitutes for leadership: their meaning and measurement', *Organisational Behaviour and Human Performance*, Dec. 1978, 375–403.

Kotter, J.P. and Schlesinger, L.A. (1979), 'Choosing strategies for change', *Harvard Business Review*, March-April 1979.

Lawrence, P.R. and Lorsch, J.W. (1967), *Organisation and Environment*, Harvard University Press, Harvard, 1967.

Legge, K. (1989), 'Human resource management: a critical perspective', in Storey J. (Ed.), *New Perspectives on Human Resource Management*, Routledge.

Levinson, D.J. et. al. (1978), *The Seasons of a Man's Life*, New York, Knopt.

Lewin, K. (1948), *Resolving Social Conflict*, Harper.

Lewin, K., Lippitt, R. and White, R.K. (1939), 'Patterns of aggressive behaviour in experimentally created social environments', *International Journal of Social Psychology*, vol. 10.

Likert, R. (1961), *New Patterns of Management*, McGraw-Hill.

Luft, J. (1961), 'The Johari Window', *Human Relations Training News*, 5 (1), 6–7.

McClelland, D.C. (1961), *The Achieving Society*, Van Nostrand Reinhold.

McGregor, D.V. (1960), *The Human Side of Enterprise*, McGraw-Hill.

Manz, C. and Sims, H. (1987), 'Leading workers to lead themselves: the external leadership of self-managing work teams', *Administrative Science Quarterly*, Vol. 32, 106–107.

Maslow, A.H. (1954), *Motivation and Personality*, Harper and Row.

Mayo, G.E. (1945), *The Human Problems of an Industrial Society*, Harvard University Press.

Mintzberg, H. (1973), *The Nature of Managerial Work*, Harper and Row.

Mintzberg, H. (1979), *The Structuring of Organisations*, Prentice Hall.

Morrison, J.H. and O'Hearne, J.J. (1978), *Practical Transactional Analysis in Management*, Addison-Wesley.

Moult, G. (1990), 'Under new management', *Management Education and Development*, 21 (3), 171–182.

Ouchi, W. (1981), *Theory Z: How American Business Can Meet the Japanese Challenge*, Addison-Wesley.

Parker, S.R. (1971), *The Future of Work and Leisure*, MacGibbon and Kee.

Perrow, C. (1970), *Organisational Analysis: A Sociological View*, Tavistock Publications.

Polya, G. (1945), *How to Solve It*, Princeton, University Press.

Popper, K.R. (1963), *The Growth of Scientific Knowledge*, Routledge.

Porter, L.W. and Lawler, E.E. (1968), *Managerial Attitudes and Performance*, Irwin-Dorsey.

Salaman, G. and Butler, J. (1990), 'Why managers won't learn', *Management Education and Development*, 21 (3), 183–191.

Schein, E.H. (1965), *Organisational Psychology*, Prentice-Hall.

Schein, E.H. (1985), *Organisational Culture and Leadership*, Jossey-Bass.

Schneider, B., Parkington, J.J. and Buxton, V.M. (1980), 'Employee and customer perceptions of service in banks', *Administrative Science Quarterly*, Vol. 25, 252–267.

Schramm, W. (1954), *The Process and Effects of Mass Communication*, University of Illinois Press.

Shannon, C. and Weaver, W. (1949), *The Mathematical Theory of Communication*, University of Illinois Press.

Sherif, M., Harvey, O.J., White, B.J., Hood, W.R., and Sherif, C. (1961) *Intergroup Conflict and Co-operation*, University of Oklahoma Press.

Simon, H.A. (1960), *Administrative Behaviour*, Macmillan.

Skinner, B.F. (1953), *Science and Human Behaviour*, The Free Press, New York, 1953.

Sorge, A. and Streeck, W. (1988), 'Industrial relations and technical change', in Hyman, R. and Streeck, W. (Eds.), *New Technology and Industrial Relations*, Blackwell, 19–47.

Soujanen, W.W. (1966), *The Dynamics of Management*, Holt, Rinehart and Winston.

Stubbs, D.R. (1985), *How to Use Assertiveness at Work*, Gower.

Tannenbaum, R. and Schmidt, W.H. (1958), 'How to choose a leadership pattern', *Harvard Business Review*, March-April, 1958.

Taylor, F.W. (1911), *The Principles of Scientific Management*, Harper.

Tolman, E.C. (1932), *Purposive Behaviour in Animals and Men*, New York, Appleton Press.

Training Commission: Occupational Standards Branch, (1989), *Classifying the Components of Management Competencies*, Training Agency, Sheffield.

Trist, E.L. and Bamforth, K.W. (1951) 'Some social and psychological consequences of the Longwall method of coal getting', *Human Relations*, Vol. 4.

Tuckman, B.W. (1965), 'Developmental sequences in small groups', *Psychological Bulletin*, June 1965, 384–399.

Vroom, V.H. (1964), *Work, and Motivation*, Wiley.

Warde, A. (1990), 'The future of work', in Anderson, J. and Ricci, M. (Eds.) *Society and Social Science*, Open University Press.

Waterman, R.H. (1987), *The Renewal Factor*, Bantam.

Weber, M. (1947), *The Theory of Social and Economic Organisation*, The Free Press.

Weiner, N. (1948), *Cybernetics*, MIT Press.

Woodward, J. (1965), *Industrial Organisation*, Oxford University Press.

Wyatt, S., Frost, L., and Stock, F.G.L. (1934), *Incentives in Repetition Work*, Medical Research Council, HMSO.

INDEX